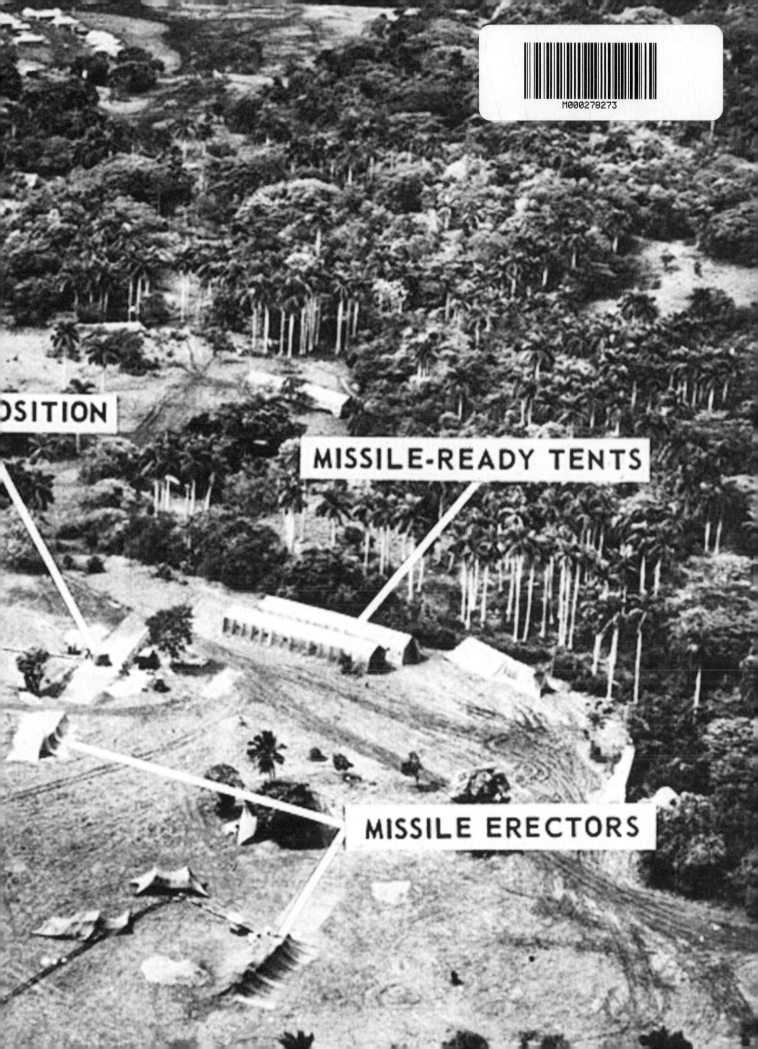

OSITION

MISSILE-READY TENTS

MISSILE ERECTORS

SPYPLANES

SPYPLANES

THE ILLUSTRATED GUIDE TO MANNED RECONNAISSANCE AND SURVEILLANCE AIRCRAFT FROM WORLD WAR I TO TODAY

BY NORMAN POLMAR

AND

JOHN F. BESSETTE

WITH

HAL BRYAN

ALAN C. CAREY

MICHAEL GORN

CORY GRAFF

AND

NICHOLAS A. VERONICO

VOYAGEUR
PRESS

CONTENTS

PERSPECTIVE

A LA FRONTIÈRE DE GALICIE

Des sentinelles autrichiennes tirent sur des aviateurs russes qui font des reconnaissances nocturnes à la frontière avec des aéroplanes munis de projecteurs électriques

Austrian guards on the Galician border take aim at Russian aviators making reconnaissance flights in aircraft fitted with electric searchlights. The military potential of aerial observation had been noted as far back as the eighteenth century, but it saw its first true expression with fixed-wing aircraft in World War I. *Private Collection/© Look and Learn/Bridgeman Images*

To "spy" is to acquire information that another nation—enemy, neutral, and sometimes allied—does not want one to obtain. Spyplanes have been invaluable in obtaining such information for more than a century. And despite the advent of satellites and unmanned aerial vehicles for this role, manned aircraft continue to have great importance as spyplanes. This book is about the development and operations of those aircraft.

The terms *observation, reconnaissance*, and *surveillance* are closely related, with definitions that differ depending upon the source and perceived function.

Observation: Gathering information about the target area from above, primarily using visual means. The term emerged during World War I—especially in the US military—and survived into World War II, when it was largely replaced by "reconnaissance."

Surveillance: Gathering information, but usually when the targets or goals are not well defined. Good examples are maritime surveillance missions, in which aircraft search broad expanses of ocean seeking possible shipping or naval activity.

Reconnaissance: Similarly gathering information, but increasingly using more technical means, such as photographic, electronic, and communications intercept systems as well as visual sightings. Usually reconnaissance missions have specific targets or at least specific goals in mind (that is, to determine the frequencies of a specific radar set). Within "reconnaissance," there are two broad types of missions—tactical and strategic:

Tactical reconnaissance involves operations in the vicinity of, or in direct support of, ongoing or impending battles.

Strategic reconnaissance covers all other aspects of information gathering in this context, for example, monitoring borders of hostile or potentially hostile entities during times of tension, or gathering information on political, economic, and military aspects away from the battlefield.

Determining which aircraft to include in this volume became an exercise in deciding which aircraft to *exclude*. In the broad sense, virtually all military and many civilian aircraft have had a role in "aerial spying" at some time in some place. From the very beginning of armed flight, nations have asked (or ordered) their aircrews—whether on combat missions such as fighter escorts or nuclear strikes, or airlift large and small—to report their observations of the enemy to an intelligence officer. Thus, all aircraft are in some sense "spyplanes."

Some spyplanes are covert—innocent-appearing transport aircraft, commercial/civil or military—with hidden electronic surveillance gear. These include Sydney Cotton flying covert photo missions in a Lockheed 12A over Germany in the 1930s on behalf of the British government, and US Air Force C-97G Stratofreighters flown over East Germany during the Cold War. Most spyplanes are *overt*, like the high-flying, highly publicized US U-2 and SR-71, or the lumbering, graceful Soviet/Russian Bear.

A major issue when describing spyplanes is the "cut" between tactical and strategic aircraft. An aircraft such as the LTV RF-8 Crusader was primarily a tactical recon aircraft, but during the Cuban missile crisis of 1962, the RF-8s from Navy light photograph squadron VFP-62 were employed to obtain strategic-level intelligence of Soviet missile emplacements. Similarly, the Lockheed RF-80 Shooting Star, another tactical recon aircraft, flew strategic missions into Manchuria to ascertain the status of Chinese and Soviet airfields during the 1950–1953 Korean conflict. Thus, the lines between tactical and strategic spyplanes often become blurred. We have decided to address both types of "spyplanes," in part because of this overlap in missions and assignments.

The officially recognized American short term for reconnaissance is "recon," which is used in this book, while the British tend to use the term "recce."

ABBREVIATIONS

AAF	Army Air Forces (US, 1941–1948)
AFB	Air Force Base
AWS	Air Weather Service (US)
ASW	anti-submarine warfare
CIA	Central Intelligence Agency (US)
COMINT	communications intelligence
CV	aircraft carrier
CVA	attack aircraft carrier
CVAN	attack aircraft carrier (nuclear-propelled)
CVS	anti-submarine aircraft carrier
ECM	electronic countermeasures
ELINT	electronic intelligence
FEAF	Far East Air Forces (US)
FLIR	forward-looking infrared
HASP	high-altitude sampling program
JCS	Joint Chiefs of Staff
LPH	amphibious assault ship
Mach	speed of sound (named for Ernst Mach)
MAD	magnetic anomaly detection
NATO	North Atlantic Treaty Organization
PACAF	Pacific Air Forces (US)
PARPRO	Peacetime Aerial Reconnaissance Program (US)
RAF	Royal Air Force (UK)
RPA	remotely piloted aircraft
SA-( )	Soviet surface-to-air missile (NATO designation)
SAC	Strategic Air Command (AAF command, 1946–1947; USAF/US Specified Command, 1947–1992)
SENSINT	sensitive intelligence
SIGINT	signals intelligence (includes COMINT and ELINT)
SLAR	side-looking aircraft radar
TV	television
UAV	unmanned aerial vehicle
USAF	US Air Force (1948–)
USAFE	US Air Forces Europe
USN	US Navy
VFP	light photographic squadron (US Navy)
VQ	fleet air reconnaissance squadron (US Navy)

The French used the observation balloon *L'Entreprenant* to great effect at the Battle of Fleurus in 1794—much to the chagrin of Austria's General Friedrich Josias von Saxe-Coburg. This color litho commemorating the events was published more than a century later in 1898. *Private Collection/© Look and Learn/Bridgeman Images*

PART I
SPYPLANE OPERATIONS

By Norman Polmar and John F. Bessette

"There's a spy in that thing and I can't get at him to have him hanged!" So declared General Friedrich Josias von Saxe-Coburg in June 1794 after the Austrian defeat in the Battle of Fleurus. Frustrated by the French use of a balloon for observation, the general inadvertently summed up aerial reconnaissance's military value for all time.[1]

But this may not have been the first use of aerial vehicles in such a way. Attempts at aerial reconnaissance may have first occurred about 500 BCE, with one source crediting the Chinese with using man-lifting kites to gain a height advantage for observation.[2]

In the modern era such efforts to "look down on the enemy" began at almost the very beginning of manned flight, traceable to the Montgolfier brothers' first balloon activity in France in September 1783. On October 15 that year in Paris, Joseph-Etienne Montgolfier was credited with being the first human to become airborne in a balloon. The American innovator Benjamin Franklin observed the early Montgolfier flights and was among the first to comment on the possibility of military use. However, it was not until 1794, during the French Revolutionary Wars, that the French Aerostatic Corps was formed. Reconnaissance missions began in June 1794, and at the Battle of Fleurus on June 26, balloon observers dropped notes to troops on the ground, and also used hand signals.[3]

Despite the rising popularity of ballooning in the first half of the nineteenth century, its perceived military value was limited. Even the first known aerial photographs from balloons—in France in 1858 and Boston, Massachusetts, in 1860—did not prompt extensive military interest. During the early years of the American Civil War, both the Union and the Confederacy employed balloons for visual reconnaissance, chiefly in northern Virginia and the Hampton Roads area, but also in the central Mississippi River basin. Union balloon observers occasionally used a telegraph key in the balloon basket connected by wire to the ground, thus providing the first aerial examples of "real-time intelligence." But neither side expended much effort to exploit this asset, and US military balloon activity had ceased by 1863.

There was no known balloon reconnaissance in the Spanish-American War of 1898. Later, extensive balloon reconnaissance was used in World War I, especially after the conflict had reached a stalemate on the Western Front in the static situation known as "trench warfare." Both sides of the conflict turned to balloons to "look over the hill" into the enemy's trenches. These used wire communications to report changes to the enemy lines. But enemy fighter planes soon began sighting on these highly flammable hydrogen-inflated balloons as targets, and balloon reconnaissance had ceased by the war's end.

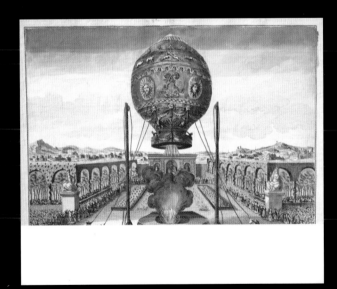

Efforts to "look down on the enemy" began at almost the very beginning of manned flight. On 15 October 1783, in Paris, Joseph-Etienne Montgolfier was credited with being the first human to become airborne in a balloon. Benjamin Franklin observed early Montgolfier flights and was among the first to comment on the possibility of military use.
Archives Charmet/Bridgeman Images

THE FIRST SPYPLANES

The first aerial photographs taken from a heavier-than-air machine were probably taken in 1909 near Rome, Italy, from a biplane built by the Wright brothers. But the French soon advanced the technique with high-quality aerial photos.

The first "spyplane" used in combat came in 1911, when Italy and Turkey fought for the provinces of Tripolitania and Cyrenaica (the main parts of present-day Libya). Italy had developed a fixed-wing military aviation component—the Italian Aviation Battalion—and sent the unit with nine aircraft to Tripoli. On 23 October, Captain Carlo Piazza flew the first heavier-than-air reconnaissance mission in a Bleriot XI monoplane, observing Turkish troops and positions in the Benghazi area on his one-hour flight. Nine days later, Italian planes made history's first aerial bombing raid on an enemy, using Captain Piazza's observations to target the Turks.

In the same campaign, on 24 and 25 February 1912, Captain Piazza again made history by taking the first aerial photographs of enemy positions from an aircraft.[4] Then, on 19 April, a colleague of Piazza's took the first aerial motion-picture films of an enemy encampment while flying the airship P.3.

(Captain Piazza, having qualified as a pilot at age 40 in 1911, soon took command of the aviation detachment in Libya. He was killed on the Austrian-Italian Front in 1917.)

Aerial reconnaissance was taking off as a major factor in military affairs, with Italy introducing the technique into warfare in 1911. In the same year, Great Britain, France, and the United States introduced it in military exercises. In Britain, the army maneuvers of 1912 and 1913 featured aircraft observing "hostile" forces and reporting back after landing. One appraisal made after the 1912 exercise stated, "It seems to me impossible for troops to fight while hostile aeroplanes are able to keep up their observations . . . warfare will be impossible unless we have mastery of the air."[5]

During World War I (1914–1918), the initial collection of intelligence by manned aircraft was made by the pilot's own visual observation. Subsequently, handheld cameras were provided for a second crewman. Larger cameras were later mounted on the rear machine gun ring. Still later, a hole was cut in the rear fuselage bottom for cameras. "The aerial photograph is born of trench warfare," a French source said in 1918.[6] This simple statement summarizes the decisive role aerial reconnaissance would play in transforming the nature of combat.

The airplanes of the Allies and the Central Powers (Germany and Austria-Hungary) carried out extensive aerial photography as well as general visual

LEFT: Images created over Boston, Massachusetts, by Samuel Archer King in 1860 were among the first successful aerial photographs. *Private Collection/Archives Charmet/Bridgeman Images*

OPPOSITE: During the American Civil War, both the Union and the Confederacy used balloons for visual reconnaissance. Here, Thaddeus S. Lowe observes a battle from his balloon *Intrepid*, in 1862. *Universal History Archive/UIG/Bridgeman Images*

reconnaissance, or "observation," during the conflict. One efficient reconnaissance aircraft could provide more intelligence for a field commander than could several hundred horse cavalry. Recon aircraft went aloft throughout daylight hours, often escorted by fighters to protect them from enemy air attack. They took photos of enemy troops on the move, their extensive trench system, and important towns. Specialists—soon known as photo interpreters—examined the photos to discern minute changes in the landscape that could indicate an enemy's movements or, just possibly, intentions. This new intelligence source "reinvented the way that modern battle was envisioned, planned, and executed."[7]

By the end of World War I, the Germans were taking about 4,000 aerial photographs per day; the Allied effort was at least as great. David Kahn, an authority on German military intelligence, observed, "After 1917, both Allied and Central Powers so feared [aerial reconnaissance] that neither dared

OPPOSITE: Airplanes on both sides carried out extensive photography and visual recon during World War I. This artwork depicts the first aerial reconnaissance carried out by the Royal Flying Corps. The two aircraft are a Bleriot XI (foreground) and a BE 2b (background). *Private Collection/© Look and Learn/Bridgeman Images*

BELOW: On 23 October 1911, Italian Captain Carlo Piazza flew the first heavier-than-air reconnaissance mission in a Bleriot XI monoplane like this one, observing Turkish troops and positions in the area around Benghazi, Libya. *Dorling Kindersley/UIG/ Bridgeman Images*

FRANCE 1918

DE HAVILAND "4"

The Geoffrey de Havilland–designed Airco DH.4 was one of the most popular reconnaissance aircraft of World War I. *Burton Historical Collection, Detroit Public Library*

Designer Igor Sikorsky's Ilya Muromets bombers, the world's first operational four-engine aircraft, were among the most impressive recon aircraft of World War I. Here Sikorsky demonstrates his aircraft in 1914. *Sovfoto/UIG/Getty Images*

This artwork depicts two crewmen attempting to extinguish an engine fire in an Ilya Muromets. *Private Collection/© Look and Learn/Bridgeman Images*

move troops in daylight hours."[8] Both sides developed extensive (and widely publicized) fighter aircraft, at first largely to destroy opposing recon aircraft and to protect their own.

Two of the most popular reconnaissance aircraft of the war were the British Geoffrey de Havilland–designed DH.4 and the French Salmson 2A2, both modified for photo reconnaissance. The most impressive reconnaissance aircraft, though, were the Russian Ilya Muromets bombers, the world's first operational four-engine aircraft. Some 40 of these planes made about 440 bombing raids over enemy territory from 1915 to 1917. On all of their missions—bombing as well as reconnaissance—the planes carried a still-frame camera that provided the Russian Army with about 7,000 aerial photographs during their operational service.

Developed by aviation genius Igor Sikorsky, the Ilya Muromets bombers could be considered the world's first "strategic reconnaissance" aircraft, seeking intelligence on German activities far behind the front lines. Aircraft like the DH.4 and the Salmson 2A2 sought information on frontline defenses, supply dumps, and troop movements as well as ship movements, collecting what became known as "tactical intelligence."

When the United States entered the war in April 1917, the US Army had some aerial reconnaissance experience. The first training exercise in which aircraft had taken part was in Kansas in 1911; the following year, a large war game centered in Connecticut included four aircraft reporting visual observations, in one case via wireless radio.[9] In 1916, extensive photorecon missions were flown when Major General John J. (Blackjack) Pershing led a punitive expedition into Mexico. About 15 Curtiss-built Jenny biplanes were used for visual and photo reconnaissance in that campaign. In France, US aerial observation squadrons used both the DH.4 and the 2A2 in considerable numbers during World War I. ■

World War I airmen aboard aircraft like the French-built Salmson 2A2 sought "tactical intelligence" on defenses and troop and ship movements. *National Archives and Records Administration*

BETWEEN THE WARS

Between the world wars, several nations made significant progress in the development and clandestine use of aerial photography. As early as 1930, Germany began "spy flights," initially over Poland. The leader of this effort was Theodor Rowehl, a World War I reconnaissance veteran who initiated the flights as a civilian.[10]

Back in uniform in 1934, Rowehl created an organization that flew many peripheral and occasional overflights of Poland, France, Britain, Czechoslovakia, and the Soviet Union. His favorite aircraft before the war was the civilian version of the Heinkel 111 bomber. The cover story for these aircraft flights was that the German airline Lufthansa was expanding its operations and investigating new routes. These "air routes" covered large swaths of territory from eastern England across northern Europe and the Baltic Sea to Leningrad (now St. Petersburg) in the Soviet Union.

The Heinkel 111, which first flew in 1935, was developed in Germany in violation of the Treaty of Versailles, which dictated the terms for Germany's surrender in World War I. It was designed as a high-speed medium bomber for the German Air Force (*Luftwaffe*), though it was originally flown as a civilian transport aircraft to disguise its potential military role.

The French Air Force began photo flights over western Germany in the 1920s, but these ceased in 1929 for reasons that are not clear.[11] The French resumed the flights in 1936 and sought British cooperation as the German threat increased. The resulting British-French effort featured Sidney Cotton, an enterprising Australian flier. Beginning on 25 March 1939, he made several photographic flights over Germany, Italy, and Libya. Sponsored by British and French intelligence agencies, Cotton flew these missions under the cover of a firm called the Aeronautical Research and Sales Corp.

Cotton's aircraft—a secretly modified Lockheed 12A twin-engine passenger plane—was fitted with up to three cameras in the fuselage, with shutters that hid the cameras being controlled from the cockpit. After the outbreak of war in September 1939, Cotton continued his flights over German ports in his modified civilian aircraft, because Royal Air Force (RAF) photo planes were relatively ineffective. Cotton flew three successive Model 12A aircraft on his aerial spying missions. As the war deepened, at Cotton's urging, RAF Spitfire fighters—and then Mosquito light bombers—were employed in photoreconnaissance missions, with great success.[12] ∎

An American pilot in a Salmson 2A2 shows off the aircraft's camera equipment. *National Archives and Records Administration*

Beginning in 1939, Germany adapted bombers like the Dornier Do 215 (opposite) and Do 17 to specialized high-altitude recon roles. The Do 17 above is being serviced by a Finnish Air Force ground crew in January 1942, amid the Finns' Continuation War with the Soviet Union. *Heinrich Hoffmann photo/ullstein bild/Getty Images and SA-kuva*

THE WORLD AT WAR—AGAIN

When the European war began in September 1939, the Germans shifted to specialized, high-altitude versions of several bombers for strategic reconnaissance, primarily the Dornier Do 215 and Do 217, as well as the Junkers Ju 86 and Ju 88. Especially useful was the Ju 86P version of the obsolescent Ju 86 bomber. From 1940 to 1943, these aircraft—which could operate at extremely high altitudes—roamed far and wide, especially deep into the Soviet Union and over the Middle East and North Africa.[13] No fighter aircraft could intercept them at their high altitudes until 1942, when the British, using specially modified Spitfires, shot down three Ju 86P spyplanes over the Eastern Mediterranean at altitudes reported as high as 42,000 feet.

During World War II, most belligerent countries used aircraft for tactical reconnaissance and intelligence collection. Initially standard aircraft were fitted with cameras, usually at the expense of guns. Particularly successful in British service were variants of the Spitfire and Mosquito, designated FR for "fighter-reconnaissance" and PR for "photoreconnaissance," respectively. The twin-engine Mosquito—a multirole aircraft constructed mostly of plywood—was noted for its range, speed, and altitude, which enabled it to evade hostile fighters easily.

The Japanese also had been active with spyplanes in the 1930s. Besides missions flown in support of their war against China and their battles with the Soviet Union in Manchuria, the Japanese flew clandestine recon missions against the British-held islands in the Central Pacific using the Kawanishi H6K2 Type 97 flying boat (later given the Allied codename Mavis). They also undoubtedly flew similar missions against Malaya, the Philippines, Guam, Wake Island, the Dutch East Indies, and possibly Hawaii.[14]

The Japanese Army and Navy continued to use existing bomber and flying boat aircraft for recon purposes; the only specialized aircraft flown in that role was the army's Mitsubishi Ki.46 Dinah, a streamlined, twin-engine aircraft with thin, low-mounted wings, and a dorsal hump containing separate crew compartments for the pilot and radio operator. The crew positions were separated by a camera bay and a large,

440-gallon (1,666-liter) fuel tank. The main landing gear retracted into the engine nacelles and the tail wheel was also retractable.

The design and powerful twin engines provided greater speed, allowing the Dinah to pull away from pursuing Allied fighters. Only later in the war would skillfully handled Lockheed P-38 Lightnings and Supermarine Spitfires prove consistently successful against the Ki-46. The recon aircraft had a single, aft-firing machine gun in the radioman's cockpit. No radar was fitted in any variants.

The Dinah flew missions over Manchukuo (Manchuria) and China, as well as Southeast Asia. Long-range recon flights continued throughout the

Variants of the Supermarine Spitfire were successfully repurposed for reconnaissance roles. This PR (photoreconnaissance) Mk IX was photographed in October 1943. *National Archives and Records Administration*

Pacific War, including overflights of northern Australia from bases in the East Indies and, in 1945, US B-29 Superfortress bases in the Mariana Islands. Recon of US and British naval task forces provided information that resulted in more destructive kamikaze attacks.

After World War II several surrendered Dinahs were flown briefly by the French in Indochina and by Communist Chinese forces.

The principal German tactical reconnaissance aircraft were variants of Messerschmitt's Bf 109—the top-performing fighter at the start of the European conflict—and the twin-engine Bf 110 and Me 210 fighters. Several German tactical bomber-type aircraft were employed in the recon role, with the Ju 88—flying throughout the war and on every front—being the most prominent. The Arado Ar 234 Blitz (Lightning), the world's first jet-propelled bomber, was often employed as a long-range recon aircraft during the last year of the war, including several missions over England at almost 40,000 feet.[15] Recon variants of the huge Junkers Ju 390 and Messerschmitt Me 264 had ranges that were theoretically sufficient to reach the United States from occupied France, but they were only in planning and development by the time of the German surrender in 1945.[16] Reports that perhaps one recon flight had reached New York City have not been substantiated. Such missions, whether bombing or recon, would have required midair refueling, a technique the Germans had just begun testing when the European war ended.

The Soviet Union entered World War II with no specialized reconnaissance aircraft and no personnel with experience in military aerial photography.[17] Few of the aircraft assigned to the reconnaissance role had factory-installed cameras. The demand for "precise and authentic reconnaissance data, which could be obtained only with the help of aerial photography," led to several steps being undertaken by the air force high command. The 15th Separate Reserve Reconnaissance

TOP: At the outset of World War II, standard fighter and bomber aircraft were fitted with cameras, usually at the expense of guns. The twin-engine, multirole de Havilland Mosquito was notable for its ability to evade enemy fighters. *Royal Air Force photo*

CENTER AND BOTTOM: Mitsubishi's streamlined Ki.46 was one of the rare World War II–era aircraft designed for a reconnaissance role. It featured low-mounted wings and a dorsal hump containing separate compartments for the pilot and radio operator. *Both public domain*

The Junkers Ju 88 was the most prominent German bomber adapted for a recon role. *National Archives and Records Administration*

Regiment with Petlyakov Pe-2 aircraft was activated in November 1941. The Pe-2 was a twin-engine, multirole aircraft, in several respects analogous to the de Havilland Mosquito.

More recon units were formed and courses established for photo interpreters. Still, the recon demands led to non-specialized air units continuing the efforts to spy out German positions and forces. As the war progressed and photo reconnaissance became more important, though, improved aircraft and well-trained personnel became available. Beginning in 1943, when Soviet forces went on the offensive, every operation was preceded by extensive recon flights.

Throughout the war, aerial photography only grew in importance. In 1941, some 10 percent of the recon missions were photographic; by 1945, this number had risen to 87 percent.

The US Army Air Forces (AAF) entered World War II with no significant aerial reconnaissance capability, but planning had already begun. In the summer of 1941, the army, recognizing the increased Japanese threat in the Pacific, began modifying a few new B-24 Liberator long-range bombers with cameras to reconnoiter the Japanese islands in the western Pacific. The first such B-24 was in Hawaii preparing for a mission when the Japanese attack on Pearl Harbor destroyed it on the ground.[18]

When the US Army entered the Mediterranean Theater with the invasion of North Africa in November 1942, the AAF flew British-provided Spitfire photo aircraft. Later, the US Eighth Air Force, operating from England, had two squadrons equipped with the Mosquito for high-altitude reconnaissance (designated F-8 in US service). During the war, the AAF modified a variety of American aircraft for reconnaissance purposes. They were designated "F," for "fotographic," since the "P" designation was already being used for "pursuit" (fighter) aircraft.

US Navy combat aircraft converted to the recon role—primarily for use in the Pacific Theater—included the camera-laden PB4Y-1P (a variant of the B-24 Liberator bomber) as well as the F4F-3P Wildcat (flown by the marines) and the F6F-5P Hellcat carrier-based fighters. At the end of the war, the F7F Tigercat

The Arado Ar 234, the world's first jet-propelled bomber, was employed as a long-range recon aircraft in 1945, including several high-altitude missions over England. *National Archives and Records Administration*

In November 1941, the Soviet Union activated the 15th Separate Reserve Reconnaissance Regiment, which it outfitted with the twin-engine multirole Petlyakov Pe-2. *Private Collection/© Look and Learn/Bridgeman Images*

The US Navy also converted combat aircraft for recon, primarily for use in the Pacific Theater. These included the camera-laden PB4Y-1P, a variant of the B-24 Liberator bomber. This aircraft was photographed in March 1945. *National Archives and Records Administration*

entered service; it was the first twin-engine aircraft accepted by the navy for carrier operation. The F7F-3P recon version was quickly developed, although the plane saw only limited service.

Only two US specialized photographic recon aircraft were developed during the war: the Hughes F-11 and the Republic F-12. The former was a twin-engine aircraft designed by aviation pioneer, industrialist, and film producer Howard Hughes. Two F-11s were built with competitive powerplant arrangements; Hughes crashed and was almost killed flight testing one of these prototypes. The F-12 Rainbow was a long-range, four-engine aircraft with an onboard capability for developing film; only one prototype was built. Neither aircraft entered production or service.

Photo reconnaissance became a component of virtually every military operation in the war. The US Ninth Air Force, operating from bases in Britain (and later in northwestern Europe) flew an average of more than 20 photo missions a day in support of ground and air forces during the last year of the war. British planes provided comparably extensive photo coverage of the region, and the results were shared through the Joint Allied Air Reconnaissance Centre at Medmenham in southeast England. ■

ARMY AIR FORCES AIRCRAFT DESIGNATIONS

The US Army designated photoreconnaissance aircraft with the prefix letter "F" from 1924 to 1946. The F-series designations were assigned to existing aircraft that had been modified or—in two instances—built for the recon role.

In 1946, the aircraft reverted to their "basic" designations, usually with the letter "R" prefix. Thus, in 1946, the F-13 Superfortress became the RB-29.

A pilot with his Lockheed F-5. *Cory Graff collection*

RECON VARIANT	BASIC TYPE	NAME
XF-1	Former XC-8	—
YF-1	Service text XF-1; became C-8	—
F-1A	Became C-8A	—
F-2	B-18	Bolo
F-2A	UC-45A/B	Expeditor
F-2B	C-45F	Expeditor
F-3	A-20	Havoc
F-4	P-38E/F	Lightning
F-5	P-38G/H/J/L	Lightning
F-6	P-51A/B/C/D/K	Mustang
F-7	B-24D/H/J	Liberator
F-8	DH.98 (Canadian)	Mosquito
F-9	B-17F/G	Flying Fortress
F-10	B-25D	Mitchell
F-11	New design	—
F-12	New design	Rainbow
F-13	B-29A	Superfortress
F-14	YP-80A	Shooting Star
F-15	P-61A/E	Black Widow
FA-20C	A-26C	Invader
FP-80A	P-80A	Shooting Star

ELINT AND COMINT

On the eve of World War II, the newly built German passenger airship *Graf Zeppelin* was used in an attempt to "spy out" the new British air defense radar installations. She was employed by the Luftwaffe in the spring of 1939 to measure the wavelengths of British radars and pinpoint the location of the radar sites, a role that would come to be called electronic intelligence (ELINT) or "ferret" operations. The airship was used because airplanes at the time lacked the endurance and space for the electronic equipment necessary for such work.

Based at Frankfurt, the *Graf Zeppelin* made its first surveillance flight in late May 1939. No useful data were acquired because of equipment problems. The second flight, in early August 1939, also failed to acquire useful information. While the *Graf Zeppelin* was tracked by British radar on her first flight, she escaped unnoticed on the second. The airship was sighted visually, however, and after the London *Daily Telegraph* newspaper revealed the flight, the German government denied that the airship had left Germany or approached the coast of England. Thus ended the first known attempt at aerial ELINT collection. The airship was scrapped soon afterward and the aluminum used in aircraft production. She never entered commercial service and was the world's last passenger zeppelin.

During the war, the British pioneered the use of aircraft for ELINT missions in support of their bomber offensive against Germany. At first they installed devices on bombers to monitor German radar emissions; later, by jamming and deception, they helped bomber formations to penetrate air defenses.

The first US effort in this field came in the fall of 1942 when a joint Navy-AAF team—with the codename Cast Mike Project No. 1—began using a modified B-17 Flying Fortress bomber on ELINT missions over the Solomon Islands in the Southwest Pacific. Based on Espiritu Santo in the New Hebrides Islands, the plane carried out eight long-range missions with both American and New Zealand flight crews. Subsequently, the Cast Mike team flew PBY-5A Catalina flying boats in the ELINT role during the Solomons–New Britain campaigns of 1942 and 1943; by mid-1944, they were flying up to the Philippines to detect Japanese radar emissions. The navy also employed carrier-based TBM Avengers in the ELINT role.

The US Army Air Forces commenced ELINT operations when a modified B-24D Liberator searched out radars on the Japanese-occupied Aleutian islands of Attu and Kiska, flying three long-range missions from Adak, Alaska, in March 1943. Extensively modified AAF B-17F Flying Fortress bombers also carried out ELINT missions in the Mediterranean area from bases in North Africa beginning in May 1943. In that role, they worked alongside British twin-engine Wellington bombers modified for the ELINT role.

The importance of detecting and classifying enemy radar emissions was not universally understood, and when the first ELINT-configured AAF B-24 Liberators reached the Southwest Pacific in late 1943, the local commanders ripped out their "black boxes" and used the aircraft as standard bombers. Additional ELINT-configured B-24s sent out in October 1943 were "protected" from misuse and were employed for their intended purpose. The planes flew against Japanese forces in the Pacific, including the home islands in 1945. These ELINT B-24s paved the way for the B-29 Superfortress raids against Japan, especially the atomic strikes on Hiroshima and Nagasaki, by pinpointing Japanese air defense radars.[19]

By the end of World War II, electronic intelligence collection had joined photo reconnaissance as a vital intelligence tool. Aerial communication intelligence (COMINT) collection also was beginning to be recognized as important in both Europe and the Pacific. This effort took the form of language-trained personnel who would fly in bomber formations to intercept, jam, and/or deceive the enemy's air defense communications network. Their intercepts of enemy air-to-ground and air-to-air communications allowed fighter escorts to be vectored to intercept enemy fighter formations, significantly reducing bomber losses.[20] ∎

The F-12 Rainbow was a long-range, four-engine aircraft with an onboard capability for developing film; only one prototype was built and the model was one of only two recon-specific types developed during World War II (the other being the Hughes F-11). The F-12 was redesignated the XR-12 when the US Army Air Forces separated from the US Army. *National Archives and Records Administration*

On the eve of World War II, the German passenger airship *Graf Zeppelin* was employed by the Luftwaffe to measure the wavelengths of British radars and pinpoint the location of the radar sites, a role that would come to be called electronic intelligence (ELINT) or "ferret" operations. The airship is seen here above the harbor entrance of Lindau, Bavaria, in 1928.
© SZ Photo/Scherl/Bridgeman Images

EARLY COLD WAR RECONNAISSANCE

During the long Cold War (1945–1991), aircraft were used extensively for both strategic and tactical reconnaissance. US and British aerial spying efforts were driven mostly by the extremely secretive nature of the Soviet Union. Western political and military leaders were desperate to know everything possible about the Soviet, Chinese, and other Communist Bloc military forces. Both ground-based and airborne collection systems were critical. Human intelligence collection remained important, but extensive efforts to insert agents behind the Iron Curtain largely failed, with most agents killed or captured almost as soon as they arrived. These losses were due mainly to the betrayal of agents by British traitors Donald McLean and Harold (Kim) Philby, who had access to the majority of US and British insertion plans.

The first major aerial ferret (ELINT) missions of the Cold War occurred in September 1946, when the Army Air Force's newly created Strategic Air Command (SAC) fitted a B-17 Flying Fortress with electronic analyzers and recorders to overfly a Soviet ice station in the Arctic. US military commanders were concerned that the Soviet facility might have a military purpose. Operating from bases in Greenland and Iceland during several flights over the area, the B-17 detected no signs of Soviet radar emissions.[21]

At virtually the same time, two shootdowns in Yugoslav airspace impelled US Air Forces in Europe (USAFE) to begin its own ELINT program. On two days in August 1946, army C-47 Skytrain courier transports flying from Vienna, Austria, to Venice, Italy, were shot down by Yugoslav fighters when they inadvertently penetrated Yugoslav airspace during bad weather. Once the survivors were released and the crisis died down, USAFE sought to discover how the Yugoslavs had been able to find and destroy the C-47s in such poor weather conditions. Two B-17s were hurriedly equipped with ferret gear and flew several missions along the Italian-Yugoslav frontier. They discovered that the Yugoslavs had used German-made "Wurzburg" radar for this purpose. USAFE promptly used these ELINT aircraft to track the emerging Soviet air defense network in central Europe.[22]

Cold War photo reconnaissance also began in 1946. SAC-modified B-29 Superfortress bombers (designated F-13s) operating from Alaska flew "peripheral" reconnaissance missions, using both photo and ELINT aircraft, along the Soviet Pacific coast. In 1948, temporary SAC RB-29 deployments to both Japan and Great Britain increased coverage from the Soviet-Norwegian border as far as the Kuril Islands, north of Japan. These missions became easier and more productive when the RB-29s were replaced by longer-range RB-50s.

The Army Air Forces theater commands—USAFE in Europe and Far East Air Forces (FEAF) in Japan— also launched their own aerial reconnaissance efforts. Besides USAFE's ELINT B-17s, camera-carrying B-17s conducted periodic photo missions along the Iron Curtain from the Baltic to the Aegean. Especially important and fruitful were photo and ELINT missions in the "Berlin corridors," the air routes from western Germany to the divided city of Berlin, from which observations of Soviet activity in East Germany were perfectly legal (and highly productive).

By 1948, when the USAF had been established as a separate service and the Berlin Airlift had begun, aerial reconnaissance was a major source of intelligence in the theater. For corridor missions, RB-26 Invaders and C-47 Skytrain transports were fitted with cameras, while outdated B-17 bombers were converted for both photo and ELINT work along the borders of communist-controlled Europe.

In the late 1940s, the US Navy also began flying extensive reconnaissance missions along the Soviet periphery, initially employing patrol bomber (PBM) Mariner flying boats and PB4Y-2 Privateers, the latter the much-improved version of the B-24 Liberator bomber.[23] The Baltic and Mediterranean Seas—as well as the Sea of Japan and the North Pacific—saw extensive naval aerial reconnaissance throughout the Cold War. The navy's primary targets were Soviet Bloc naval bases, among other maritime facilities and installations. ∎

The Joint Navy–Army Air Forces Cast Mike team used PBY-5 Catalina Flying Boats like this one in an ELINT role during the Solomons–New Britain campaigns of 1942 and 1943 and in the Philippines in 1944. Here aviation machinist's mates work on the starboard engine of a PBY-5A at an East Coast naval air station in the early 1940s. *PhotoQuest/Getty Images*

PEACEMAKER "PARASITE" EXPERIMENTS

In an effort to overcome the perceived vulnerability of the B-36, the air force developed the diminutive McDonnell F-85 Goblin "parasite" fighter to be carried recessed in the bomber's lower fuselage, released when enemy fighters threatened, and subsequently taken back aboard the bomber. This XF85 was flight tested from a modified B-29 Superfortress but never from a B-36. That scheme was quickly discarded (although SAC did operate its own land-based escort fighters until 1957).

Republic RF-84 Thunderflash recon aircraft also were evaluated in a parasite role, to be carried beneath a B-36 and released to extend the reconnaissance range of the "system." One YRF-84F was tested in this role with one RB-36F modified for the carrier role (redesignated GRB-36F). Subsequently, seven RB-36D Featherweight aircraft were converted to the GRB-36D configuration and 23 RF-84K aircraft were modified to be carried by "mother" aircraft. After flight trials from December 1955 to February 1956 this scheme also was discarded.

In another project, a B-36 was evaluated carrying two RF-84 aircraft attached to the bomber's wingtips (another discard).

The term FICON (Fighter Conveyer) was used for these concepts.

The Republic RF-84 Thunderflash was evaluated as a parasite to be released from beneath a B-36, thus extending the

EARLY CONFRONTATIONS

Before the Korean War, a series of aerial confrontations occurred when American reconnaissance aircraft flew close to Soviet, Chinese, and satellite airspace. These incidents depended on several factors: whether the Soviets detected the aircraft, whether they thought the aircraft had penetrated their airspace (the Soviets claimed 12 nautical miles out to sea as their territory), and whether they had fighters based close enough to intercept the US aircraft.

The first known attack on a US reconnaissance aircraft occurred as early as 15 October 1945 against a US Navy PBM Mariner flying boat on a reconnaissance flight to monitor ships evacuating Japanese troops near Soviet-occupied Port Arthur in northern China. A Soviet fighter buzzed the PBM when it was approximately 2 miles (3.2 kilometers) off the China coast and opened fire when the PBM was out some 45 miles (72.4 kilometers) south of Port Arthur. The PBM dived to wave-top level and escaped; there were no casualties.

On 8 April 1950, Soviet fighters shot down a US Navy PB4Y-2 Privateer patrol aircraft on an ELINT reconnaissance mission over the Baltic Sea. The unarmed aircraft was over international waters off the coast of Latvia when it was attacked by Soviet La11 piston fighters. The Soviets later claimed that the plane had flown 13 miles (20.9 kilometers) inland from the Latvian coast before it was intercepted. The plane had a crew of ten, none of whom survived, although later unsubstantiated reports claimed some were alive and being held by the Soviets.[24] This was the first US spyplane known to be shot down during the Cold War. ■

NUCLEAR AERIAL SAMPLING

Another aspect of aerial intelligence collection was initiated in September 1947 when the USAF was directed to establish a program of high-altitude air sampling. Its objective was "the determination of the time and place of all large explosions which might occur anywhere in the world and to ascertain in a manner which leaves no question, whether or not they were of nuclear origin."[25]

Within a year, 55 RB-29 and WB-29 Superfortress aircraft were fitted with filter devices to collect airborne debris from nuclear tests. A year later, on 3 September 1949, a WB-29 weather reconnaissance aircraft flying from Japan to Alaska on a sampling mission detected the first signs of a Soviet nuclear test. During a two-week period, 92 such flights collected hundreds of air samples in the region. Analysis of these samples determined that "there was no room for doubt that an atomic explosion had occurred somewhere on the Asiatic mainland and at some date between 26 and 29 August."[26] In fact, the Soviet Union had detonated its first nuclear device on 25 August 1949.

These missions by specially equipped B-29s were the precursors to the high-altitude sampling program (HASP) later flown by U-2 aircraft. Other aircraft types used for nuclear sampling during the Cold War were the RB-50, RB-57/WB-57 Canberra, RB-47 Stratojet, WC-130 Hercules, and WC-135 Stratolifter. Modified B-36 Peacemaker and B-52 Stratofortress strategic bombers supplemented the effort. The Air Force Tactical Applications Center controlled this nuclear fallout detection and analysis effort—which continues to this day—under the codename Constant Phoenix.[27] ■

STRATEGIC PHOTO RECONNAISSANCE

In many respects, high-altitude photography offered the most important means of intelligence collection during the 45 years of the Cold War. During World War II, aerial photography had been used mostly to locate enemy forces for targeting and for post-attack bomb damage assessment. Initial post–World War II applications of high-altitude photography were primarily for domestic photomapping and surveying for highway construction and mineral and oil exploration.

In Operation Leopard (1948), USAF camera-fitted RB-29s crossed the Bering Strait to take oblique photos of the Chukotski Peninsula in the Soviet Far East. This area was thought to possibly contain Soviet bomber bases targeted against North America. Subsequent

USAF peripheral missions of this kind in the Far East had codenames such as Overcalls, Rickback, and Stonework. They could confirm no bomber bases, but they did detect the beginnings of a Soviet air-defense system. The RB-29s could fly missions up to 30 hours in duration without aerial refueling.

The air force needed both medium- and long-range reconnaissance aircraft, the latter to overfly the Soviet Union in advance of potential strategic bomber strikes and for post-strike damage assessment. General Curtis E. LeMay, who had taken command of the new Strategic Air Command (SAC) in October 1948, was particularly dissatisfied with the air force's strategic reconnaissance capability.[28] In the late 1940s, only RB-29s were available for that role.

Improved strategic reconnaissance aircraft were proposed. At first, modifications of existing bomber aircraft were undertaken with the RB-50 following the RB-29. Two new aircraft were seriously considered for the strategic reconnaissance role: the Republic F-12 Rainbow (a four-engine piston aircraft) and the RB-49 version of the Northrop B-49 Flying Wing (a six-engine turbojet aircraft of radical design). Air force plans called for 73 F-12s to be built by 1952, but that project was soon dropped in favor of the Flying Wing. Eventually, the entire B-49 program—both bombers and recon aircraft—was terminated.

Further cancellations took place. In May 1949, work was halted on the RB-54, which would have been a reconnaissance variant of the proposed B-54 upgrade of the B-50 Superfortress. All of these programs were cancelled in favor of the advanced jet-propelled bombers already being planned and tested, as well as the very-long-range B-36 Peacemaker. The air force now concentrated on specialized reconnaissance variants of the giant B-36. This aircraft would be ideal for the post-strike reconnaissance role, at least in the near-term (early to mid-1950s).

With only four exceptions, all US military spyplanes have been adopted from existing military or civilian aircraft. The exceptions were the World War II –era Hughes F-11 and Republic F-12 Rainbow, and the Cold War–era Lockheed U-2/TR-1 Dragon Lady and the A-12 Oxcart/SR-71 Blackbird. The reasons for adopting existing designs are lower development cost, earlier deployment time, and more efficient and economical support in the field. The decision to employ primarily modified bomber aircraft for the strategic recon role was due in part to the demands of General LeMay, head of SAC from October 1948 to June 1957 and Chief of Staff of the Air Force from 1961 to 1965. General LeMay believed that using modified bombers would simplify logistics, training, and operations. Indeed, he rejected the proposed U-2 spyplane for SAC use in favor of adopting existing bomber designs. ■

EARLY PEACETIME OVERFLIGHTS

The first US overflights of the Soviet Union took place in August and September 1948 by USAF RB-29 Superfortress recon aircraft from Alaska on shallow penetrations of the Soviet Siberian coast. These overflights may have been inadvertent. In March 1950—three months before the outbreak of the Korean War—a pair of RF80A Shooting Star photo planes, fitted with auxiliary fuel tanks, intentionally overflew the Soviet Sakhalin and Kuril Islands and areas near the major port/military complex of Vladivostok.[29] It is not clear if US national leadership was aware of or approved these missions.

These are the earliest known *deliberate* US overflights of the Cold War, with the purpose of assessing Soviet aviation capabilities. When the Korean War erupted in June 1950, President Harry S. Truman restricted overflights as well as reconnaissance missions anywhere

along the Soviet periphery that might be considered provocative. Once the Soviet Union and China had intervened in the Korean War, these restrictions ceased and President Truman approved deep-penetration overflights of the Soviet Far East *outside* the conflict area. There was particular concern about airfields in the Soviet Far East that could be used as bomber bases for overt Soviet participation in the Korean War—or for long-range bomber attacks against the United States. In December 1950, the president personally authorized two deep-penetration flights to seek out such bases. These flights were not flown because the aircraft, a brand-new B-47B Stratojet specially fitted with cameras for the missions, caught fire and burned on an airfield in Alaska on 15 August 1951. The next such missions would not be undertaken until the following year.

Believing modified bombers preferable for the reconnaissance role, Gen. Curtis LeMay rejected the proposed U-2 spyplane for the SAC. *Underwood Archives/UIG/Bridgeman Images*

These Far East overflights, in the spring of 1952, saw an unusual teaming of US Navy and Air Force piston-engine aircraft—a P2V-3W Neptune patrol aircraft and an RB-50 Superfortress. The Neptune, with two piston engines and a crew of ten, had a very-long-range capability. Its main features for electronic reconnaissance were the large AN/APS-20 search radar and specialized ELINT gear. This was an unpressurized aircraft with a top speed of only 345 miles per hour (555 kilometers per hour) and a ceiling of 32,000 feet (9,750 meters). The RB-50, with four piston engines, was a pressurized aircraft with a maximum speed of 395 miles per hour (635 kilometers per hour) and a ceiling of some 37,000 feet (11,300 meters). It was fitted for photographic reconnaissance.

After the P2V-3W flew test flights against Alaskan air defense radars, the two-plane team took off from Kodiak or Shemya in the Aleutian Islands and overflew Soviet airfields and air defense sites (mainly radar installations). The planes flew inland some 15 to 20 miles (24 to 32 kilometers), with the navy aircraft using its electronic intercept equipment to locate targets for the other aircraft's cameras. The P2V-3W flew at 15,000 feet (4,570 meters) with the RB-50 following above and behind. From 2 April to 16 June 1952, the two planes flew eight or nine missions against Soviet installations from the Kamchatka Peninsula north to the Bering Straits and Wrangel Island. Soviet MiG-15 fighters intercepted the US aircraft on two of these overflights, once over the Bering Strait near St. Lawrence Island and once over Soviet territory. In both instances, the MiGs flew alongside the American aircraft and took photographs, but did not fire on them.[30]

In this period, US radio intercepts indicated that Soviet Tu-4 bombers—direct copies of the US B-29 Superfortress—were being deployed to airfields in the Far East. If nuclear weapons were available, the Tu-4 bomber (given the NATO codename Bull) could reach the northwestern United States on one-way bombing missions.

Subsequently, the US Air Force and the Central Intelligence Agency (CIA) proposed deep-penetration overflights. A plan for two missions by camera-carrying aircraft was given to President Truman on 12 August

From April to June 1952, a US Air Force RB-50 Superfortress like this participated in overflights of the Soviet Far East alongside a US Navy P2V-3W Neptune. *National Archives and Records Administration*

1952. He approved a mission over the Chukotka Peninsula but refused support for a more southern route—over Anadyr, Magadan, and the Kamchatka Peninsula—as too dangerous.

In July and August 1952, SAC modified two B47B Stratojet bombers with special cameras for the overflight. The B-47B, which had entered service with SAC in October 1951, was powered by six turbojet engines and could reach a maximum speed of 516 miles per hour (830 kilometers per hour) and an altitude of 41,000 feet (12,500 meters). One of these B-47B aircraft made the first USAF deep-penetration overflight of the Soviet Union on 15 October 1952. Both modified aircraft took off from Eielson AFB at Fairbanks, Alaska, the second a backup in the event that the first aircraft experienced problems. The planes were refueled in flight by two KC-97 Stratofreighter tanker aircraft.

While the backup plane circled over the Chukchi Sea collecting ELINT, the lead B-47B proceeded to fly over the most northeastern portion of Siberia at altitudes above 40,000 feet (12,200 meters). Soviet radar detected the plane and fighters attempted an intercept, but without success. The B-47B mission took almost eight hours and covered a 3,500-mile (5,630-kilometer) route, of which some 800 miles (1,290 kilometers) were over Soviet territory, with the plane reaching as far west as the city of Igarka. Although some of the area was covered by clouds, the mission collected valuable photographs. Both B-47s returned safely to Eielson.[31]

Because of the difficulty in gaining Washington's approval for American crews to overfly the European Soviet Union, SAC approached the British government for assistance. The command had an urgent need for radar-scope images of potential targets in the USSR. General Nathan B. Twining, air force chief of staff, and General LeMay, then head of SAC, asked the Royal Air Force (RAF) to undertake the first deep-penetration flights over the Soviet Union. The RAF might have been flying some shallow-penetration flights over Soviet territory since at least late 1948, although publicly available evidence is limited. Using the wooden, twin-engine Mosquito PR.34, British pilots had reportedly overflown portions of the southern Soviet Union from airfields in Iraq, Crete, and perhaps elsewhere.[32]

In spring 1951, three RAF aircrews had been sent to the United States to train on the RB-45, returning to Sculthorpe later that year with four USAF RB-45C

Tornados. With RAF markings applied to the planes, British crews prepared to fly night-penetration missions to obtain radar pictures of potential targets for SAC and British Bomber Command. The planes flew a trial mission over East Germany on the night of 21–22 March, 1952.

The first RB-45C overflights of the Soviet Union were flown on the night of 17–18 April with three aircraft, their targets being Soviet long-range bomber bases and air defenses. The planes took off from Sculthorpe and were refueled over Denmark and West Germany by USAF KB-29 tankers. The RB-45C spyplanes then streaked eastward, entering Soviet airspace at three different points. They flew three different routes: the northern one overflying the Baltic states, the second flying as far east as Moscow, and the third heading southeast over the Ukraine. The flights took up to 10.5 hours, with the planes overflying their targets in darkness at about 35,000 feet (10,670 meters). While over Soviet territory, they were tracked by radar and fighter intercepts were attempted, but without success. They were again refueled by KB-29s on their return flights.

In marked contrast to U-2 flights several years later, the RAF crews had been given cover stories—that they had become lost—and they carried bags of false navigation plots and maps. All three planes returned safely to base, their overflights providing SAC and RAF Bomber Command planners with invaluable target information. General LeMay himself congratulated the lead RAF crew. Intelligence historian R. Cargill Hall summarized the flights:

> In approving the mission, [Prime Minister Winston] Churchill took a breathtaking political risk. . . . If any of the RB-45Cs had been brought down, the resulting outcry probably would have led to Churchill's unseating as prime minister. But balanced against this was the need of Western intelligence to acquire radar-scope photographs of specific military installations.[33]

The British were developing their own high-altitude reconnaissance aircraft in the early 1950s. A remarkable aircraft, the English Electric Canberra twin-turbojet light bomber became operational in early 1951. The

The remarkable English Electric Canberra light bomber became operational in early 1951. The PR.3 photorecon variant entered squadron service in late 1952. *National Archives and Records Administration*

PR.3 photorecon variant entered squadron service in late 1952. (There is some disputed evidence that Canberra overflight missions took place in 1953.) The first target proposed to the RAF was the reported missile test facility at Kapustin Yar on the Volga River, near Stalingrad (now Volgograd). Although Prime Minister Churchill had briefly halted RAF RB-45C overflights, his concern about Soviet missile developments apparently led to approval of the mission.

RAF Canberras reportedly flew two penetration missions over Kapustin Yar as part of Operation Robin. Details of these missions are still held secret by the British government, but at least one reportedly flew in August 1953.[34] The daylight flights originated from Giebelstadt, West Germany—and they were tracked from takeoff by Soviet radar. Fighters made several attempts to intercept the first Canberra flight and the plane suffered some damage, but it was able to land safely in Iran. The photos, however, were blurred because of vibrations caused by the damage to the aircraft and were of little value.

There would be one more RAF overflight series flown with RB-45C Tornado aircraft on loan from the United States: On the night of 28–29 April 1954, three planes took off from Sculthorpe. Two flew photo missions over the central Soviet Union and the third flew a southern route toward Kapustin Yar. The two aircraft on the central route encountered fighters but were able to take radar photos of their targets and return safely to Sculthorpe.

The Kapustin Yar RB-45C flight encountered heavy and accurate anti-aircraft fire as it streaked over the southern route at 36,000 feet (10,970 meters). The pilot decided to abort the mission short of its principal target but still obtained valuable photographs. As the lone RB-45C flew toward its home base, it rendezvoused with a USAF KB-29 tanker over West Germany. The planes were unable to connect properly, though, and the RB-45C landed at an airfield near Munich instead of returning to Sculthorpe. Years later, the CIA concluded that the operation had been compromised by Kim Philby, one of the major Soviet moles operating within the British government at the time.[35]

Meanwhile, SAC sponsored the development of a specialized photoreconnaissance variant of the B-47 bomber, which had been in service as a strategic bomber since November 1953. Flown by a crew of three, the B-47 was, in the words of aviation historian Bill Gunston, "a design so advanced technically as to appear genuinely futuristic."[36] The B-47, he continued, "ended up as the foundation of America's strategic power in the Jet Age and the most important single weapon in the world through the perilous years of the 1950s."

In April 1954, SAC deployed several RB-47E spyplane variants to Fairford, near Oxford, England. The SAC leadership decided to fly a deep-penetration of the Soviet Union to evaluate the feasibility of such flights as well as strategic bomber strikes. Early on 8 May, three of these aircraft launched from Fairford toward the Kola Peninsula in the Arctic, which contained several Soviet air and naval bases. The mission followed by one week the overflights carried out by the three RAF-flown RB-45C aircraft over the central and southern Soviet Union.

The three RB-47Es were refueled in flight. Two of the aircraft turned back toward their base before overflying Soviet territory, as their crews had been briefed. The third penetrated Soviet airspace, passing over Murmansk at noon and flying at just over 500 miles per hour (800 kilometers per hour) at 40,000 feet (12,200 meters). The RB-47E flew across the Kola Peninsula, over the shipyard complex at Arkhangel'sk, and then turned southwest, returning on a route that took the plane over Finland, Sweden, and Norway. It refueled again over the North Sea before landing at Fairford. Several MiG fighters attempted to intercept the spyplane, and the RB-47E suffered minor damage from cannon fire. The aircraft's twin 20mm tail guns had jammed after firing a single burst at the plane's pursuers.

A year later, in March 1955, three RB-45C Tornados made another nighttime reconnaissance flight over the Soviet Union. This time the planes were flown by USAF crews. Taking off from Sculthorpe, they flew routes generally similar to the previous RAF flights, although the specific targets differed. All three planes returned safely to the British base. ∎

THE KOREAN WAR

When the Korean War began in June 1950, the United States used RB-29 piston and, later, RB-45C Tornado turbojet aircraft for strategic photoreconnaissance of North Korea. As early as 22 August 1950, antiaircraft guns from north of the Yalu River—which divides North Korea from China and Russia—fired at RB-29s reconnoitering the border from *south* of the river. This was the first hostile Chinese action against US aircraft. From the autumn of 1950, these US aircraft required fighter escorts to protect them from the Soviet-piloted MiG-15 interceptors—with Chinese markings—that plagued the North Korean skies. They did attack and damage some US recon aircraft over North Korea, but no aircraft were lost.

On occasion, US spyplanes overflew northeast China, Manchuria, and the Vladivostok area of the Soviet Union during the conflict. The United States, when engaged in a United Nations–sanctioned operation, could legally overfly sanctuaries used by an unannounced "cobelligerent" state. Nevertheless, the US government exercised close control, since such flights could provoke international political crises and possibly escalate military crises.[37]

These overflights became imperative because of the massive Communist Chinese intervention that began in the fall of 1950, including the MiG-15 fighter buildup north of the Yalu River. In response, Truman began authorizing overflights north of the Yalu in winter 1950–1951. RF-80 Shooting Star photo aircraft first penetrated the area, providing valuable intelligence of airfields just north of the Yalu.

In 1952 and 1953, special recon versions of the F-86A Sabre—RF-86s that could fly up to 55,000 feet (16,800 m)—took over these missions. Some 20 such missions were able to reach photo targets as far as Harbin, Manchuria. That coverage was especially important for revealing Soviet support to the Chinese and North Koreans. The camera-armed RF-86s normally flew north with F-86 fighter sweeps; once the fighters engaged MiGs *south* of the Yalu, the photo planes would evade the melee and streak north on their reconnaissance runs. A few RF-86 flights also were flown over the important Soviet port city of Vladivostok. Chinese and Soviet air defense reaction was considerable, but no RF-86s were lost.

ABOVE AND OPPOSITE: RF-80 Shooting Star photo aircraft provided valuable intelligence of Communist Chinese airfields just north of the Yalu River in winter 1950–1951. *National Archives and Records Administration*

Also important were SAC-operated RB-45C Tornado overflights, which extended down into central China and were flown at night because, like the RB-29, the RB-45 was vulnerable to MiG-15 interception. On 4 December 1950, an RB-45C on a routine mission was shot down by MiG-15 fighters while flying along the Yalu River. In late 1952, there was at least one reported low-level, daytime RB-45C overflight of Vladivostok. These RB-45 and RF-86 missions were vital in assessing the Chinese and Soviet support of North Korea.[38]

Thousands of USAF tactical reconnaissance missions over the Korean peninsula—flown mainly by RF-51 Mustangs and RF-80s in the daytime and by RB-26 Invaders at night—provided vital intelligence for UN ground forces. Together, air force strategic and tactical aircraft in the Korean theater flew 2,400 photo sorties in May 1952 (a peak performance), and then averaged almost 1,800 sorties per month through March 1953. These flights provided US ground forces with 64,657 photographic negatives in March 1953 alone. This effort was in addition to extensive navy and Marine Corps photo missions, most by F2H-2P Banshees flown from aircraft carriers and from land bases.[39]

During this period, US Navy F2H-2P Banshee turbojets also overflew mainland China, which had been controlled by the communists since 1949. In late 1952, Banshees from the aircraft carrier *Kearsarge* (CV 33) flew several missions, some as far as 200 miles (320 kilometers) into China, primarily to search out the status of airfields.[40] US carrier-type reconnaissance aircraft would again overfly China in 1955. Between 11 May and 12 June 1955, F2H-2P Banshees from a land-based marine photo squadron overflew Fukien (Fujian) Province. The unarmed photo planes, some escorted by marine-piloted F2H-2 fighters, flew from Tainan airfield on Taiwan, seeking evidence that China was planning an amphibious assault against Taiwan. A total of 27 overflights were flown by the marines, whose photo aircraft were normally based in South Korea.[41] ■

MASS OVERFLIGHTS

Massive US military overflight operations against the Soviet Union were flown between 21 March and 10 May 1956. SAC flew 156 overflights from Thule, Greenland, in Operation Homerun. Supported by 28 KC-97 tankers, 16 RB-47E photo planes and 5 RB-47H electronic reconnaissance aircraft were used. The aircraft took off almost daily, overflew the Arctic Ocean, and penetrated Soviet Arctic territory in pie-shaped sectors from the Kola Peninsula in the west to the Bering Strait in the east. The planes that overflew the eastern areas landed at Eielson AFB in Alaska to refuel before returning to Thule.

The missions, averaging more than three per day, were normally some 3,400 miles (5,470 kilometers), with an RB-47E and RB-47H sometimes flying as a team. On 6–7 May 1956, six RB-47Es flew abreast over their Soviet targets in a "massed overflight," mapping the nuclear test site on Novaya Zemlya Island, searching out airfields and radar sites along the coast, and gathering data on Soviet Arctic industries. The Soviets made few attempts to intercept the US planes. These remote areas apparently were not yet as well guarded by Soviet radars as the European and Far Eastern borders. At the time, US intelligence analysts believed that those areas held the advance airfields from which Soviet strategic bombers would be launched against the United States.

Perhaps the best comment on Project Homerun was that of historian Cargill Hall: "To this day, the

SAC Thule missions remain one of the most incredible demonstrations of professional aviation skill ever seen in any military organization at any time."[42]

SAC crews would fly only one more Soviet overflight mission. In November 1956, SAC deployed six of the new RB-57D Canberra aircraft, a big-wing modification of the American RB-57A version of the British Canberra, to Yokota Air Base outside of Tokyo, Japan. In contrast to RB-57 missions flown by US Far East Air Forces, SAC flew all six aircraft on a single mission on 11 December. Three aircraft acted as decoys while the others photographed the Vladivostok area. This operation resulted in a serious Soviet diplomatic protest, the most severe in a string of them that year. Apparently, before President Dwight D. Eisenhower had approved this SAC mission, he had been told the Soviets could not detect the Canberras. "On 18 December 1956, an agitated president ordered a cessation of all American overflights of denied territory. . . . The Air Force SENSINT (sensitive intelligence) program ended with his December edict," wrote Hall.[43] An overflight program using balloons, which had also garnered a series of vehement Soviet protests, was also halted. ▪

Extensive US Navy and Marine Corps photo missions over Korea were conducted from aircraft carriers and from land bases, most by F2H-2P Banshees. *Nicholas A. Veronico collection*

Massive SAC overflight operations against the Soviet Union between 21 March and 10 May 1956, from Thule, Greenland, were supported in part by 16 RB-47Es. *National Archives and Records Administration*

OTHER PACIFIC OVERFLIGHTS

SAC was not the only USAF command conducting overflights. After the Korean War ceasefire in July 1953, the Far East Air Forces (FEAF, later Pacific Air Forces) remained intensely interested in Soviet, North Korean, and Chinese air power.[44] Beginning in early 1954, Eisenhower approved occasional overflights of the Vladivostok, Khabarovsk, Sakhalin, and Kurile Island areas of the Soviet Far East. North Korea was overflown several times, and spyplane missions also covered targets from Harbin in the north to Shanghai in central China. From March 1954 until December 1955, the improved RF-86F Sabres—dubbed Haymakers—flew at least 14 overflights of these countries.

Beginning in late 1955, the US Air Force introduced highly specialized recon versions of the B-57 Canberra bomber and North American F-100 Super Sabre fighter to the Pacific. Three RF-100As deployed

to Yokota, Japan, and took over the RF-86 mission. Under Project Slick Chick, these modified birds could reach over 55,000 feet (16,800 meters) and a combat radius (at a lower altitude) of up to 700 miles (1,130 kilometers), allowing them to cover the same areas as the RF-86, but with a better camera system and a supersonic dash capability.

The other new air force program featured a special version of the RB-57A, itself the first reconnaissance version of the B-57 bomber adapted by the Martin firm from the British Canberra. Under Project Heart Throb, Martin provided FEAF four lightened RB-57A aircraft with a special high-altitude camera configuration. These RB-57s had a higher altitude capability and increased range compared to the RF-100s. An early mission illustrates the recon tactics. On 26 November 1955, a Heart Throb RB-57A launched from northern

Three RF-100As were deployed to Germany in May 1955. These "Slick Chicks" had a combat radius sufficient to cover East Germany and western Czechoslovakia. Note the side bulges to accommodate the camera. *US Air Force photo*

Japan, flew north at a 100-foot (30-meter) altitude to the east of Soviet-occupied Sakhalin, a 600-mile-long (965-kilometer) island bristling with military facilities. Northeast of Sakhalin, having escaped detection by Soviet radar and thus gaining surprise, the RB-57 climbed to more than 55,000 feet (16,800 meters) and streaked south at maximum speed down the full length of Sakhalin, gaining photography of the entire island. In the Pacific Theater, four successful Heart Throb missions were flown out of six attempted before the military overflight missions ended in December 1956. ■

OTHER EUROPEAN OVERFLIGHTS

The European Theater also received Slick Chick RF-100A and Heart Throb RB-57A aircraft. Three Slick Chicks deployed to Europe in May 1955. To keep them inconspicuous, they were located at Bitburg Air Base in Germany, home of a USAFE F-86 fighter wing. These RF-100s had a combat radius sufficient to cover East Germany and western Czechoslovakia from above 50,000 feet (15,240 meters). If deployed to a base near Munich, they could reach western Hungary and northern Yugoslavia. Penetrations into "denied" airspace paid unexpected dividends when the entire Soviet air defense radar and communications network activated in response to these flights: US SIGINT collectors had a field day. As in the Pacific, the RF-100's supersonic speed and high-altitude capability protected the aircraft from Soviet interception.

In August 1955 the four European Heart Throb RB-57A Canberras deployed to Rhein-Main Air Base in

West Germany. They operated at altitudes up to 66,000 feet (20,120 meters) at high-subsonic speeds out to the Polish-Soviet border. The notorious European weather, as well as other limits on overflights, meant that only about 25 productive overflights (6 Slick Chick and 19 Heart Throb) were flown before the two programs were cancelled in August 1956.

The US Navy also sought intelligence on potential targets in the Soviet Union from the European side. The staff of the US Sixth Fleet in the Mediterranean proposed using carrier-based F2H-2P Banshee photo aircraft to overfly potential nuclear targets in Caucasus, Crimea, and Ukraine. At the time, US aircraft carriers deployed to the Mediterranean carried nuclear strike aircraft. Under the plan—called Operation Steve Brody—at least four F2H-2P photo planes were to be launched from a carrier operating south of Thessaloniki, Greece, in the Aegean Sea. The mission would have required the aircraft to fly for about four hours over the Soviet Union to obtain the needed coverage. The proposal for the highly sensitive photo mission was hand-carried to Washington in May 1952, but Secretary of Defense Robert Lovett refused to take the proposal to the president.[45] ■

ENTER THE U-2 SPYPLANE

There was a highly significant reason that the Slick Chick and Heart Throb overflights were cancelled in the summer of 1956: a remarkable replacement aircraft had just arrived in Western Europe. Long before the 1956 cessation of military overflights, President Eisenhower had expressed serious concern that the loss of a military aircraft and the possible capture of its crew could precipitate a major crisis, or even war. An alternative aircraft offered by the CIA answered his concerns—the new, very-high-altitude Lockheed U-2.

The U-2 would transform the overflight reconnaissance process and greatly increase the hitherto grossly inadequate knowledge of the Soviet Union and other denied countries. It ostensibly was not a military vehicle, but its origins were military. In 1952, the air force had generated a requirement for a high-altitude reconnaissance aircraft. Among the responding designs was the eventual winner, the Martin RB-57D big-wing, a redesigned Canberra. An unsolicited company proposal from the Lockheed "Skunk Works"—headed by legendary designer and engineer Kelly Johnson—proposed a single-engine, glider-like aircraft that could collect intelligence from altitudes above 70,000 feet (21,300 meters).

The air force resisted this aircraft, preferring multiengine spyplanes derived from bomber designs. But the CIA embraced it. U-2 performance would exceed that of the RB-57D, and the CIA saw it as the ideal vehicle for overflights, closing the still-vast geographic gaps in photographic coverage inside that secretive nation. Other information indicated that the Soviets were beginning to develop ballistic missiles—but where, how, and how soon this hugely significant capability could become operational were vital, unanswered questions. Further, many Soviet defense industries were as yet unlocated and in many cases unknown.

The U-2s were deployed first to Lakenheath in Britain in May 1956, then to Wiesbaden in West Germany in June. The first operational U-2 mission, flown over East Germany and Poland on 20 June 1956, was deemed a major success.[46] Two more flights over Eastern Europe were flown in early July.

With President Eisenhower's approval, the CIA flew its first U-2 mission over the Soviet Union on the Fourth of July. The second Soviet overflight took place the next day. The Soviets detected these and the ensuing three missions, and launched not only fighters but protests. CIA photo interpreters were immediately impressed with the product: "For the first time we had the capability to derive precise, irrefutable, up-to-date data on the vast land mass and physical installations of our principal adversary," noted top CIA photo analyst Dino Brugioni.[47]

Eisenhower was also highly impressed with the intelligence that these missions produced, and more overflights were cautiously authorized and executed in the next four years. Then-CIA Special Assistant Richard M. Bissell recalled that the president would study each proposed route in detail and occasionally eliminate a flight leg or make other corrections.[48]

The CIA quickly moved its West German base to Giebelstadt and obtained the use of several overseas bases, notably in Turkey, Pakistan, and Japan. The vast, unknown Soviet spaces were slowly revealed, mission by mission, and the United States gradually learned the emerging truth: the bomber and missile "gaps" existed not in favor of the Soviet Union, but of the United States.

By 1959, the focus of US strategic intelligence had shifted to Soviet ballistic missile systems. U-2 missions had provided intelligence on several test and development centers and were probing for operational missile bases. Soviet Premier Nikita Khrushchev had boasted that they were "producing missiles like sausages," thus adding fuel to western concerns that a "missile gap" existed. Missile target coverage was so effective that, by the time of the Gary Powers shootdown on 1 May 1960, leading experts and Eisenhower himself stated that the missile gap was in the favor of the United States. The U-2 aircraft had done excellent work, solidifying the sense that the United States must rely on reconnaissance, by air and space, to monitor its major adversaries carefully—a fact that remains true today.[49]

The U-2 piloted by Powers was shot down by a V-75 Dvina missile—known in the West as the SA-2 Guideline. When the U-2 entered service in July 1956, the CIA projected that it could not be detected by radar over the Soviet Union and that it would be invulnerable to Soviet air defenses until about 1960. Contrary to this position, every flight over the Soviet Union was detected, and most were fully tracked.

When the first U-2 fell to an SA-2 missile, the event occurred precisely at the time estimated by the CIA. Before Gary Powers was shot down, though, there had been 25 successful U-2 overflights of the Soviet Union (two flown by RAF pilots).

Soviet development of the SA-2 strategic air defense missile had begun in 1952–1953 and prototype tests occurred about 1954, with initial deployments three years later. Thousands of SA-2 missiles were deployed in the Soviet Union around key military, industrial, and scientific installations as well as major cities. On 1 May 1960, eight SA-2s from three batteries at Sverdlovsk (now Yekaterinburg) were fired, a salvo that, in addition to disabling Powers's aircraft, scored a direct hit on a Soviet fighter sent aloft to intercept the U-2. (Colonel Oleg Penkovskiy—the Soviet military intelligence officer who spied for the West—reported that 14 SA-2 missiles were fired at the aircraft, but later sources revealed that the number was 8.)

The resulting public furor over the U-2 shootdown, including the collapse of a four-power summit meeting that summer, led President Eisenhower to prohibit further overflights of the Soviet Union. He knew that the US intelligence community was about to enter the era of space satellite photography with the first images from the Corona satellite returned to earth soon after, in August 1960. While it took time for satellite imagery to approach the quality and the responsiveness of the U-2's product, it eventually made the Soviet and other threats to the West better understood.

CIA-piloted U-2s were also collecting intelligence elsewhere. Allen Dulles, the head of the CIA from 1953 to 1961, reported to Eisenhower that, as of July 1960, CIA U-2s had flown 38 missions over the Soviet Union and Soviet Bloc countries, photographing about 1,752,000 square miles. Also, they had flown 13 missions over Communist China and Tibet, covering another 1,061,000 square miles, and 239 missions over non-bloc nations, providing photography of some 12,310,000 square miles.[50] Soon the Strategic Air Command obtained U-2 aircraft and, in the 1960s, supplanted CIA as the American operator of the spyplane. ■

PERIPHERAL RECONNAISSANCE CONTINUES

The US peripheral recon program begun in 1946 was expanded greatly in the 1950s as the SAC RB-50s were supplanted by the newer spyplane versions of the B-47 Stratojet bomber. By the mid-1950s, specialized SAC RB-47s were flying SIGINT and photo missions around almost the entire periphery of the Soviet Union, continuing the collection on the improving Soviet air defense network, a vital concern if SAC was to fight a nuclear conflict with the Soviet Union.

SAC's RB-47 fleet was gradually replaced by the new, more capable RC-135, which entered service in the early 1960s. RC-135s, developed from the Boeing 707 commercial airliner, collected both COMINT and ELINT, recording radio and radar transmissions. By 1967, the last RB-47 had been withdrawn from intelligence collection. Into the twenty-first century, the RC-135 remains the centerpiece of US airborne SIGINT collection.

Similarly, US Navy patrol aircraft flew peripheral reconnaissance missions in the various sea areas from the Baltic to the Black and Mediterranean Seas, off the Soviet Pacific coast from Vladivostok up to the Bering

In the early 1960s, SAC's RB-47 fleet was gradually replaced by the new, more capable RC-135, developed from the Boeing 707 commercial airliner. This is an RC-135V. *Dana Bell collection via Walter Wright*

The US Navy's WV-2/EC-121 airborne early-warning aircraft collected high-priority SIGINT on Soviet and other nations' naval targets worldwide. The aircraft were, of course, built on Kelly Johnson's and Hall Hibbard's stylish Lockheed Constellation airframe. *National Archives and Records Administration*

Strait, and off the coasts of North Korea and China. Seeking out intelligence primarily related to Soviet naval facilities were, initially, PB4Y-2 Privateers, followed by the more advanced P4M Mercator and P2V Neptune. All were piston-engine aircraft, with the P2V-5F and later Neptune variants having two turbojet pods to provide higher "dash" speeds. In time, two specialized squadrons were established to operate the navy's land-based spyplanes: VQ-1 and VQ-2. Squadron VQ-1 was established as Electronic Countermeasures Squadron 1 at Naval Air Station Iwakuni, Japan, on 1 June 1955, initially flying P4M1Q Mercator aircraft; VQ-2 was established as ECM Squadron 2 on 1 September 1955, at Port Lyautey, Morocco, first flying the P4M-1Q and the A3D-1Q (later EA-3B) aircraft. The twin-turbojet A3D Skywarrior was a carrier-based aircraft, at 35 tons the largest aircraft to operate from carriers. Both VQ-1 and VQ-2 eventually received Lockheed WV-2Q long-range maritime recon aircraft, later redesignated EC-121M. These, modifications of the navy's WV-2/EC-121 Constellation airborne early-warning aircraft, continued collecting high-priority SIGINT on Soviet and other nations' naval targets worldwide. A VQ-1 EC-121M was shot down by MiG-21s on 15 April 1969 off the eastern North Korean coast while on a peripheral mission; all 31 navy and marine crewmen were killed. This was the last recon aircraft lost to hostile action during Cold War recon operations.

National-level control of these sensitive flights occurred from the beginning, although it was somewhat loose at first. Initially, the main tasking and operational control originated at the air force and navy theater level, with guidance from the services' national-level headquarters.

Defense Department and presidential interest began in 1947, formalized in what came to be known as the Peacetime Aerial Reconnaissance Program (PARPRO). This covered not only the peripheral missions, but also the overflights. A Joint Chiefs of Staff (JCS) directive on 9 April 1947 noted the "necessity of conducting reconnaissance in close proximity to Communist territory and fully recognizes the risk of shooting incidents which may result." This directive laid out basic rules that the services were expected to follow.[51] Over time, the JCS, secretary of defense, and president exercised increasing control over the peripheral flights as it became manifest in the 1950s and into the 1960s that, while these missions collected vital intelligence, they were very sensitive to the countries being spied upon and were fraught both with military and political risks.

Besides the SAC and Navy PARPRO missions, USAFE and FEAF (later renamed PACAF) flew spy missions around the Iron Curtain. By 1952, USAFE was coping with mounting requirements for recon information that swamped the command's few, aging specialized aircraft. That year, USAFE sent a high-priority request to Air Force Chief of Staff Gen. Hoyt S. Vandenberg for an aircraft with photo capability for high-altitude peripheral missions. General Vandenberg established a special organization to find, equip, and rapidly deploy such an aircraft. That organization, ultimately given the name Big Safari, produced a modified Boeing C-97A Stratocruiser cargo aircraft with a highly secret camera featuring a 240-inch (6,096mm) focal length, originally designed for the RB-36 strategic bomber. This system, given the codename Pie Face, was deployed to USAFE within a year and collected high-resolution peripheral photography from altitudes above 30,000 feet (9,140 meters) until late 1962.

In the early 1950s, USAFE also received special photo and ELINT collection versions of the C-54 Skymaster, the widely flown military version of the Douglas DC-4 four-engine transport. These modifications also were the responsibility of Big Safari, and the aircraft would be very active in the European Theater through the early 1960s. The burgeoning USAFE intelligence requirements demanded ever more technical solutions and expanded aerial recon efforts. Consequently, the European PARPRO program led to the creation of the 7499th Support Group at Wiesbaden, with three subordinate squadrons:

- 7405th Support Squadron (formerly the 7499th Squadron; photo and ELINT C-54s, then CT-29s and C-97s, and later C-130s)

- 7406th Support Squadron (aerial COMINT, RB-50s and later C-130s)

- 7407th Support Squadron (high-altitude photo RF-100s and RB-57s

These units supplied the European Theater's need for peripheral reconnaissance of the Warsaw Pact and other potentially hostile nations in Europe and the Middle East. In combination with their counterpart units in the Pacific Theater, and SAC and navy assets, they would also contribute toward solving national-level intelligence requirements. By the mid-1970s, however, as photo and SIGINT satellites became more capable and responsive—and as SAC acquired additional RC-135 aircraft and could expand theater SIGINT collection—the need for the 7406th and 7407th Squadrons diminished, and they were deactivated. However, the 7405th, which had been bolstered in the early 1960s by specialized photo and ELINT C-97 transports as well as CT-29 "courier" photo aircraft, soldiered on because of its unique collection capability in the Berlin corridors, where the spyplanes could legally overfly many of the massive Soviet garrisons and airfields in East Germany, collecting intelligence every day if required. Indeed, in 1976, the 7405th acquired three C-130E Hercules aircraft capable of multisource, near-real-time collection, which provided unique coverage almost to the day of German reunification on 3 October 1990, when the corridors were abolished. At that time, the German government took responsibility for watching the diminishing Soviet presence in the area until final withdrawal in 1994.

The more than 15,000 corridor missions flown from 1946 through 1990 were remarkable because, despite their collecting on very large and important Soviet military dispositions, the corridor-flying aircraft were seldom harassed and never attacked. The same applied to the similar British and French corridor missions, coordinated with the US effort. The reasons for Soviet tolerance of these missions probably included the legality of Allied flights in the corridors, the Soviet ability to monitor the flights closely, the Western ability to keep their intelligence activities very secret (thus avoiding public embarrassment to the Soviets), and the fact that the flights almost never strayed outside the corridor boundaries.

US Air Force theater PARPRO missions in the Pacific generally followed the pattern in Europe. When the Korean War ended, SAC inactivated its recon squadron in the theater, and FEAF's 6091st Reconnaissance Squadron was created. The 6091st inherited SAC's RB-29s and picked up the COMINT/ELINT mission, continuing to fly recon missions from Yokota, Japan, along the Soviet Pacific coast as well as off the coast of China. In 1956 and 1957, the RB-29s were replaced by five RB-50 Superfortresses, which specialized in airborne COMINT collection. These, in turn, were replaced by 1960 with C-130 Hercules, having greatly improved COMINT collection capability.

By the early 1960s, the 6091st also acquired a pair of C-97s configured for photo collection, one of which also had an ELINT capability. The principal mission for these aircraft was to fly against targets in Southeast Asia nations such as Indonesia, Burma, Laos, Cambodia, and North Vietnam, as well as North Korea. Clark AFB in the Philippines was the major base of operations for these specialized RB-50, C-130, and C-97 spyplanes, all of which were products of the Big Safari program. Indeed, some of the aircraft were assigned over time to both the European and the Pacific Theaters.

In 1964, the increasingly violent conflict in Vietnam required 6091st aircraft to deploy frequently to Southeast Asia. The first COMINT aircraft to collect in the Tonkin Gulf in July 1964 was a C-130B Hercules. The 6091st Squadron became so heavily involved in the Vietnam conflict that, for several months in 1967, the 7406th Squadron from Europe provided additional C-130s and crews to keep up the required collection against Soviet, Chinese, and North Korean targets.

As in Europe, by the late 1960s SAC had acquired enough of the ubiquitous RC-135 recon aircraft to enable it to conduct the Pacific Theater COMINT and ELINT PARPRO missions, and the 6091st—with its propeller-driven C-97s and C-130s—was inactivated. ■

BRITISH AND FRENCH PERIPHERAL RECONNAISSANCE

Like their US Air Force counterparts, the RAF Bomber Command recognized the need for airborne SIGINT missions along the periphery of the Soviet Union and the Warsaw Pact to gain detailed insight into their air defense capabilities. In the early postwar years, the two countries agreed to work closely to collect and share this data. Thus, SAC and Bomber Command cooperated to build a target and air defense database.

But in the early 1950s, the British had neither a very-long-range bomber nor a comparable ELINT reconnaissance aircraft. Several aircraft were in development for these roles, but as an interim

A 7405th Operations Squadron C-130E SIGINT and imagery collector lands at Berlin Tempelhof Airfield in November 1978 after a recon flight in the Berlin corridors over East Germany. Note Military Airlift Command markings to hide its intelligence role. *Peter Seemann via John F. Bessette*

solution, the United States loaned the British 87 B-29 bombers and 3 RB-29 recon variants, all of which were given the RAF name "Washington." The three recon Washingtons were modified in 1952 and 1953, with their first operational mission flying out of an RAF base in Iraq, over Turkey, and against the Soviet Black Sea coast on 18 December 1952. ELINT Washingtons would fly many missions along the Soviet/Warsaw Pact periphery until their withdrawal in 1957. One also flew at least one mission against Egypt in support of the 1956 Anglo-French-Israeli invasion of the Suez Canal.[52]

The British quickly realized that a more advanced ELINT aircraft was needed, because the Washington would soon be vulnerable to the improving Soviet air defenses. Noting the high speed and altitude capabilities of the new Canberra bomber, they modified several for the task. The first Canberra ELINT missions were flown in September 1953 over the Baltic, with subsequent missions over the Black and Caspian Seas from a base in Iraq. Despite its capacity for only two ELINT operators, the Canberra would be an important asset for 21 years, flying its last operational mission in June 1974.[53]

The need for more SIGINT operators aboard the aircraft led the British to develop a version of the de Havilland Comet airliner. From 1958 until 1974 Comet R Mk 2s flew peripheral missions along the Soviet frontier, collecting COMINT and ELINT. The main effort was along the East-West German border and the Baltic and Barents Seas, but especially interesting were missions flying from Iraq, then Iran, along the Soviet-Iranian border and into the Caspian Sea. UK/US coordination of flight schedules and the sharing of the intelligence "take" from the missions were force multipliers for both countries.

In 1974, three R.1 variants of the Hawker Siddeley Nimrod maritime patrol aircraft supplanted aged Comets and Canberras in the British strategic reconnaissance effort. *Dan Davison, CC Attribution 2.0 Generic*

RC-47s were redesignated EC-47s in the early 1960s when they began carrying ELINT gear consisting of signal intercept and emitter location equipment. They were put to great use during the Vietnam War. *National Archives and Records Administration*

As the Soviet air defense system developed and the Comets and Canberras aged, the British realized they needed yet another aircraft. They chose a specialized recon version of the Hawker Siddeley Nimrod maritime patrol aircraft. In 1974, three Nimrod R.1 variants supplanted the Comets and Canberras. These Nimrods sustained the British strategic reconnaissance effort until 2011.

Like the United States, the British and the French operated reconnaissance aircraft in the Berlin corridors and Control Zone throughout the Cold War, until just before German reunification in October 1990.[54] The British effort was modest compared to that of the United States, with fewer flights per week and a concentration on photography rather than SIGINT. A mix of de Havilland Mosquito and Douglas Dakota (C-47) missions were flown from 1945 to 1947. From 1948 to 1958, the British concentrated on the Avro Anson twin piston–engined light transport, because it was a widely used courier aircraft and its flights could look like normal air transport missions. In the late 1950s, they replaced the Ansons with more modern Hunting Percival Pembrokes. These missions were also easily disguised as courier flights, and they continued in the photo recon role for over 30 years.

By the mid-1980s, the Pembrokes were old and wearing out, their load-carrying capacity too small. The British replaced them with Hawker Siddeley Andover twin-engine turboprop transports, featuring a more sophisticated camera setup and plans to incorporate thermal imaging. The Andover began operational corridor missions in early 1990, just as the Berlin Wall collapsed. The last British corridor mission was flown on 6 September of that year. The program officially ceased at the end of the month.

French corridor missions were considerably different. The French emphasized airborne SIGINT collection rather than imagery, and the missions were more integrated into their larger peripheral reconnaissance program. For example, a French aircraft would fly via one of the corridors to Berlin, remain overnight, and the next day return via the north corridor. Turning north, the route would take the aircraft over the Baltic Sea, where collection would take place along the Polish and Soviet coasts before the aircraft returned home.

The first known French corridor flights were made by Douglas C-47s beginning in 1957. These were replaced beginning in 1962 by Nord Noratlas twin-engine medium transports, with photo collection and enhanced SIGINT collection capability.

Like the British transition from the Pembroke to the Andover, the French moved to a more modern aircraft in the 1980s. Also like the British, they introduced a new SIGINT/photo variant of their latest twin-turboprop transport, the C-160 Transall, almost too late, flying its first corridor mission on 3 July 1989. In tandem with the United States and Britain, France ended corridor flights shortly before the 3 October 1990 reunification of Germany.

France always viewed its recon aircraft as national assets, often redirecting them for tasks in its colonies (and later countries) of interest and concern. Thus its efforts in the corridors and along the Iron Curtain were less intense than those of the British and especially the United States. The withdrawal of France from the military arm of NATO in 1966 also played a part in this de-emphasis. For its overseas missions, the French employed two Douglas DC-8 four-turbojet long-range transports converted for SIGINT collection. Carrying up to 23 "back-end" operators, DC-8s operated from 1976 to 2004. ■

EXOTIC MISSIONS

The May 1960 shootdown of Gary Powers ended the CIA's overflight program against the Soviet Union and its Warsaw Pact allies, but it did not halt U-2 missions elsewhere. From 1949, the CIA supported operations of the Nationalist Chinese government on Formosa (now Taiwan) against mainland China. Beginning in June 1958, a CIA U-2 detachment based in Japan flew missions along and sometimes over the Chinese mainland.

During the 1958 Taiwan Straits crisis, CIA-operated U-2s flew a number of missions in that area to support US and Nationalist activities.[55] Also, U-2 missions over China had often been flown from the CIA's base in Peshawar, Pakistan. Eventually, the CIA handed over U-2 operations to the Taiwanese government, though the United States retained a firm hold on mission tasking and the exploitation of the resulting imagery.

With SAC gaining its own U-2 fleet beginning in 1957, it was increasingly able to monitor nuclear detonations. The U-2s patrolled at first outside Soviet airspace in the Arctic and North Pacific to target Soviet activities, but as nuclear weapons testing proliferated, the U-2s also targeted China.[56] Carrying sensor packages similar to those first deployed on RB-29s in the late 1940s—but to a much higher altitude—the U-2s were extremely valuable for this mission. U-2 sampling missions became a major tool as nations such as France and Israel developed nuclear capabilities. The efforts against France included U-2s operating from US aircraft carriers in 1964. ■

THE CUBAN MISSILE CRISIS

Although various aspects of secret US reconnaissance efforts were occasionally reported in the press, the extent of spyplane operations was largely unknown to the public. That changed dramatically in 1962, when the Soviet Union deployed strategic missiles and troops to Cuba, a newly hostile island nation some 90 miles from the Florida Keys. After a revolution culminating in the emergence of a new regime in Cuba, its leader, Fidel Castro, having been rejected by the US government, cultivated ties with the Soviet Union. As Cuba began receiving Soviet military aid, President Eisenhower authorized occasional CIA U-2 flights over the island, the first successful one on 27 November 1960. Seventeen such missions were flown in April and May 1961 in support of the abortive CIA-sponsored Bay of Pigs invasion, after which overflights took place roughly once a month. SAC also began flying peripheral photo and ELINT RB-47 missions around the island, and the navy increased air and surface-ship surveillance in the area, the latter including SIGINT collection assisted by the National Security Agency.

The Kennedy administration became apprehensive of overflying Cuba, and for a while suspended the overflights. By July 1962, however, other intelligence indicated unusual Soviet activity in Cuba and the overflights resumed. Between early August and 25 October, at the height of the Cuban crisis, 16 successful U-2 overflights furnished to President John F. Kennedy and his advisers vital, detailed information on the buildup of Soviet strategic missiles, tactical missiles for repelling a US invasion, light bomber aircraft, and an extensive air-defense network of fighters and advanced SA-2 surface-to-air missiles. As the crisis intensified and the possibility of a U-2 shootdown, as well as military operations against Soviet forces, became real, U-2 overflights became "militarized," with SAC pilots taking over U-2 flights from the CIA on 12 October.

The navy assumed a major role in the crisis when directed to establish a "quarantine" around Cuba, using aircraft as well as surface ships to detect, photograph, report on, and, if so ordered, prevent Soviet merchant ships from delivering missiles and other offensive weapons to the island. Navy Lockheed P-2 (P2V) Neptune and P-3 Orion patrol aircraft had a key role in these surveillance operations. Air force aircraft, including RB-47s, flew a few of these missions.[57]

However good the U-2's photography was, it was not detailed enough for the analysis required for this all-important verification task. Thus, very-low-level overflight reconnaissance missions were initiated. On 23 October, navy photo recon squadron VFP-61 from Jacksonville, Florida, began flying RF-8A Crusaders on missions over suspected missile sites and other Soviet installations. The results were "spectacular," providing unprecedented detail to the analysts and immediately understandable photos to Kennedy and his advisers. On 26 October, the RF-8s were joined by air force RF-101C Voodoos from Shaw AFB, South Carolina. Together, these planes, with Crusaders flown by marine and navy pilots, flew five to ten missions per day, uncovering finite detail of the Soviet buildup.[58]

Then on 27 October, as Kennedy and Khrushchev were on the verge of an agreement, an SA-2 missile shot down a SAC U-2 over Cuba, killing its pilot, Maj. Rudy Anderson. The missile's Soviet crew had fired on the authority of the local commander, who violated Khrushchev's directive. That and an unrelated, inadvertent SAC U-2 overflight of Soviet Siberia while on a nuclear sampling mission elevated the crisis between the two super powers. Kennedy ordered all U-2s grounded, but the RF-8s and RF-101s continued their low-level overflights. Some were

Lockheed P-2 (P2V) Neptune patrol aircraft played a key role in surveillance operations during the run-up to the Cuban Missile Crisis. The Army's AP-2E version, seen here, would be used by the US Army's 1st Radio Research Company at Cam Ranh Bay Air Base. *National Archives and Records Administration*

fired on by Cuban-manned antiaircraft guns, but none of the aircraft were damaged or shot down.

The crisis wound down with an agreement that required the Soviets to withdraw their missiles, bombers, and support equipment. The recon mission became one of verifying the Soviet withdrawal, with low-level flights continuing through mid-November. SAC U-2s resumed overflights on 4 November, and the heavy pace continued through March 1963. The intensity decreased over time, but Cuba remained an overflight target for most of the remainder of the Cold War.

A highly significant finding of these recon activities was that neither the U-2 high-altitude fights nor the low-level flights by the RF-8 Crusaders and RF-101 Voodoos had revealed any indication that the Soviets had landed nuclear warheads in Cuba. In reality, the Soviets had secretly placed 134 nuclear weapons in the island nation, with another 24 offshore aboard a Soviet merchant ship. Similarly, based on aerial photos, US intelligence estimated there were some 8,000 Soviet troops and advisers in Cuba—in reality, roughly 40,000 were present on the island.

The intensive strategic and tactical spyplane activity had failed in these very important matters.[59] ■

The CIA-sponsored RB-69A—developed from the P2V Neptune variant—was outfitted with the latest American COMINT and ELINT collection gear. Missions began in Europe in 1957 and would continue in the Far East. *National Archives and Records Administration*

TARGET CHINA

After World War II, the Communist Chinese insurgents led by Mao Zedong intensified their campaign against the government of Nationalist leader Chiang Kai-Shek. In 1949, the "Reds" succeeded in driving Chiang's forces from the mainland to the island of Formosa (Taiwan).[60]

As mainland China became enmeshed in the Korean War in late 1950, the CIA was authorized to work closely with the Nationalist government on Taiwan to penetrate Red China's secrets. A close partnership emerged, with the CIA funding and helping operate Nationalist (or Republic of China) intelligence assets. These efforts sought both to hinder Chinese efforts during the Korean conflict and to penetrate secrets

of the new Chinese regime. The main role of CIA-Taiwanese air operations, beginning in the late 1940s, was to insert and sustain agents and to encourage guerrilla warfare on the mainland.

These covert operations originally used transport aircraft such as the C-47 Skytrain and C-46 Commando, converted bombers such as the B-17 Flying Fortress and the B-26 Invader, and ex-navy PB4Y-2 Privateers. Their missions were not primarily reconnaissance, but they depended heavily on good maps and intimate knowledge of China's air defenses, and reconnaissance became vital for all CIA-Nationalist air operations. Indeed, many US and Taiwanese peripheral recon missions along

China's coast directly supported the covert operations/ recon overflights. Electronic gear was also installed in these converted cargo planes and bombers, and into the 1960s, these missions became more reconnaissance and less guerrilla support, especially in the eyes of the CIA, which saw that the agent and leaflet drops were less important, ineffective, and dangerous.[61]

By the mid-1950s the CIA sponsored the development of a special variant of the Lockheed P2V Neptune patrol bomber that could support agent activities in European and Asian regions. The US Air Force agreed to provide "cover" for the CIA project; this specialized aircraft—designated the RB-69A— was outfitted with the latest American COMINT and ELINT collection gear. RB-69A missions began in 1957 in Europe and a year later over China, the latter missions launched from Taiwan. Not long thereafter, the CIA diverted its European-based RB-69s to join the operation in the Far East.[62]

Meanwhile, the United States provided the Taiwanese regime with modern tactical recon aircraft, the RF-84F Thunderflash and RF-86 Sabre; Nationalist pilots were trained in the United States. These aircraft flew missions along and often over Chinese coastal areas. Later, in 1958, Taiwan acquired RF-100A Super Sabres and RB-57D Canberras, which began deep-penetration overflights.[63] One such RB-57D overflight, on 7 October 1959, was shot down by a Chinese SA-2 missile battery. This marked the first time a surface-to-air missile shot down a hostile aircraft.[64]

The CIA began U-2 overflights of mainland China in June 1958, collecting intelligence to cover the burgeoning Taiwan Straits crisis. Subsequently, a joint CIA-Taiwanese U-2 program was established, and Nationalist pilots and support personnel were trained on the aircraft. Increasingly over the program's life, the Nationalists proved very adept at film processing and analysis. The extensive U-2 overflight program began with the first Taiwanese-piloted mission taking place in January 1962. By that time, a prime intelligence objective of the United States was to ascertain Chinese nuclear weapons development and strategic missile programs. Taiwanese-piloted U-2s flew missions over China, while CIA pilots began flying Taiwan-based U-2s over North Vietnam and Laos in February 1962 as conflicts erupted in Southeast Asia. Through 1 March 1968, the Nationalists flew 102 U-2 missions over the mainland, suffering five losses. Among these missions were several flights against nuclear test ranges in northwest China, including one on 7 May 1967 that featured the drop of a sensor package that could transmit needed data from the site (unfortunately, the package failed). After the overflights were halted in 1968, the Taiwanese-manned U-2s flew 118 peripheral missions around the Chinese mainland until the program's end in 1974.

The US–Taiwanese spyplane collaboration continued throughout this period, each partner participating for different reasons: some Taiwanese leaders still harbored ambitions to "liberate" the mainland, while the United States found the reconnaissance product to be invaluable, especially concerning Chinese nuclear weapons and offensive ballistic missile systems development. Updates to the RB-69s had kept them useful, and plans were made to have a newer aircraft as their eventual replacement, most likely the navy Lockheed P-3 Orions, which would later be flown as spyplanes by the United States and Japan.

But several factors—including heavy Taiwanese losses in aircraft and aircrews (including the five U-2s lost to SA-2 missiles), ineffectiveness, and other emerging reconnaissance sources (namely satellites)—conspired to end these US-Taiwanese aerial spy operations. Also, the US was opening up politically to the Communist Chinese regime. The Taiwanese squadron flying the RB-69 was disbanded in early 1973, and the last Taiwanese U-2 mission took place on 24 May 1974.[65]

The five U-2 shootdowns over China (one before the incident with Gary Powers) were scored by Soviet-provided SA-2 missiles. Counting the loss of Powers's U-2 over the Soviet Union and the Anderson shootdown over Cuba, the Soviet missile was responsible for the loss of seven preeminent US spyplanes.

Besides a large number of recon aircraft lost to accidents, the emerging Chinese air defense capabilities—both fighters and surface-to-air missiles—had taken an increasing toll. The cost to Taiwan was 142 aircrew killed and others captured, while a large number of agents attempting to be inserted were lost. These programs, however, did provide valuable intelligence on mainland China and adjacent countries at a very important time. ∎

US STRATEGIC RECON, 1962–1976

In the 1960s, both the CIA and SAC expanded U-2 operations worldwide. SAC increased its nuclear sampling flights to areas beyond the Arctic as weapons testing proliferated. SAC coverage of Cuba remained intense following the missile crisis of 1962, varying with indicated Soviet activity. (After withdrawing strategic missiles and Il-28 light bombers in late 1962, the Soviets maintained a ground combat brigade in Cuba, as well as a massive SIGINT facility at Lourdes, just south of Havana's José Martí Airport.)

The U-2 was used from another type of airfield in the early 1960s: an aircraft carrier. The US Navy and the CIA together developed the ability to carrier-launch and recover a U-2, extending the aircraft's ability to cover targets in remote parts of the world. This ambitious but difficult attribute was used just once. France was developing a nuclear capability and testing it in a remote area of the South Pacific in 1964. On 19 and 22 May 1964, a CIA U-2, launched from the carrier *Ranger* (CVA 62) flew missions over the Mururoa Atoll in French Polynesia, the site of the testing. The photographic take was flown by navy courier from the carrier to Hawaii and on to the mainland for advanced processing and readout. Although highly successful, this carrier-based capability was never used again operationally because of navy objections.[66] (Significantly, several U-2s were produced with removable wings and strengthened fuselages for carrier stowage and operation.)

Although the U-2 was not used by the United States during the 1967 Arab-Israeli War, it did fly missions over Suez during the 1970 crisis. After the October 1973 Middle East conflict, CIA U-2s were used, by agreement with Israel and Egypt, to monitor the ceasefire.

A major roles-and-missions decision related to the U-2 took place in the early 1970s. As US-Chinese relations warmed and the CIA overflight mission in Taiwan ended, the rationale for a CIA-operated U-2 program grew weaker. There were very few missions for the U-2 that required a "civilian" cover. Increasingly, the U-2 was viewed as a military asset, and, in 1974, the CIA transferred its remaining U-2s to SAC. ∎

THE ULTIMATE SPYPLANE

Even before the U-2 began operations in the late 1950s, the CIA was planning for its successor. Again using great imagination, Lockheed's Skunk Works produced the A-12, a very-high-altitude, triple-sonic, recon aircraft—almost a space vehicle. The Lockheed design was selected for development in 1959. The program was dubbed Oxcart and the first A-12 aircraft was delivered in 1962.[67]

Developed simultaneously was a ramjet-powered recon drone, the D-21, intended to be launched from the A-12 to attain even higher altitudes and speeds while avoiding the potential loss of aircrew lives over target areas. The first D-21 launch from an A-12 was in March 1965. Extensive problems with the combination resulted in D-21 recon drones being launched from B-52 strategic bombers. That program led to four D-21 flights over China from 1969 to 1971. Continuing technical problems, however, led to cancellation of the D-21 program.[68]

Not so the CIA-operated A-12: with its speed in excess of Mach 3 and altitude above 80,000 feet (24,400 meters), it became operational in 1967, when it first flew missions over North Vietnam from Kadena, Okinawa. Immediately following the North Korean capture of the US spy ship *Pueblo* (AGER-2) in 1968, the A-12 overflew that country three times.[69]

The unprecedented capabilities of the A-12 led to a decision to create two military variants: the F-12 fighter-interceptor and the SR-71 strategic recon aircraft. By March 1968, SAC-operated SR-71s took over the A-12 missions. They also were used for SIGINT collection, and one SR-71 performed a high-priority imagery and ELINT mission against a Soviet Pacific Fleet exercise in the Sea of Japan on 27 September 1971.[70] SR-71s deployed in England beginning in April 1976 were also very useful in supporting NATO with unique intelligence on its Warsaw Pact adversaries over the next 13 years.[71]

Another highly capable US spyplane emerged in the 1960s: the RC-135. In its many "Rivet Joint" recon variants, this version of Boeing's successful KC-135 Stratotanker became the vastly improved successor to

SAC-flown Okinawa-based SR-71s provided intelligence coverage of North Vietnam and contributed greatly to the success of 1972 B-52 raids on the North. *US Air Force photo*

SAC's EB/RB-47 fleet. Carrying many more specialists than the four men in an RB-47, the RC-135 expanded COMINT and ELINT collection enormously. Only gradually could enough airframes be built or modified to replace the RB-47s, but by the end of 1967 the last of the specialized Stratojets, an EB-47L, was retired.[72] The RC-135s dramatically increased the quantity and timeliness of airborne SIGINT and other collection operations. In the same period they took over most theater airborne SIGINT missions.

The Korean peninsula posed a strategic problem for intelligence collection. A high-altitude platform was needed to observe North Korean developments closely, often, and in depth. Recon drone developments during the Vietnam conflict (see page 60) provided an interim answer. A SAC program using C-130 Hercules transports (modified as DC-130s) to launch and control such drones along the north-south Korean border had begun in 1970, but problems forced the use of RC-135s until SAC U-2s took over in 1976.[73] In that year, SAC shed the drone program, which

was shifted to the Air Force's Tactical Air Command (TAC). Operational, technical, and cost difficulties forced TAC to end the recon drone program in 1979.[74]

The US Navy benefitted from a similar increase in aircraft and equipment capability in this period. From 1962 it began receiving the P-3 Orion long-range maritime patrol aircraft as successor to the P-2 Neptune. As with the RC-135, the P-3 was an adaption of another airframe, the Lockheed Electra turboprop airliner. Besides its significant anti-submarine and overall maritime patrol missions, the P-3 evolved into the EP-3E specialized electronic reconnaissance variant, which provided national intelligence as well as information for fleet support.

The same era saw the modification of the A-3 Skywarrior carrier-based bomber into the EA-3B and RA-3B recon aircraft, capable of providing direct ELINT and photo recon support to the fleet. It also could fly national-level missions in areas accessible to carrier aircraft, where a land-based aircraft would be more difficult to employ.[75] ■

WAR IN SOUTHEAST ASIA

After the eviction of the French from Indochina, Communist North Vietnam began a carefully orchestrated takeover of the US-supported South. The United States gradually increased its political, economic, and military support in the late 1950s, and by 1960 and 1961, it was heavily involved in the growing conflict, which was also spreading into neighboring Laos and Cambodia. Intelligence of Communist activities in North Vietnam and Laos was needed.

In January 1961, the CIA deployed U-2s to the airbase at Takhli, Thailand; they then flew five successful missions over North Vietnam and Laos. U-2s did not return to Thailand until September 1963, when the CIA again flew several missions over Southeast Asia. In early 1964, by mutual agreement, SAC U-2s gradually assumed these missions. Based at Bien Hoa near Saigon (now Ho Chi Minh City), they began almost daily coverage of the region. The SAC U-2 missions increased after the Gulf of Tonkin incident in August 1964 and the resulting US military buildup.

In response to the increased US air operations in the area, both China and the Soviet Union began providing North Vietnam with air-defense fighters and SA-2 missiles, as well as radar/ground-control facilities to counter the increasing US recon and eventual combat missions over the North. As the North's air defense system grew, the SAC U-2s were forced to restrict their missions to Laos and to the far northwestern area of North Vietnam. By October 1968, the North became completely off limits to U-2s, which were still collecting important information over South Vietnam, Laos, and Cambodia.

By 1971, the U-2s, now based at U Tapao, Thailand, had new recon packages. On 13 August, a SAC U-2 flew a mission over the Gulf of Tonkin with COMINT receivers and recorders together with an electronic datalink. As soon as the U-2 recorded its electronic take, it transmitted the data to a ground station, thus flying the first operational real-time manned airplane recon mission in history. Such instantaneous and quickly processed coverage was important to many US air operations, especially the B-52 bomber raids against the North in 1972.[76]

After the withdrawal of US ground combat troops in 1973, US air activity gradually wound down, the last major operational support taking place in the May 1975 operation to recover crewmen from the merchant ship *Mayaguez*, which had been seized by Cambodian guerrillas. The last SAC U-2s departed the theater in April 1976.

Beginning on 31 May 1967, CIA-flown A-12s, followed by SAC-flown SR-71s, began providing intelligence coverage of North Vietnam. Based on Okinawa, CIA A-12s flew 22 missions that year and 17 in early 1968. SAC SR-71s took over that spring, flying an average of two flights per week. Missions over the North were flown with impunity, although SA-2 missiles were fired and MiG fighters launched in vain shootdown attempts. SIGINT, photography, and imaging radar all improved in timeliness and quality and, like their U-2 brethren, the SR-71s contributed greatly to the success of the 1972 B-52 raids on the North.[77]

Throughout the decade-long Vietnam conflict, SAC maintained extensive airborne SIGINT collection, first using the RB-47H Stratojet, then the RC-135M variant known as Combat Apple. An early example of coordinated collection resulting in important information was the effort in 1965 and 1966 to gain complete SIGINT on an SA-2 missile launch-to-impact sequence. On 16 February 1966, a high-altitude drone was deliberately flown into an SA-2 protected area in order to provoke a launch. An SA-2 was launched and shot down the drone. However, orbiting within collection range was an RB-47H, which acquired vital data on the guidance and warhead fusing sequence, to include blast overpressure. This information contributed significantly to the survival of US aircraft exposed to SA-2 missiles the remainder of the war.[78]

These "strategic" missions also provided valuable intelligence for tactical commanders. Another example of this—and a harbinger of things to come in the 1990s—was the deployment and use of unmanned recon drones, or unmanned aerial vehicles (UAVs). In this first successful use of these vehicles, SAC deployed DC-130 variants of the Hercules transport to Bien Hoa in South Vietnam in August 1964. These "Herk" transports air-launched Teledyne Ryan Model 147 Buffalo Hunter drones—adapted from target drones—on ELINT and photo missions over North Vietnam and southern China. The early years were rife with operations and maintenance problems, but by 1972 these drones were highly reliable and productive, gathering low-level imagery from the North impossible to obtain from manned aircraft, except at great cost in aircraft and aircrew lives.[79]

Tactical reconnaissance was a vital asset for ground and air units alike, and the take from many of these missions also was important at the national level. The first such missions were flown beginning in late 1961 by air force RF-101 Voodoos and navy carrier-based RF-8 Crusaders.[80] The air force and marine RF-4 recon variant of the F-4 Phantom fighter-attack

SAC-deployed DC-130s based in Bien Hoa, South Vietnam, air-launched Buffalo Hunter drones on ELINT and photo missions over North Vietnam and southern China. *US Air Force photo*

Variants of the F-4 Phantom became the dominant tactical/operational-level reconnaissance aircraft of the US Air Force and Marine Corps in Vietnam. *US Air Force photo*

aircraft became dominant in tactical/operational-level reconnaissance, being flown from carriers and land bases. The navy flew the North American RA-5 Vigilante as well as the RA-3B and EA-3B Skywarrior from carriers, and the air force operated the RB-66 and EB-66 Destroyer from bases in Thailand. It also flew specialized versions of the RB-57 Canberra, equipped with forward-looking infrared radar (FLIR) and other imaging devices for night recon.

By the time the Vietnam conflict ended, the major technical strides in recon collection and evaluation had set the stage for enormously improving intelligence gathering for decades. (The A-5 Vigilante, like the A3D Skywarrior—later A-3—was developed as a nuclear-capable, carrier-based strike aircraft.) ■

SOVIET AERIAL RECONNAISSANCE

The Soviet Union, which lacked overseas airbases from which to fly reconnaissance missions against the United States, was limited in long-range aerial intelligence collection during the Cold War prior to the development of satellites. The Soviets partially compensated for this shortcoming with an extensive espionage network in the West, the deployment of a fleet of intelligence collection ships (designated as AGI in naval parlance), the use of submarines to collect intelligence, and land-based SIGINT collection stations (the latter including a massive complex at Lourdes in Cuba). Like the United States and Great Britain, the Soviet Union adopted bomber-type aircraft for the long-range reconnaissance role, principally the Tu-16 Badger medium-range bomber (counterpart of the US B-47 Stratojet) and the M-4 Bison and Tu-20/95/142 Bear long-range bombers. The Badger and Bison were turbojet aircraft; the Bear was the only turboprop aircraft to achieve operational status as a bomber with any air force. This large, graceful aircraft, with four engines fitted with contra-rotating propellers, has continued to be used for long-range maritime reconnaissance in the Bear-D/E/F variants. The Bear has a range in excess of 7,500 miles (12,000 kilometers), which can be extended with in-flight refueling.

Beginning in March 1963, Soviet naval Badgers and then Bears carried out extensive overflights of US and NATO ships on the high seas. Initially operating from bases in Soviet Siberia, these flights ranged over the Pacific as far as the outer Hawaiian Islands, serving as training flights and spying on Western naval forces. The Soviet flights soon extended to the Atlantic and Mediterranean areas, often "escorted" by US and NATO fighters flying intercept missions. From the late 1960s until the early 1970s some Soviet Badger flights originated from bases in Egypt, and, with other Soviet aircraft (including MiG-25 Foxbat recon variants) flew with Egyptian markings. Some of these MiG-25s were flown by Soviet pilots over Israel in the period before the October 1973 Israeli-Arab War. Syrian bases also were used in this period.

A major series of Soviet reconnaissance flights began during the Okean multi-ocean exercises of April–May 1970, when a pair of Tu-95RT Bear-D reconnaissance planes took off from the Kola Peninsula and flew around North Cape and down the Norwegian Sea, over Soviet ships operating in the Iceland-Faeroes gap, and then south to land in Cuba. This nonstop flight of more than 5,000 miles (8,050 kilometers) marked the first time that Bear aircraft had landed outside an Eastern Bloc country. This established a regular pattern for such operations, with several such flights occurring every year through the 1980s. Until the end of the Cold War, the Bears conducted general surveillance and ELINT collection along the coast of North America, usually flying 200 to 250 miles (320 to 400 kilometers) offshore.

US Navy recon flights in Vietnam were conducted with the North American RA-5C Vigilante, among other aircraft. *US Navy photo*

In 1973, pairs of Bear-D aircraft began flying into Conakry, Guinea. On several occasions, Bears in Cuba and others in Conakry appear to have carried out coordinated reconnaissance flights over the south and central Atlantic. Bears changed their African base from Conakry to Luanda, Angola, in 1977, with occasional flights across the Atlantic between Cuba and Angola.

Several specialized strategic reconnaissance aircraft were developed by the Soviet Union during the Cold War era. The most ambitious Soviet spy aircraft was the RSR strategic reconnaissance jet—a craft that never flew. The Tsybin design bureau started development in 1954, just a year after US U-2 development began. The Soviet program was far more ambitious: a plane to fly greater than Mach 2 at altitudes above 65,000 feet (19,810 meters; the subsonic U-2 operated at some 70,000 feet, or 21,300 meters). The advanced-design RSR was so radical that the NM-1, a slower technology demonstration aircraft, was built first, flying in 1959. The NM-1 revealed a number of problems, as was

Postwar, the Soviet Union relied on existing bomber designs for recon duties, principally the Tu-16 Badger (above) and M-4 Bison (below). *US Navy National Museum of Naval Aviation (above) and Kaboldy, CC Attribution-Share Alike 3.0 (below)*

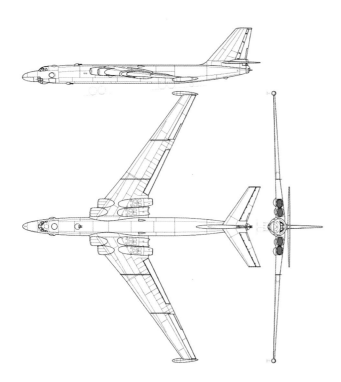

to be expected with such an advanced design. The problems persisted and appeared insurmountable, so Premier Khrushchev cancelled the program in April 1961.[81]

More akin to the American U-2 in concept—essentially a powered glider—was the M-17 Mystic-A, developed by the Myasishchev design bureau. First flown in the early 1980s, the aircraft operates above 70,000 feet (21,300 meters). But, like its improved variant, the M-55 Mystic-B, as well as the U-2, it is slow, flying at about 470 miles per hour (760 kilometers per hour). Also like the U-2, the Russian aircraft has been employed for scientific research missions, both variants having flown in the Arctic and Antarctic.

The Soviets were late in developing a regional border reconnaissance capability akin to that of the United States and NATO. In the mid-1970s they began deploying their counterpart aircraft, a version of the Il-18 Coot transport known as the Il-20 Coot-A. This four-turboprop, long-endurance aircraft could collect SIGINT as well as imagery (including side-looking radar) intelligence. First seen flying the East-West Germany border area collecting intelligence on NATO's

The Soviets utilized the Il-18 "Coot," seen here, as the basis for the long-endurance, SIGINT-collecting Il-20 "Coot-A" and the Il-38 anti-submarine and maritime patrol. *National Archives and Records Administration*

air-defense radar network, the Coot-A eventually was found in other military districts opposite potential hostile countries.[82] The Il-18 also was configured for the maritime patrol/anti-submarine role as the Il-38 May, an aircraft similar in concept to, but less capable than, the US Navy's P-3 Orion.

The Soviets also modified several aircraft for tactical reconnaissance. Two were particularly significant in the East-West confrontation: the Yak-25R Mandrake and Yak-28R Brewer-D. The Mandrake was a long-range reconnaissance aircraft, adapted from the twin-jet, swept-wing Yak-25 Flashlight air-defense fighter, capable of all-weather and night operations. The Mandrake was provided with a straight wing (to increase range and lift) and a variety of sensors. The plane's ceiling may have approached 70,000 feet (21,300 meters). The Yak-25R reconnaissance aircraft—most or all are believed to have been converted from Yak-25 fighters—entered service about 1959.

The widely used Yak-28R Brewer-D tactical recon version was a multisensor aircraft that entered service about 1969, with five interchangeable pallets containing various fits, both cameras and electronic sensors. The Brewer-D made several overflights of China as the two Communist countries periodically confronted one another.

Tactical reconnaissance also was the mission of the MiG-21R Fishbed-H version of the ubiquitous MiG-21

The Soviets' widely used Yak-28R Brewer-D tactical recon aircraft entered service about 1969. The Yak-28-64 prototype, below, was an ill-fated attempt to reconfigure the engine placement and intakes. *Hugo Mambour photo (above); Kaboldy, CC Attribution-Share Alike 3.0 (below)*

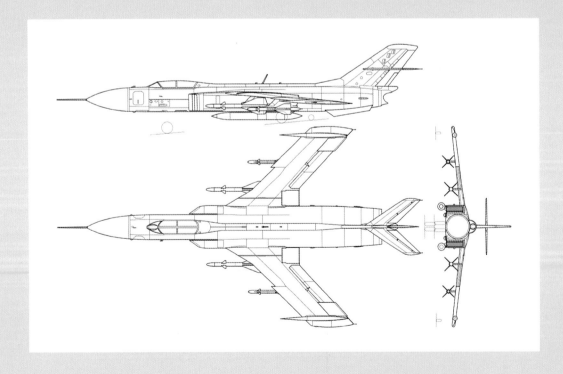

fighter from the 1960s into the 1980s. Beginning in the 1970s, the Soviets replaced their Brewer-D aircraft with several recon variants of the MiG-25 Foxbat fighter that, with its high-altitude and supersonic speed capabilities, was used against NATO forces into the early 1990s and remained in the Russian Air Force inventory until late 2013.[83]

The most advanced reconnaissance aircraft developed in the Soviet Union was the Su-24MR Fencer-E variant of the Fencer strike aircraft, which is still in significant use by the Russian Air Force. Besides the modern navigation suite, it can employ TV, side-looking aircraft radar (SLAR), and infrared sensors.

The Soviet civil airline Aeroflot played a large, if covert, military reconnaissance role. Some transports on international routes, like the long-range Ilyushin Il-62 Classic, had cameras and SIGINT gear installed. One report had an Aeroflot Il-62 flying an airline route near a recently upgraded British air defense radar station; it descended rapidly, then just as suddenly climbed back to normal altitude. It was collecting ELINT on the radar system's capability.[84] Numerous similar instances occurred in many NATO nation airspaces.

Some other Warsaw Pact nations had reconnaissance aircraft, usually variants of Soviet aircraft, such as the Fishbed-H. One significant exception was the German Democratic Republic (East Germany), which worked closely with the Soviets to monitor the western Allies in Berlin. Beginning in the 1970s, East German-modified An-2 Colt and An-26 Curl light transports—and at least one Mi-8 Hip helicopter—flew frequently around West Berlin to collect Allied communications. The Soviets had East German operators aboard their Il-20 Coot-A SIGINT aircraft patrolling the Iron Curtain from the East.[85]

Soviet naval recon aircraft regularly overflew US and other Western warships during the Cold War. Before 1963, there had been occasional overflights, but in late January of that year the Soviets initiated a series of overflights of US carriers, mostly by Tu-95 Bear-D aircraft. Between 27 January and 27 February, Soviet planes flew over the carriers *Constellation* (CVA 64), *Enterprise* (CVAN 65), *Forrestal* (CVA 59), *Kitty Hawk* (CVA 63), and *Princeton* (LPH 5). The overflights occurred in both oceans—the *Constellation* was observed by Soviet planes some 600 miles (965 kilometers) south of Midway Island, the *Forrestal* just southwest of the Azores. In all cases the carriers were

in international waters. Shipboard radar detected the snoopers some 200 miles (320 kilometers) out and, in the case of the attack carriers, Phantom and Crusader fighters escorted the Soviet planes while they were in the vicinity of the American ships. In some instances, US Air Force fighters also escorted the Soviet planes on their overflights when they passed near US air bases in Iceland and elsewhere.

Secretary of Defense Robert S. McNamara revealed the overflights to the press on 28 February 1963, stating that he saw no cause for alarm and that any nation had the right to photograph ships in international waters. Navy officials pointed out that the carriers were steaming on normal sailing routes with their schedules published and no effort was being made to keep radio silence. Vice Admiral William A. Schoech, the Deputy Chief of Naval Operations (Air), declared that the Soviet purpose was twofold: (1) to undermine the confidence of the American public in the carrier as a striking force, and (2) to convince the Soviet people that carriers were obsolescent, thus justifying the Soviet Navy's lack of such ships. Undoubtedly, the Soviets also made overflights to provide realistic training for their naval aviators.

In June 1963 the *Ranger* became the sixth US carrier overflown by Soviet aircraft in 1963. Six Tu-16 Badger turbojet bombers flew near the ship as she steamed about 330 miles (530 kilometers) east of Japan. In all, there were 14 overflights of US carriers in 1963. The number dropped to four in 1964 as the Soviets returned to the more mundane practice of sending electronics-laden intelligence ships or destroyers to trail US aircraft carriers during fleet exercises. Still, Soviet planes periodically returned to streak over the carriers.

On May 25, 1968, a Tu-16R Badger streaked over the *Essex* (CVA 9) during operations in the Norwegian Sea. One of the Badger's wings touched water as it turned, and the plane crashed and exploded. There were no survivors from its crew of six or seven. The *Essex* suffered no damage.

Periodic Soviet overflights continued. In May 1979, two Il-38 May recon aircraft flew so close to the carrier *Midway* (CVA 41) operating in the Arabian Sea that aircraft in the ship's landing pattern had to take evasive action.

Reviewing the Soviet overflights, Vice Adm. Gerald E. Miller, a veteran aviator and fleet commander,

The Tu-95 Bear was a key player in several Soviet overflights of US aircraft carriers commencing in January 1963. Here, a US Navy F-4J Phantom meets a Bear over the Atlantic near the carrier *Franklin D. Roosevelt* (CVA 42). *US Navy photo*

later observed the overflights by Soviet Bear and Badger aircraft were of great concern to US naval aviation, not because they posed a threat to the carriers but because they provided ammunition to the US Air Force for use in their traditional contention that the carriers were vulnerable to air attack and therefore a waste of US taxpayer money. It was a case of US interservice rivalry. Consequently, any carrier commanding officer or embarked admiral transiting the Atlantic or operating in the Mediterranean or Western Pacific was enjoined to take special precautions to avoid the overflights. Many tactics were employed to counter the event, including high transit speeds, longer ocean routes, and electronic silence.[86]

Soviet overflights continued on a periodic basis throughout the Cold War and afterward. In the fall of 2000, Russian Su-24 Fencer and Su-27 Flanker aircraft overflew the *Kitty Hawk* in the Sea of Japan. Photos taken of the ship's flight deck were emailed to the carrier's commanding officer. ∎

RECON OUTSIDE THE NATO ARENA

During the Cold War, many nations used aerial reconnaissance to monitor real or potential adversaries, whether or not it was relevant to the East-West confrontation. For example, the British made vigorous use of their recon assets around the world, especially while policing the drawdown of their empire. These included extensive recon over Malaya in the 1950s in an attempt to pinpoint rebel opposition. The 1963–1967 confrontation between the newly independent Malaysia and Indonesia had RAF Canberra photo recon aircraft overflying potential Indonesian targets and SIGINT Comets probing Indonesian air defenses. Monitoring Mediterranean nations such as Egypt, Syria, Israel, Libya, and Algeria was a constant requirement. From other bases in the Persian Gulf area, the RAF eyed countries of interest, such as Iraq, Yemen, Ethiopia, and Somalia.[87]

One example illustrates how many nations, otherwise lacking dedicated recon assets, used what was available when requiring intelligence about an opponent. In the late 1940s, the Dutch, attempting to retain their East Indies possessions, used locally built recon pods fitted to their P-51 Mustang fighters to reconnoiter their Indonesian opponents.[88]

Sweden, after the end of World War II, enhanced its intelligence collection against the Soviets, especially in the Baltic Sea area, using several Supermarine Spitfire PR.XIX photo recon variants to fly recon missions in 1948–1949 over several Baltic ports as well as areas along the Soviet-Finnish border. The Soviets failed to engage these flights, and valuable intelligence was gained.[89]

Also among Swedish efforts were dedicated aerial SIGINT missions against the Soviet Baltic coast to monitor naval and air defense activity. Beginning in 1946, the Swedes flew missions using a Junkers Ju 86, replaced in 1948 by two modified C-47s. However, as the Soviets built up their military capabilities in the Baltic, they became increasingly sensitive to all Western activity. This was manifest when the Soviets shot down a US Navy PB4Y-2 over the Baltic in April 1950 (see above). Even though the Swedes became more cautious, the Soviets tried to intimidate them by shooting down one of the SIGINT C-47s over international waters on 13 June 1952; the crew was lost. Nevertheless, Swedish operations in the area continued throughout the Cold War, gradually employing more capable aircraft like the Canberra.[90]

In 1982, the British became embroiled in conflict over the Falkland Islands in the South Atlantic, claimed by Argentina as the Malvinas. After the Argentines occupied the islands, the British dispatched a large naval force, led by two small aircraft carriers and several nuclear-propelled submarines. The initial British effort was to recapture the South Atlantic island of South Georgia. Lacking long-range in-theater reconnaissance assets, the British employed Victor tankers for surveillance, the large jets using their navigational radar to verify that no Argentine surface ships were near South Georgia. A single Nimrod R.1 was deployed to the theater and flew several ELINT missions from the Chilean-owned island of San Felix Island *west* of the Chilean mainland.[91] Subsequent tactical recon was undertaken by Harrier vertical-takeoff/landing aircraft embarked in the two British carriers; these were flown by both Royal Navy and RAF pilots.

The Argentines also were versatile. They modified two of their Boeing 707 transport aircraft with photo and ELINT gear and sent them, along with a Neptune maritime patrol plane, to scout the approaching British fleet. The resulting intelligence alerted them in time to respond to the British forces, although it did not change the outcome of the conflict. ∎

THE END OF THE COLD WAR

In 1976, SAC consolidated its two premier spyplanes—the U-2 and the SR-71—into the 9th Strategic Reconnaissance Wing at Beale AFB, northeast of San Francisco, California. The requirements for the U-2s continually increased, driven by conflicts and crises in the Middle East, Somalia, Yemen, the Caribbean, and elsewhere. U-2s also continued nuclear sampling missions along the periphery of the Soviet Union and China.

Also in the 1970s there appeared a new role for, and variant of, the U-2. Despite the daunting air defense environment in the Soviet-held areas in Europe, a 9th

The TR-1 ("tactical reconnaissance") was a U-2 variant developed to conduct flights along the East-West borders in Europe. Throughout the 1980s, TR-1s provided near-real-time intelligence for US and NATO forces. *Dana Bell collection via Walter Wright*

SRW U-2 began operational test missions in Western Europe in 1976. The results were excellent, including a series of U-2 flights in April 1980 over the Norwegian and Barents Seas that provided near-real-time SIGINT data on Soviet merchant and naval ship activity near a US Navy warship.[92]

Planning went ahead for the TR-1 (for "tactical reconnaissance") U-2 variant to conduct flights along the East-West borders. Over the next few years, a complex working arrangement between SAC and USAFE evolved to support NATO. Throughout the 1980s the TR-1s, flying from Alconbury, England, used increasingly sophisticated collection equipment to provide a multisource, near-real-time intelligence capability for US and NATO forces confronting Soviet and Warsaw Pact forces. In 1989, U-2 capabilities were expanded even further with the addition of an electro-optical system and the ability to communicate data via satellite datalink.

The SR-71 also operated in the European Theater from Mildenhall, England. Besides flying missions along the East-West German border, the SR-71 flew missions carefully coordinated with SAC RC-135 SIGINT collectors over the Baltic and Barents Seas. The SR-71 flew a profile to make Soviet air defense commanders believe that it was about to penetrate their territory, thus exciting the Soviet air defense system. The RC-135 Rivet Joint, meanwhile, would be in position off the Soviet coast collecting valuable SIGINT information on the Soviet responses. This technique became especially useful as the Soviets deployed their new SA-5 air defense missile system, designed especially to track and destroy fast, high-flying aircraft, including the SR-71. In the 1980s, the Soviets made futile attempts to use this missile in coordination with MiG-25 Foxbat and MiG-31 Foxhound interceptors to catch and possibly destroy SR-71s, but they were unsuccessful.

The RC-135 platform was continuously upgraded during this period. A variant known as the RC-135U Combat Sent was tasked against various new Soviet air defense radars, including the SA-5 radars mentioned above. The deployment of it and the other Rivet Joint aircraft to collect SIGINT continued worldwide.

Together and separately, these three aircraft often flew coordinated missions with Royal Air Force Hawker Siddeley Nimrod and West German Breguet Atlantic SIGINT collectors over the Baltic Sea, taking advantage of NATO allies' capabilities.

One RC-135 mission inadvertently contributed to a tragedy in the air. On 1 September 1983, an RC-135 Cobra Ball, the variant that collected against Soviet ballistic missile tests, had completed a mission opposite the Kamchatka Peninsula in the Soviet Far East. At the same time, a South Korean Boeing 747 airliner was approaching the Kamchatka coast—a place it was not supposed to be. It had experienced a navigation system malfunction, of which the 747 crew was unaware. The Soviet air defense forces in the area misidentified the 747 as the RC-135 and launched fighters to shoot down the supposedly hostile target. Eventually a Su-15 Flagon interceptor destroyed the 747, resulting in the deaths of 269 passengers and crew.[93]

During the 1980s, the SR-71 became uniquely useful during several Middle East crises. It overflew Lebanon following the Beirut bombing of an American military barracks in 1982 and Libya during and after the 1986 US air strikes, with more missions over Libya following in 1987. But the SR-71's days were drawing to a close. Because of its high operating costs, the inability to transmit data from a supersonic SR-71 to a ground station (unlike the early U-2s), and the increased flexibility of surveillance satellites, the air force decided in 1989 to terminate the program. The last operational mission over Europe was flown 20 September 1989, and over the Far East five days later. The program was reactivated—due mainly to congressional action—in the 1990s, but no operational missions were flown. However, several SR-71s were used by the National Air and Space Administration (NASA) for research, the last such mission being flown on 9 October 1999. ∎

THE MIDDLE EAST: HOTBED OF AERIAL SPYING

During the Cold War, Great Britain, the United States, and the Soviet Union all flew reconnaissance missions over Israel and the Arab states. In the 1948–1949 Israeli War of Independence, British and Egyptian aircraft flying from Egypt flew reconnaissance flights over Israeli territory. The British effort was mainly to inform themselves of both Arab and Israeli activity, but it is possible that some intelligence was shared with the Trans-Jordan Arab Legion, commanded by British officers.

During the summer and fall of 1948, RAF Mosquito aircraft made several overflights of Israeli territory at about 30,000 feet (9,140 meters). At first they flew with

immunity, as available Israeli fighters could not reach that altitude in time to engage them. On 20 November 1948, the fledgling Israeli Air Force shot down an RAF Mosquito with a newly acquired P-51 Mustang, and several RAF and Egyptian Spitfires on tactical recon flights in 1949 were also downed.[94]

Following the 1948–1949 war for Israeli independence, the Arab states began preparations for the next conflict with Israel. But this would be more complex, as Britain and France attacked Egypt—with Israeli collusion—following nationalization of the Suez Canal in July 1956. As British and French air and ground forces struck, British Canberra PR.7 and French RF-84F Thunderchief recon aircraft based on Cyprus overflew the canal area.

On the morning of 1 November 1956, following a night of bombing Egyptian bases, the RAF flew two Canberra PR.7 reconnaissance flights that were intercepted by Egyptian MiG-15 fighters. Three weeks before, the War Office had advised the RAF, "If photographic reconnaissance is undertaken by single Canberra aircraft, the chances of detection are very small. Indeed, apart from some misfortune due to engine failure or a fortuitous interception . . . the risk of interception can be discounted."[95]

The pilot of one Canberra PR.7 from No. 13 Squadron, Flying Officer Jim Campbell, reported that he and his copilot were "quite disturbed to see explosive shells sailing by the cockpit on both sides from the rear."[96] The Canberra took evasive action and suffered only minor tail damage. The British and French recon flights continued—with caution. (Canberra recon aircraft also overflew Syrian and, most likely, other Arab airfields; four Soviet Il-28 light bombers were reported at Damascus.[97])

US reconnaissance aircraft also overflew the region. In 1956, before and during the Suez crisis, the CIA flew numerous U-2 missions over the area, keeping tabs on all the belligerents. On 19 July 1963, a pair of Israeli Mirage fighters reportedly fired warning shots to force a US RB-57A Canberra to land at Lod (later Ben-Gurion) Airport outside of Tel Aviv. On another occasion, the Israelis considered employing a highly modified F-4 Phantom to intercept U-2 flights if the United States persisted after being asked to halt such missions over Israel.

The Soviets also overflew the Middle East. After the massive defeat suffered by the Arab states in the 1956 Arab-Israeli conflict, Egyptian President Gamal Abdel Nasser sought and received extensive military assistance from the Soviet Union. In the run-up to the June 1967 Arab-Israeli War, the USSR also deployed a unit of MiG-25 Foxbats, pilots, and ground crews to Egypt. This was remarkable, since the Foxbat was not yet operational at home. Undiscovered by either Israel or the US, they flew two missions over Israel (including its Dimona nuclear site) in late May 1967 before returning home after the conflict.[98]

In January 1970, Nasser made a secret visit to Moscow to seek more Soviet assistance in rearming his military, which had been devastated by Israel in the 1967 Six-Day War. The Soviets again responded generously. Among the aircraft were MiG-21 Fishbed recon variants. They also deployed a recon Foxbat air detachment of four aircraft. Two of the Mach 2+ aircraft were MiG-25R variants with advanced cameras and two were MiG-25RB variants with cameras and bomb racks. They arrived (carried in An-12 and An-22 cargo aircraft) at the Cairo-West airfield in March 1971. After reassembly and test flights, the MiGs began flying recon flights over the Israeli-occupied Sinai and the blocked Suez Canal, and then over Israel itself.

Israeli fighters made an effort to intercept the MiG-25 flights, without success. Similarly, the US-provided Hawk surface-to-air missiles could not reach the MiG-25s, flying as high as 75,000 feet (22,900 meters). About 20 recon missions were flown before President Anwar Sadat (who had succeeded Nasser in 1970) forced the Soviet "advisors" out of Egypt in July 1972 as he planned another assault on Israel. All but one of the missions were flown by pairs of MiG-25s; that single mission was over Israel's Mediterranean coastal waters. After these missions, the MiG-25s were disassembled and flown back to the Soviet Union.

The pictures brought back by the MiGs clearly showed the positions of Israeli troops. The Egyptian high command was very impressed by the high level of photo detail, since their own MiG-21RFs had cameras with a narrow field of view.

Egypt and Syria again unleashed their forces against Israel in the so-called Yom Kippur War, or Ramadan War, on 6 October 1973. Soon in trouble and needing information on Israeli troop movements, the Egyptians again welcomed the Soviets. On 19 October, Soviet An-22 cargo aircraft began landing in Egypt with a new detachment of MiG-25RB aircraft. Israeli tanks were approaching Cairo as the giant transports touched down. Contingency plans were readied to fly the MiG-25s back to the Soviet Union if they were threatened; if evacuation were not possible, they were to be destroyed on the airfield. Even as the truce arrangements between the cobelligerents were being negotiated, the MiG-25s began making photorecon flights. The conflict ended on 25 October with another Israeli victory over its Arab antagonists, but the success of the MiG-25 in the arduous combat conditions of the Middle East demonstrated the excellence of the MiG design bureau and aircraft builders.

The Soviets also deployed Tu-16R Badgers to Egyptian bases from 1967 until 1972. From there, wearing Egyptian markings, they reconnoitered the Mediterranean, keeping an eye on the Sixth Fleet—while being closely watched themselves by US and Allied aircraft.

The Israelis in turn flew camera-equipped British Meteors, then French Mirages, and later US RF-4 Phantoms to spy out targets in surrounding Arab countries. One specific incident involved a slower and lower aircraft. In the 1960s, the Israelis had acquired at least 14 Boeing Stratofreighters, most of them former KC-97 tankers, for airlift and air refueling purposes.[99] At least one was outfitted with a 66-inch focal-length camera, suitable for long-range oblique photography. On 17 September 1971, this aircraft had finished flying north-south several miles east of the Suez Canal when it was shot down by two SA-2 missiles. All but one of the eight-man crew were killed. This loss accelerated the Israeli desire for high-and-fast recon aircraft like the F-4 Phantom fighter—a desire that was quickly fulfilled by the United States.[100]

The 1974 agreements between Israel and Egypt, brokered by the United States after the end of the October 1973 conflict, included periodic flights by US U-2s over the Sinai Peninsula. These aircraft, flying from Akrotiri in Cyprus, provide high-quality imagery to both parties as a confidence-building measure to ensure a stable peace, at least in that area. These missions have continued unchecked for more than 40 years, undoubtedly the longest continual aerial reconnaissance series in history. ■

AERIAL RECONNAISSANCE CONTINUES

The Cold War is considered to have ended with the collapse of the Soviet Union in December 1991, but the events following the August 1990 Iraqi invasion of Kuwait are more properly seen as harbingers of the post–Cold War world of conflict. Responding swiftly to this crisis, the United States formed a coalition force with NATO nations as its core, but quickly involving other nations, including Eastern Europe. Aerial recon became vital to the defense of Saudi Arabia (Operation Desert Shield) as well as to the ensuing offensive campaign to liberate Kuwait (Desert Storm).

Among the first American aircraft to respond to the crisis were two U-2s from the United States, which deployed to Saudi Arabia; they were augmented by TR-1s from Britain. Together, they flew hundreds of photo-collection missions both before and after the Allied ground attack on 17 January 1991. These aircraft showed their new capabilities by providing immense amounts of tactical recon info to ground and air forces. One source credits 50 percent of all recon imagery during the conflict and 90 percent of the useful target information provided to ground forces, to the U-2/TR-1 effort.[101]

In the 1990s, as the ethnic conflicts in the former Yugoslavia intensified and festered, U-2s were also involved in supporting national and international efforts to resolve them. From early 1993 through the Kosovo crisis of 1999, U-2s covered the entire region, working for the United Nations as well as the allied armed forces to police the agreements that came into being. And after the September 2001 attacks on the New York City World Trade Center and the Pentagon, the U-2s were again deployed to support the invasions, occupations, and stabilization operations in Iraq and Afghanistan.

Throughout these various post–Cold War crises and all the other confrontations since—including Arab Spring movements—RC-135 SIGINT aircraft have been active. The capability and flexibility that the RC-135 SIGINT collector crew brings to its missions is virtually irreplaceable, even today. The U-2, with its now-unique ability to shoot very high-resolution "wet film," has likewise been extremely useful. Despite the ubiquitous use of satellite imagery and SIGINT, and the meteoric rise of reconnaissance drones, manned platforms will be with us for the foreseeable future.

However, as the saying goes, "all good things must end." In 2014—in the face of draconian budget cuts—the air force reluctantly made public its decision to terminate U-2 operations in favor of the Northrop Grumman RQ-4 Global Hawk UAV much earlier than

ABOVE AND OPPOSITE: The Hawker Beechcraft MC-12W Liberty is a greatly advanced variant of the long-serving RC-12 Guardrail.
National Archives and Records Administration and US Army photo

planned. That decision was based strictly on financial grounds, as the U-2 still had greater recon capability than its proposed successor.

The US Navy had its own replacement issues, with the EP-3 recon version of the veteran P-3 Orion maritime surveillance aircraft approaching retirement in the second decade of the twenty-first century. The leading candidate for replacement was a recon version of the turbojet Lockheed Martin P-8 Poseidon.

Other Western nations' strategic reconnaissance capabilities have been threatened, as post–Cold War defense budgets have been slashed. The Germans and French have phased out the Breguet Atlantic, and the British grounded their Nimrods, settling on acquiring their own RC-135 Stratotanker manned SIGINT collectors; the first of these was delivered in late 2013.

US manned tactical recon assets have also been cut. The McDonnell Douglas RF-4 Phantom, ubiquitous in the US Air Force, Navy, and Marine Corps, has vanished from the forces' inventory. The air force has coped with these changes by mounting specialized recon pods on both the McDonnell Douglas F-15 and the General Dynamics F-16. Fewer of these modified fighters have been needed because much of the recon mission has been absorbed by UAVs, the so-called "drones," known to the air force as remotely piloted aircraft (RPAs). These vehicles, equipped with highly advanced electronics, have come to dominate recon in virtually every US conflict from the late 1990s to present.

There is one significant exception: the Hawker Beechcraft MC-12W Liberty, a greatly advanced variant of the long-serving RC-12 Guardrail aircraft, is a low-level, quick-response, tactical collection aircraft.

The Liberty demonstrated its efficacy during the lengthy Afghanistan conflict.

Many other nations also have had to cut their tactical recon assets. However, several believe they must retain this capability. Examples include the Greek and Turkish Air Forces, which have kept RF-4 Phantoms active for years past the Phantom's scheduled departure. Some former Eastern Bloc nations, having rearmed and joined NATO, have also kept their recon ability alive.

After the fall of the Soviet Union in December 1991, the Russian armed forces were severely reduced. Thousands of aircraft were destroyed or left to rot throughout the former Soviet republics. Twenty years later, the reconnaissance capability of the Russian air and naval air arms has been drastically reduced. At the end of 2013, the Russian Air Force finally grounded its recon MiG-25s. It has kept several Su-24 Fencer variants active and retains a nominal recon ability with its few Il-20 Coot-As.

Despite these reduced capabilities, Russia has retained an edge over most of its neighbors. Nations like Ukraine, which has experienced major aggression from Russia, have almost no recon ability and will depend on Western resources to provide the vital intelligence they need.

In the Asia-Pacific area, reconnaissance remains a vital need as well in an uncertain world. Since the 1980s, China's military has risen in strength and capability to an extent far beyond its past. Emblematic of this is its development of the recon and electronic warfare variants of the Shaanxi Y-8 transport aircraft. As India and Pakistan keep a cautious eye on each other (and on China), the "eye" in many cases includes reconnaissance aircraft. Australia and New Zealand both contribute to and are reliant on US recon ability in this theater, while smaller nations rely explicitly on alliances, South Korea and Japan, among others, valuing their defense agreements with the United States.

With many examples in the past 20 years and more to illustrate that reconnaissance is a necessity, and the lack of it can contribute to a nation's fall, there is a need, stretching far into the future, for nations to keep aerial recon assets, along with their normal armed units, active and ready to defend their interests.

PART II
THE SPYPLANES

GERMANY

Junkers Ju 86s. © SZ Photo/Scherl/Bridgeman Images

JUNKERS JU 86

The Junkers Ju 86 was a twin-engine medium bomber. Six military variants were produced by Junkers Flugzeug und Motorenwerke AG: the Ju 86 D, E, G, and K bomber series and the Ju 86 P-2 and Ju 86 R-1 reconnaissance variants.

The aircraft was originally designed as a high-speed, ten-passenger civilian plane and medium bomber with a four-man crew based on Luftwaffe specifications. It was in competition for Luftwaffe contracts with the Dornier Do 17 and Heinkel He 111; all three received contracts, but Heinkel dominated the industry with He 111 production ultimately reaching 6,556 aircraft while Junkers built 910 Ju 86s.

DESIGN

Engineers for Junkers Flugzeugwerke AG designed a bomber similar in construction to those built by the company's competitors and characterized by all-metal construction; a broad, rounded fuselage tapering toward the rear and ending at a twin-stabilizer-and-rudder system; and a low-wing design featuring double flap and aileron configuration. The series went through several cockpit configurations in size, shape, and glazing. The early Ju 86 A and D variants were powered by Junkers Jumo 205C diesel engines; later variants were fitted with BMW 132N radial engines.

Two Ju 86 D airframes were converted in 1939 as prototypes for the Ju 86 P-2 Höhenbomber (high-altitude bomber) and the Ju 86 P-1 Aufklärer (reconnaissance) aircraft. Structural modifications to the Ju 86 P-2 included a smaller two-man pressurized cockpit that reduced overall length by three feet. Three vertical cameras were installed in the bomb bay. Defense armament consisted of a single fixed, rear-firing MG 17 machine gun. The P-2 was powered by two 1,000-horsepower turbocharged Junkers Jumo 207A-1 diesel engines providing a maximum speed of 224 miles per hour (420 kilometers per hour). Approximately 40 P-1s and P-2s were built.

ID silhoutte of Junkers Ju 86 P. *Public domain*

The unarmed Ju 86 R-1 followed with four-bladed propellers powered by 1,100-horsepower 207B-3/V diesel engines with nitrous oxide injection boosters for the superchargers. Wingspan was nearly 21 feet (6.4 meters) longer than that of the P-2. Conflicting information confuses the record on specific performance data of the reconnaissance variants, especially the R-1's maximum service ceiling; some sources cite the aircraft as capable of reaching more than 49,000 feet (14,935 meters), some 10,000 feet (3,048 meters) higher than the P-2's rated ceiling.

OPERATIONS

The Ju 86's service life as a frontline bomber was rather brief, as it was outperformed by the He 111B, which was approximately 50 miles per hour (80 kilometers per hour) faster. In addition, the diesel engines of the A and D were difficult to maintain in the field. Most Ju 86 bomber variants were taken out of frontline service during 1939. However, demand for high-altitude bombers and recon aircraft remained strong, and the Luftwaffe requested that between 37 and 40 Ju 86 Ds be converted to the Ju 86 P bomber and Ju 86 P-1 photo intelligence platform. The Ju 86 P-2 prototype (W.Nr. 0421) first flew in February 1940. Luftwaffe units equipped with the aircraft began reconnaissance operations that summer. The P-2's rated service ceiling was 39,300 feet (11,980 meters), but there were instances in which 42,000 feet (12,800 meters) was obtained, an altitude that was beyond the capacity of conventional enemy fighters for some two years. Approximately 16 Ju 86 Ps were upgraded to the Ju 86 R-1 recon variant, with W.Nr. 5132 becoming the first of that type delivered to the Luftwaffe in early 1942.

Aufklärungsgruppe (Aufkl. Gruppe; reconnaissance group) (F)/Ob.d.L. was equipped with the Ju 86 P-2. Some of these aircraft bore Lufthansa markings and began unmolested flights over Britain in the summer of 1940, followed by missions over Soviet territory during the winter of 1940 and 1941 from bases in Poland and Hungary. On 15 April 1941, a Ju 86 P2 suffered engine failure and was intercepted by a Soviet fighter near Rovno, Poland. The Russian plane opened fire, damaging the port engine and forcing the German pilot to make a crash landing. The pilot and observer were caught by Soviet authorities but later escaped and joined advancing German forces at the opening of Operation Barbarossa. Between 1942 and 1943, 1./Versuchsverband Ob.d.L. (Experimental Unit) conducted recon flights over Soviet territory with the Ju 86 P-2; Aufkl. Gruppe (F)/Ob.d.L overflew the Middle East with the Ju 86 R-1.

When Aufkl. Gruppe Ob.d.L. was disbanded, four R-2s were transferred to Crete in June 1942, followed by one more in August, for operations with 2(F)/123. To counter the German reconnaissance plane, the British and Soviets modified Spitfire V fighters by removing most nonessential equipment, including all but one wing gun. According to British records, the first successful interception took place north of Cairo on 24 August 1942, when a Spitfire of No. 103 Maintenance Unit (MU) brought down a Ju 86 from Aufkl. Gruppe 2(F)/123. However, German records show the Ju 86 R-1 returned to base safely, though damaged. One more reconnaissance variant was lost to the RAF on 6 September and one Ju 86 R-1 was recorded by 2(F)/123 as lost due to engine failure on 29 August. Encounters with the high-altitude RAF Spitfires led to the field installation of one rear-firing M 17 machine gun in recon Ju 86s. Still, two more aircraft became operational losses during November and December 1942. The group was down to one Ju 86 R-1 by October 1943 when it completed conversion to the Ju 88 recon variant.

STATUS

Retired. The Ju 86 P-2 was withdrawn from frontline service by mid-1943; the Ju 86 R-1 was withdrawn in July 1944, as within months of acceptance by Luftwaffe units, it, too, could be intercepted by aircraft such as the Spitfire IX. Junkers exported the Ju 86 K bomber to several countries but none of the reconnaissance variants were sent abroad. The only known survivor is a Ju 86K in the Swedish Air Force Museum. ∎

—*Alan C. Carey*

JUNKERS JU 86 P-2

CREW:	2
ENGINES:	2x Junkers Jumo 207A-1 turbocharged diesels; 1,000 hp
WEIGHTS:	Empty: 14,685 lb (6,661 kg) Maximum: 22,930 lb (10,401 kg)
LENGTH:	54 ft (16.5 m)
WINGSPAN:	84 ft (25.6 m)
HEIGHT:	15 ft 5 in (4.7 m)
SPEEDS:	Maximum: 224 mph (360 kph) Cruise: 161 mph (259 kph)
CEILING:	approx. 39,360 ft (12,000 m)
RANGE:	625 mi (1,006 km)
ARMAMENT:	1x MG 17 machine gun

JUNKERS JU 86 R-1

CREW:	2
ENGINES:	2x Junkers 207B-3 turbocharged diesels; 1,100 hp each
WEIGHTS:	Empty: 14,771 lb (6,700 kg) Maximum: 25,420 lb (1,530 kg)
LENGTH:	54 ft (16.5 m)
WINGSPAN:	104 ft 11.75 in (32 m)
HEIGHT:	15 ft 5 in (4.7 m)
SPEEDS:	Maximum: 261 mph (420 kph) Cruise: 205 mph (330 kph)
CEILING:	approx. 48,250 ft (14,707 m)
RANGE:	980 mi (1,577 km)
ARMAMENT:	None

Dornier Do 17. *Alan C. Carey collection*

DORNIER DO 17/215/217 FLIEGENDER BLEISTIFT

The Dornier Do 17, Do 215, and Do 217 Fliegender Bleistift (Flying Pencils) operated as high-speed light bombers and reconnaissance aircraft produced by Dornier-Werke GmbH between 1934 and 1945. The Do 17 was initially designed as a civilian transport plane for Lufthansa in 1932, but its role changed to bomber as directed by the Reich Air Ministry a year later. Three dozen versions, including prototypes and subvariants, were manufactured, including five reconnaissance aircraft. The Do 215, consisting of eight variants, was originally an export version of the Do 17 Z, though all but two were delivered to the Luftwaffe. The Do 217 was essentially a larger version of the Do 17, with over 50 variants and subvariants produced.

DESIGN

The Do 17 was a twin-engine, high-wing, double-fin-and-rudder design, with a conventional tailwheel undercarriage with the main gear retracting rearward into the engine nacelles. Fuel cells were located in the wings between the engine nacelles and fuselage. The glazed pod-like cockpit canopy rested high above a wide, forward fuselage, while the aircraft's aft end was slender, the source of the model's nickname. The bombardier station located in the nose, forward of the cockpit, went through several glazed nose designs. Early models Do 17E to M were powered by inline engines, while Do 17 M-1 to Z were fitted with radial engines; thus, each had entirely different nacelles.

Prewar prototypes V-8 (W.Nr568-D-AXOM), V-10 (W.Nr.660D-AKUU), and V-11 (W.Nr.681-D-ATYA) began as Do 17 E-1s but were finished as armed, long-range reconnaissance photo-intelligence Do 17 F-1s equipped with a downward-firing MG 15 machine gun in a hatch just forward of the bomb bay and to the cockpit's rear. Increased fuel capacity and three film-strip cameras with six flare ejector tubes were housed in the bomb bay. The bombsight and bomb-release mechanism were also removed from this variant. The F was powered by BMW VI 7D3 inline engines of 650 horsepower each. V-13 W.Nr.683 D-ATAH and V-14 9W.Nr.684 D-AFOU—both former Do 17 E-2s fitted with 1,050 horsepower Daimler-Benz 600C engines—became the last prewar photo-intelligence variants. The Dornier factory at Oberpfaffenhofen in Bavaria produced 77 Do 17 F-1s.

Do 17 P-1 followed as a reconnaissance variant of the Do 17 M but was fitted with the smaller, fuel-efficient BMW Bramo 132N nine-cylinder air-cooled radial engine with 853 horsepower, which was housed in larger engine nacelles than those of the Do 17 M. Two camera packages were available, consisting of either Rb 20/30 and Rb 50/30 or Rb 20/18 and Rb 50/18 cameras. Defensive armament was made up of two to four MG 15 machine guns located in the cockpit. Do 17 P assembly was spread among five Dornier factories with 337 machines produced. Three prototypes with Daimler-Benz 600G engines and additional cockpit space for five crewmen instead of the typical three were tested as Do 17S-O armed reconnaissance platforms. These aircraft featured additional nose glazing and a prone gunner's position in the underside of the nose, and were armed with an MG 15 machine gun.

The Do 17 Z was the definitive model, with 1,700 built between 1939 and 1940. Podded wing nacelles housed the Bramo 323P-2 radial engines, giving the aircraft a maximum speed of 255 miles per hour (410 kilometers per hour). Two bomber-reconnaissance variants were part of the production series, consisting of between 16 to 22 Do 17 Z-3s equipped with Rb 20/30 or Rb 50/30 cameras; these were fitted into the crew-entry hatch, while a small number of long-range maritime Do 17 Z-5s were fitted with flotation bags in the rear fuselage and rear engine nacelles in case of a forced ditching.

Eighteen Do 215 A-1s with Daimler-Benz 601A engines ordered by Sweden were impounded at the start of the war and modified on the production line as

DORNIER DO 17 F-1

CREW:	4
ENGINES:	2x BMW VI 7D3 V12 inline; 650 hp each
WEIGHTS:	Empty: 9,921 lb (4,500 kg)
	Maximum: 15,430 lb (7,050 kg)
LENGTH:	53 ft 3.75 in (16.3 m)
WINGSPAN:	59 ft (18.0 m)
HEIGHT:	14 ft 2 in (4.3 m)
SPEEDS:	Maximum: 220 mph (237 kph); 310 mph (500 kph) in shallow dive
	Cruise: 160 mph (257 kph)
CEILING:	18,040 ft (46,063 m) approximate
RANGE:	990 mi (1,953 km)
ARMAMENT:	1x 7.92mm MG 15 machine gun

DORNIER DO 17 P-1

CREW:	4
ENGINES:	2x BMW Bramo 132N 9-cylinder air-cooled radial; 853 hp each
WEIGHTS:	Empty: 10,140 lb (4,600 kg)
	Maximum: 16,887 lb (7,660 kg)
LENGTH:	52 ft 9.75 in (16.1 m)
WINGSPAN:	104 ft 11.75 in (32 m)
HEIGHT:	14 ft 11 in (4.6 m)
SPEEDS:	Maximum: 250 mph (155 kph)
	Cruise: 180 mph (290 kph)
CEILING:	20,340 ft (6,200 m)
RANGE:	745 m (1,200 km)
ARMAMENT:	2-4x 7.92mm M 15 machine guns

Dornier Do 217. *Roger Viollet photo/Getty Images*

camera-equipped recon aircraft designated as the Do 215 B-0 (3 modified) and Do 215 B-1 (15 modified). The Do 215 B-4 apparently was similar to the B1, but offered additional camera options.

The Do 217 introduced in 1941 was a larger and faster version of the Do 17 Z, with a longer, wider fuselage and longer wingspan, and a maximum speed of 348 miles per hour (560 kilometers per hour) from the 1,750-horsepower Daimler-Benz 603A inverted V-12 engines. Only eight of the preproduction reconnaissance variant designated Do 217 A-0 with the original narrow rear fuselage and fitted with DB 601A engines were built. The Do 217 E-0 and E-1 bomber-reconnaissance aircraft, with a broader fuselage, went into service in late 1940, powered by 1,600-horsepower BMW 801A and B air-cooled radial engines.

In the photo intelligence role, the aircraft carried a Rb 20/30 camera in the fuselage and a Rb 30/50 camera in the cockpit. Defensive armament consisted of one forward-firing MG 151 cannon and five MG 15 machine guns installed on gimbal mounts. Production ended in 1943.

OPERATIONS

Maiden flights for the Do 17 F-1 began in September 1936 and ended in February 1937. The Do 17 F-1 entered Luftwaffe service in in the spring of 1936 with Aufklärungsgruppe (F)/122. In 1937, reconnaissance missions were flown by air crews of the Condor Legion during the Spanish Civil War. The F-1 was phased out during 1938. The Do 17 E, F, and P did not fare well against Soviet fighters over Spain, leading to modifications, including a higher, longer cockpit that extended downward, ending at the front of the wings. The cockpit's floor was lowered to install a Bola (gondola) casement-style ventral defensive platform. The Luftwaffe inventory of operational Do 17 P-1s was approximately 200 aircraft by September 1939.

Luftwaffe Aufkl.Gruppe units equipped with the reconnaissance variants operated day and night missions on the Eastern and Western Fronts at least through mid-1941, when the last remaining examples were replaced by the Ju 86P and R and the Ju 88. The first Do 17 P-1 was lost to enemy action on 30 October 1939, when an RAF Hawker Hurricane shot down a Dornier of 2(F) Aufkl. Gruppe/123 over France. Aufklärungsgruppe des Oberbefehlshabers der Lufftwaffe Aufkl.Gruppe Ob.d.L., a special clandestine recon group under the direct command of Hermann Goering, received Do 17 prototypes V-13 and V-14, along with approximately a dozen photo intelligence Do 215 B-0/1s and eight preproduction Do 217 A-0s. This group, also known as Rowehl-Gruppe or Kamando Rowehl Gruppe, was headed by Oberstleutnant Theodor Rowehl, who used these aircraft in reconnaissance missions of Soviet airfields from late 1940 to June 1941.

STATUS

Retired. Production of the Do 17 ended in 1940 as Dornier switched over to assembling the Do 217. The Luftwaffe began retiring the Do 17 from frontline duty by 1941 as higher-performance reconnaissance aircraft became operational. However, the machine continued as a trainer and glider tug. Dornier exported to Yugoslavia Do 17 Ms designated as the Do Kb-1 bomber and Do 17 Ka-2 and Ka-3 reconnaissance aircraft as variants of the Do 17P-1. All were powered by 14-cylinder Gnome-Rhône 14N engines. The Bulgarian Air Force received approximately 36 Do 17s between 1940 and 1943, including some Do 17 Ps. The Finnish Air Force received nine Do 17 Z-3s in 1942 during the country's Continuation War with the Soviet Union and continued to operate these after World War II, scrapping the last one in 1952. Spain inherited ex–Condor Legion Do 17 Es, Fs, and Ps, which they operated through the Spanish Civil War. ■

—*Alan C. Carey*

DORNIER DO 217

CREW:	4
ENGINES:	Do 217 A-0: 2x Daimler-Benz 601A inline; 1,100 hp each Do 217 E/E1: 2x BMW 801A/B 14-cylinder radial; 1,600 hp each
WEIGHTS:	Empty: 19,489 lb (8,840 kg) Maximum: 36,817 lb (16,700 kg)
LENGTH:	55 ft 5.25 in (16.9 m)
WINGSPAN:	62 ft 4 in (19.0 m)
HEIGHT:	16 ft 9 in (5.1 m)
SPEEDS:	Maximum: 348 mph (560 kph) Cruise: 248 mph (400 kph)
RANGE:	1,336 mi (2,150 km)
ARMAMENT:	Do 217 E/E1: 1x 15mm MG 151 machine gun; 5x 7.92mm MG 15 machine guns; 6,614 lb (3,000 kg) bomb load

DORNIER DO 17 Z-2/3 AND 215 B-0/B-1

CREW:	4
ENGINES:	Do 17: 2x BMW Bramo 323P Fafnir nine-cylinder radial; 1,000 hp each Do 215: 2x Daimler-Benz 601A inline engines; 1,100 hp each
WEIGHTS:	Empty: 11,486 lb (5,210 kg) Maximum: 19,482 lb (8,837 kg)
LENGTH:	51 ft 9.75 in (15.8 m)
WINGSPAN:	59 ft 1 in (18.0 m)
HEIGHT:	15 ft (4.6 m)
SPEEDS:	Maximum: 255 mph (410 kph) Cruise: 186 mph (162 kph)
CEILING:	26,600 feet (8,108 m)
RANGE:	205 mi (330 km) with full bomb load; 720 mi (1,159 km) with half bomb load
ARMAMENT:	5x MG 15 machine guns; 2,205 lb (1,000 kg) bomb load

FOCKE-WULF FW 200 CONDOR

The Fw 200 was an all-metal, four-engine German airliner originally developed for Deutsche Lufthansa that also saw civilian service with DDL Danish Airlines and Syndatico Condor in Brazil. One of the Danish aircraft was even operated by British Overseas Airways Corporation (BOAC) and then the Royal Air Force after it was seized by the British in 1940. Captured or interned aircraft were also used by the Soviet and Spanish air forces.

With the onset of World War II, the Condor saw military service as a long-range patrol bomber and reconnaissance aircraft. The Luftwaffe continued to use the Condor as a transport, with one airplane, named *Immelmann III*, serving as Hitler's plush personal airliner until its destruction in 1944.

DESIGN

The Condor was the brainchild of Kurt Tank, a cavalry officer turned aeronautical engineer who would go on to develop the Focke-Wulf Fw 190 fighter and its successor, the Ta 152. Tank himself was at the controls for the first flight of the Condor in July 1937. Built for the then-developing transatlantic market, the airliner version, the Fw 200A, was equipped to carry 26 passengers in two-cabin comfort over more than 1,800 miles (2,997 kilometers) at altitudes up to 9,800 feet (2,987 meters), the highest possible at the time without pressurization.

Focke-Wulf Fw 200. *Walter Frenz photo, Bundesarchiv, 146-1978-043-02, CC Attribution-Share Alike 3.0 Germany*

With additional fuel tanks fitted, a Condor became the first heavier-than-air aircraft to fly nonstop from Berlin to New York City—an all-but-astonishing feat in 1938.

The idea to use the Condor as a patrol bomber originally came from the Japanese Navy. Focke-Wulf built a military prototype, the Fw 200 V10, but it remained in Germany as the war in Europe flared up, becoming the basis for the subsequent Fw 200B and Fw 20C models and their many variants. In addition to adding hardpoints, defensive weaponry, and bomb bay doors, a distinctive gondola, common to a number of German bombers of the era, was added under the fuselage.

While the airliner prototype was originally designed to use four Pratt & Whitney R-1690s, the production models were powered by BMW Bramo radial engines, giving the airplane a cruise speed of 220 miles per hour (352 kilometers per hour), a range of 2,200 miles (3,540 kilometers), and an impressive ten-hour endurance (up to a remarkable 18 hours with extended fuel tanks).

The military variants were originally designated "Kurier" to differentiate them from the civilian airliners, but that term eventually fell out of favor and the airplane is known universally as the Condor.

OPERATIONS

The Luftwaffe originally dedicated the Fw 200 to supporting the Kriegsmarine by spotting Allied convoys and then relaying their positions to German U-boats. Once the Condors began carrying bomb loads of their own, however, they began attacking surface ships directly. Contemporary reports claimed more than 320,000 tons of Allied shipping lost to Condors in the month of April 1941 alone.

While just 276 were built, the Condor established itself as a powerful opponent in the early days of World War II. No less than British Prime Minister Winston Churchill would later write, "To the U-boat scourge was now added air attack far out in the oceans by long-range aircraft. Of these, the Focke-Wulf 200, known as the Condor, was the most formidable."

The British took the Condor threat so seriously that they developed a scheme whereby Hawker Hurricanes were carried onboard merchant ships, both military and civilian, and launched via rocket catapult to defend their convoys. This was a one-way mission, at least for the airplanes—there was no provision for the pilots to do anything other than bail out or ditch their fighters after a sortie. These "Hurricats" proved something of a deterrent, holding their own until the Royal Navy began deploying escort carriers equipped with Grumman Martlets, the British name for the F4F Wildcat. The Luftwaffe stopped attacking shipping directly in the summer of 1941 and focused primarily on maritime reconnaissance. Condors remained in this role until late 1943, when they were largely replaced by the newer Junkers Ju 290.

The final iterations of the Condor, the Fw 200C-6 and C-8, were specially adapted to carry the Henschel Hs 293 guided missile, a radio-controlled glide bomb with a rocket motor attached; these aircraft were used throughout 1943 and 1944.

Condor production ceased in early 1944.

STATUS

Retired. No complete examples survive today, though one is currently under restoration by the Deutsches Technikmuseum Berlin using wreckage recovered from two Norwegian crash sites. ■

—Hal Bryan

FOCKE-WULF FW 200

CREW:	5
ENGINES:	4x BMW/Bramo 323-R-2 Fafnir air-cooled radials; 1,200 hp each
WEIGHTS:	Empty: 37,490 lb (17,005 kg) Maximum: 50,045 lb (22,700 kg)
LENGTH:	76 ft 11 in (20.1 m)
WINGSPAN:	107 ft 9 in (32.8 m)
HEIGHT:	20 ft 8 in (6.3 m)
SPEEDS:	Maximum: 240 mph (386 kph) Cruise: 220 mph (354 kph)
CEILING:	19,030 ft (5,800 m)
RANGE:	2,200 mi (3,540 km)
ARMAMENT:	1x 20mm cannon; 1x 15mm machine gun; 3x 7.9mm machine guns; up to 4,630 lb (2,100 kg) bomb payload
RADAR:	FuG Rostock or FuG Hohentwiel (later models)

ARADO AR 234 BLITZ

The Arado Ar 234 Blitz (Lightning) was the Luftwaffe's second operational jet, the other being the Messerschmitt Me 262, and it was the first operational jet bomber and long-range, high-altitude reconnaissance aircraft. Problems with engine development and landing gear configuration design, along with fuel and material shortages, delayed production until late in World War II, and too few became operational to change the war's final outcome. Approximately 234 B and C variants were completed at Lönnewitz from December 1944 to early 1945.

DESIGN

Initial development began with Arado Flugzeugwerke engineers Walter Blume and Hans Rebeski submitting a technical proposal to the German Air Ministry. The proposal was accepted and a design team was established, led by T. Rüdiger Kosin. The aircraft was unlike any under development by the Allied Powers at the time and featured a slender fuselage, and high-wing design, with two Junkers Jumo 109-0004 turbojets housed in nacelles under the wings; these features gave it a maximum top speed of 456 miles per hour (735 kilometers per hour), outperforming any conventional radial or inline fighter. Another unusual design feature was the cockpit, which was located in the nose with a large glazed canopy affording the crew a wide viewing area. With a required combat range of some 1,300 miles (807 kilometers), the designers had to include internal tanks behind the cockpit.

The designers initially could not solve how to fit conventional landing gear due the Ar 234's high-wing design. During takeoff, the early prototypes—Ar 234V-1 to V-5 (Ar 234A series)—employed a reusable tricycle trolley that was jettisoned upon becoming airborne, while landing skis fitted to the aft fuselage and wings were lowered for landing. The first prototype was

Arado Ar 234. *National Museum of the USAF*

completed and flight-tested in June 1943, followed by two more in September; the prototypes were initially ready by the end of 1941, but engine development and production became problematic, thus delaying testing and production by two years.

The Jumo 109-0004 powered both the Ar 234 and the Me 262; because the Me 262 took precedence, supplying the engines in adequate numbers was impossible. The powerplant also required a rebuild after only ten operational hours and was known for flameouts. Prototypes Ar 234V-6 to V-8 retained the carriage ski configuration but were powered by lower-thrust BMW 1009-003-A1 engines as an alternative to the -0004. Those three aircraft went into the development of the Ar 234C, in which fewer than half of the 14 produced were fitted with engines before the war ended.

A redesign requested by the Air Ministry consisted of enlarging the mid-fuselage, along with removal of a fuel tank to accommodate a tricycle landing gear, and installation of a recessed bomb bay in the fuselage and a periscopic optical sight above the cockpit for rearward viewing. The pilot-bombardier during a bomb run switched on the Patin PDS autopilot and then swung the control column away to use the Lotfe 7K bombsight. A maximum external and internal bomb

load capacity of over 3,300 pounds (1,497 kilograms) reduced the maximum speed to 415 miles per hour (668 kilometers per hour). The three prototypes built in this fashion were designated Ar 234V-9 to V-11 (Ar 234B series) with the first test flight occurring in March 1944. Production units were designated Ar 234B.

Several of the trolley and ski prototypes and B-1 and B-2 airframes were modified as recon platforms, with the rear fuselage housing two to three vertical and oblique cameras: the Reihenbilder (Rb) 50/30, Rb 75/30, Rb 20/30 series. Two recon variants in development, consisting of the Ar 234C-1 and the two-man Ar 234D, were not completed.

OPERATIONS

V-5 and V-7 prototypes, equipped with rocket-assisted takeoff (RATO) were sent to I./Versuchsverband Oberbefehlshaber der Luftwaffe in July 1944 for operational evaluation. The first reconnaissance mission was conducted of the Allied landing areas in Normandy by Erich Summer, piloting the V-5 prototype on 2 August 1944. Special Unit Sonderkommando (SdKdo) Götz operated four Ar 234B-1s near Rheine in Westphalia, Germany, and ran reconnaissance

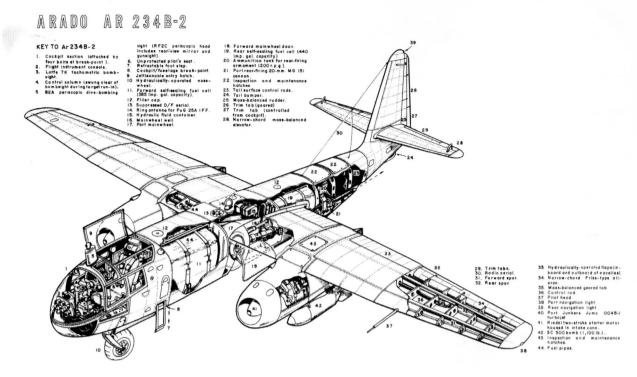

ARADO AR 234B-2

KEY TO Ar 234B-2

1. Cockpit section (attached by four bolts at break-point).
2. Flight instrument console.
3. Lotfe 7K tachometric bomb-sight.
4. Control column (swung clear of bombsight during target run-in).
5. B2A periscopic dive-bombing sight (RF2C periscopic head includes rear-view mirror and gunsight).
6. Unprotected pilot's seat.
7. Retractable foot step.
8. Cockpit/fuselage break-point.
9. Jettisonable entry hatch.
10. Hydraulically-operated nose-wheel.
11. Forward self-sealing fuel cell (385 imp. gal. capacity).
12. Filler cap.
13. Suppressed D/F aerial.
14. Ring antenna for FuG 25A IFF.
15. Hydraulic fluid container.
16. Mainwheel well.
17. Port mainwheel.
18. Forward mainwheel door.
19. Rear self-sealing fuel cell (440 imp. gal. capacity).
20. Ammunition tank for rear-firing armament (200 r.p.g.).
21. Port rear-firing 20-mm. MG 151 cannon.
22. Inspection and maintenance hatches.
23. Tail surface control rods.
24. Tail bumper.
25. Mass-balanced rudder.
26. Trim tab (geared).
27. Trim tab (controlled from cockpit).
28. Narrow-chord mass-balanced elevator.
29. Trim tabs.
30. Radio aerial.
31. Forward spar.
32. Rear spar.
33. Hydraulically-operated flaps (inboard and outboard of nacelles).
34. Narrow-chord Frise-type aileron.
35. Mass-balanced geared tab.
36. Control rod.
37. Pitot head.
38. Port navigation light.
39. Rear navigation light.
40. Port Junkers Jumo 004B-1 turbojet.
41. Riedel two-stroke starter motor housed in intake cone.
42. SC 500 bomb (1,100 lb.).
43. Inspection and maintenance hatches.
44. Fuel pipes.

Arado Ar 234. *National Museum of the USAF*

---

missions over Allied-held territory and the British Isles beginning in October 1944. SdKdo Hecht and Sperling were activated in November 1944 but deactivated and replaced by I./Fernaufklärungsgruppe (FAGr) in January 1945. SdKdo Summer operated three Ar 234B1s at Udine in northern Italy, while I./FAGr 123, based in Germany and Norway, and I./FAGr 33 flew missions over Germany and Denmark.

STATUS

Retired. The British Army transferred nine aircraft found at Sola Airbase near Stavanger, Norway, to England for evaluation. USAAF personnel confiscated four others that were flown to Cherbourg, France, for transfer to the United States. Two Arado 234s (serial numbers 140312 and 143011), were reassembled upon arrival and flown to Freeman Field, Indiana, for evaluation from August to July 1946. Ar 234B-2 (serial number 140312), formally operated by the Luftwaffe's 9./Kampfgeschwader 76, was then sent to the Accelerated Test Maintenance Section (ATMS) of the US AAF Flight Test Division at Wright Field, Ohio. It was transferred to the Smithsonian Institute and is the only surviving example of the Blitz. ∎

—Alan C. Carey

ARADO AR 234

CREW:	1
ENGINES:	2x Junkers Jumo 004B-1 axial-flow turbojets; 1,962 lbst (890 kgst) each
WEIGHTS:	Empty: 11,464 lb (5,200 kg) Maximum: 21,715 lb (9,850 kg); 22,070 lb (10,011 kg) with RATO
LENGTH:	41 ft 5 in (12.6 m)
WINGSPAN:	46 ft 3 in (14.1 m)
HEIGHT:	14 ft 1 in (4.3 m)
SPEEDS:	Maximum: 461 mph (742 kph) Cruise: 435 mph (700 kph)
CEILING:	32,810 ft (10,000 m)
RANGE:	1,340 mi (2,156 km) empty with Maximum: fuel load
ARMAMENT:	None for recon variant

Do 335, basis for the ill-fated Do 635 concept. *Nicholas A. Veronico collection*

DORNIER DO 635 PFEIL [1944]

Dornier proposed the Do 635 Pfeil (alternate designations Do 635Z and Ju 8-635) as a four-engine, high-altitude, unarmed reconnaissance variant of the Do 335 Pfeil (Arrow) fighter, but only a partial mockup had been completed before Germany's surrender. The design, consisting of two Do 335 fuselages, shared some similarities with the four-engine Heinkel He 111Z (formed with two He 111-H6s) and the later Cold War–era North American F-82 Twin Mustang (which appeared to be two F-51 Mustangs joined together). However, the F-82 went into production and remained in the USAF inventory until the early 1950s, while just two prototype Do 635s and ten Heinkel He 111Z-1s were produced.

DESIGN

In 1942, the Reich Air Ministry awarded Dornier Flugzeugwerke a contract to produce an extreme-long-range, high-speed fighter and reconnaissance platform, which evolved into the Do 335 Pfeil and the Do 635 Zwilling. The unique Do 335 is generally characterized as an all-metal aircraft, having tricycle landing gear and a low wing attached to the fuselage's midsection. Conventional descriptors end here, since the Arrow's physical attributes consist of a long nose with a setback cockpit and high aft fuselage with a ventral-vertical tail and rudder assembly. Dornier adapted a push-pull, centerline thrust configuration due to the company's experience with the concept via the Do 18 and Do 26 multiengine flying boats. The Arrow's forward tractor and backward-mounted rear pusher engines consisted of two Daimler-Benz 603E-1 liquid-cooled inverted 12-cylinders, each rated at 1,800 horsepower for takeoff, with 1,905 horsepower maximum in flight.

Germany's dwindling resources and production demands by mid-1944 forced Dornier to have Junkers take over the Do 635 project so it could concentrate on producing the Do 335. However, only 37 were completed before Germany's surrender. Erprobungskommando 335 (Operational Test Unit 335) conducted tactical evaluation of a few Do 335A1s until the unit disbanded in April 1945.

Professor Heinrich Hertel was chosen to head the design team for the Ju 635 (project 1075 01-21) due to his experience with the He 111 series including the He 111 Z01. Two Do 335 B4 airframes were to form the Do 635 and would have been powered by four 603E-1 engines. Modifications for the Ju 635 consisted of lengthening the fuselage, increasing the size of the midsection, and adding new main wheels (the same used on the Ju 352 Hercules transport). Possibly 10 to 12 fuel cells, varying in capacity, would have been located in the center section, outer wing areas, and center fuselage, with a provision for one external tank per wing. Maximum fuel capacity would have given the aircraft a range of over 4,000 miles (6,437 kilometers).

A tandem seat arrangement for both pressurized cockpits was envisioned for a three- to four-man crew. The pilot and radio operator sat in the port fuselage cockpit while the second pilot, as with the F-82, sat in the starboard cockpit (the intention was to include a navigator in the starboard side as well). A five-point landing gear configuration was planned, including a nose wheel and a main wheel for each fuselage, as well as a reusable fifth wheel under the midsection, which would be jettisoned upon liftoff. A pair of Walter rocket-assisted takeoff gear would provide additional thrust.

Photo intelligence would have been gathered with two Rb 50/30 cameras installed in the port fuselage bay, while the starboard bay could hold five 132-pound (60-kilogram) marker bombs. Wind-tunnel testing occurred in early 1945 and a cockpit mockup was created showing a multiframed canopy with a five-frame canopy hatch.

OPERATION

The air ministry ordered four prototypes and six preproduction aircraft with an expected production run of five aircraft per month. Erprobungskommando 600 N (Nebel) was selected to conduct tactical evaluation of the aircraft, but the program was abandoned in February 1945 as Allied forces neared the facility.

STATUS

None were produced, but technical details, photographs of the cockpit mockup, and schematics survive. One Do 335 is on exhibit at the Smithsonian Institution. ■

—*Alan C. Carey*

DORNIER DO 635

CREW:	2 to 4
ENGINES:	4x Daimler-Benz 603E-1 inverted V-12 liquid-cooled; 1,777 hp each
WEIGHT:	Maximum: 72,352 lb (32,818 kg)
LENGTH:	60 ft 8 in (18.5 m)
WINGSPAN:	90 ft (27.4 m)
HEIGHT:	16 ft 5 in (5 m)
SPEEDS:	Maximum: 447 mph (719 kph) Cruise: 398 mph (641 kph)
RANGE:	4,000–4,722 mi (6,437–7,600 km)
ARMAMENT:	None
RADAR:	Plans for installation on completed aircraft

GREAT BRITAIN

Airco DH.4. *NAS, San Diego, CCO 1.0 Universal Public Domain*

AIRCO DH.4

Conceived by the legendary Geoffrey de Havilland during his tenure as chief designer for the Aircraft Manufacturing Company Limited (Airco) of Hendon, England, the DH.4 was built as a recon and light bombing platform. Originally designed with a 160-horsepower Beardmore-Halford-Pullinger engine in mind, the type was ultimately fitted with a number of powerplants, including the 250-horsepower Rolls-Royce Eagle III and, later (when built under license in the United States), the 400-horsepower Liberty L-12. Paired with the then-new Liberty engine, the US-built versions quickly earned the nickname "Liberty Planes" when production began in 1917.

observer; variants included a Scarff-ring mounted Lewis gun in the rear cockpit. A pressurized fuel tank located between the cockpits had the advantage of putting the secondary cockpit further aft, thus affording greater visibility, but this arrangement also left the fuel tank vulnerable to enemy fire.

The DH.4 had no official designation, though the "Liberty Plane" moniker given to the US-built versions saw widespread use. The other nickname sometimes used was the grim, derisive, and ultimately unwarranted term "Flaming Coffin"; of the DH.4s lost in combat, the numbers that actually burned were average compared to other types.

DESIGN

The DH.4 was a fairly conventional design for the period. A two-place biplane, the DH.4 was Airco's first tractor design; their earlier aircraft all had engines mounted in the pusher configuration. The wings were fabric-covered and built around two spruce spars, along with the typical array of bracing wires. The box-girder fuselage was covered with fabric aft of the rear cockpit, with thin plywood sheeting from that point forward, providing a light but exceptionally sturdy frame. The DH.4 sported the now-classic de Havilland tail.

The DH.4 had two open cockpits: one for a pilot and the second for an optional rearward-facing gunner/

OPERATIONS

Ultimately seeing service with 15 nations, the DH.4 began its operational life with the British Royal Flying Corps (RFC) and the Royal Naval Air Service (RNAS) in early 1917. Both services used the airplane for light bombing, artillery spotting, and anti-submarine patrol (in the case of the RNAS), in addition to photographic reconnaissance. British DH.4s were operated primarily in France, but they also saw service in Mesopotamia, Macedonia, the Adriatic, the Aegean, and Russia, as well as patrol duties at home.

When the US Army first ordered the DH.4, the Aviation Section of the Signal Corps—soon to be

Airco DH.4. *National Museum of the USAF*

replaced by the US Army Air Service—had just 132 aircraft in service, none of them suitable for combat operations. Once DH.4 production had ramped up in the United States, the type was deployed to France in the summer of 1918. One crew—1st Lt. Harold Goettler and 2nd Lt. Erwin Bleckley of the 50th Aero Squadron—flew what was probably the most notable mission of the war: the discovery of more than 550 American troops who had been surrounded by German forces in the Argonne Forest, the so-called "Lost Battalion." Goettler and Bleckley were brought down by enemy ground fire, but they were awarded the Medal of Honor posthumously.

This type formed the backbone of the newly formed US Army Border Air Patrol in 1919 and saw continuous military service until its retirement from the US Army in 1932. The DH.4 also enjoyed a variety of civilian careers, most notably carrying the US Mail.

STATUS

Retired. The prototype of the DH.4 first flew in August 1916, with de Havilland himself at the controls. While 1,449 DH.4s were built in the UK by several manufacturers, the overwhelming majority were built under license in the United States, where 4,486 were produced. The US Army's initial order was for more than 12,000 of the type, though more than 7,500 of those orders were cancelled at the time of the Armistice. DH.4s were modified by multiple companies in the US after World War I, leading to more than 60 variants at one time or another.

At the time of this writing, multiple examples exist in museums around the world, with just one in flying condition; at least two other restoration projects are under way. ■

—*Hal Bryan*

AIRCO DH.4

CREW:	2
ENGINE:	1x Liberty L-12 (400 hp), among others
WEIGHTS:	Empty: 2,391 lb (1,085 kg) Maximum: 4,297 lb (1,949 kg)
LENGTH:	30 ft 5 in (9.3 m)
WINGSPAN:	42 ft 8 in (13.0 m)
HEIGHT:	10 ft 5 in (3.2 m)
SPEEDS:	Maximum: 128 mph (206 kph) Cruise: 90 mph (145 kph)
CEILING:	19,600 ft (5,974 m)
RANGE:	400 mi (644 km)
ARMAMENT:	2x .30-cal. Marlin machine guns in the nose; 2x .30-caliber Lewis machine guns in the rear; 322 lb (146 kg) bomb payload

Supermarine Spitfire PR Mk X1. *Bettmann/Getty Images*

SUPERMARINE PR SPITFIRE

Before the outbreak of World War II in Europe, the RAF relied on converted bombers and liaison aircraft for reconnaissance duties. It was soon apparent that a speedier, higher-flying aircraft would be needed to survive heavy antiaircraft fire and prowling Luftwaffe fighters in the years to come.

The RAF turned to their top-of-the-line fighter aircraft for an effective wartime photo reconnaissance (PR) machine. The Supermarine Spitfire had a racing-plane pedigree and by removing semi-necessary items, like guns and radios, the small fighter could fly reasonably far, cruise high, and move fast enough to get photographs of some of the most heavily defended areas within "Fortress Europe."

DESIGN

A pair of Spitfires was modified for "photo-recce" work in October 1939. Designated PR Mk Is, they had their guns removed and a pair of 5-inch (127mm) F.24 cameras installed in their place. The highly polished and aerodynamically clean planes flew a full 15 miles per hour (24 kilometers per hour) faster than their gun-equipped contemporaries. Additional versions (PR Mk II) substituted 8-inch (203mm) focal-length cameras and carried an additional 29 gallons (110 liters) of fuel.

The PR Mk III was the first Spitfire converted in large numbers. Some 40 aircraft received modifications to carry even more fuel and an additional camera. The PR Mk IV, nicknamed the "Browser," could fly 2,000 miles (3,219 kilometers) and carried a multitude of different photographic equipment.

Further versions operated with oblique cameras in their fuselages and a mixture of different fuel tanks. The side-facing cameras brought the planes back down to risky altitudes, which sometimes necessitated adding a complement of guns back into their airframes. The Mk IX, designated the FR Mk IX (for fighter reconnaissance) flew with standard armament and a trusty F.24 camera mounted obliquely for low-level snooping. Pilots sometimes referred to these treetop-level photo flights as "dicer" missions—meaning "throwing the dice" or "gambling with death."

About 1,000 Spitfires were modified for photo work or specially built as PR planes from the factory.

OPERATIONS

The first PR (Mk I) Spitfires were tested in combat in November 1939 with a scouting flight over the German city of Aachen. Subsequent flights necessitated the switch to larger-lensed cameras to pick up more detail on the ground.

These planes, Mk IIs, were able to shoot images of enemy ships in German port cities along the North Sea in early 1940. Browser Spitfires were able to go as far as Stettin, Germany (today Szczecin, Poland), by late 1940.

Some photographic reconnaissance units (PRUs) operated from the UK, while others flew at various times from bases in Africa, Asia, and the Mediterranean. The United States Eighth Air Force operated some 21 PR Mk XI Spitfires with the 7th Photographic Reconnaissance Group from England. PR Mk XIII aircraft famously helped shoot detailed images of the Normandy beach landing locations and defenses in the weeks before D-Day. PR Spitfires often flew several missions a day; before D-Day, they were sometimes racking up eight sorties a day if the weather was clear.

Often unarmed, "recce" Spitfire pilots commonly used speed or altitude to outrun or outfox enemy

Supermarine Spitfire PR Mk I. *Royal Canadian Air Force photo*

fighters. One flyer recorded that Messerschmitt Bf 109s twice awaited his arrival at 30,000 feet (9,144 meters) near Rheims, France. On both occasions, he was able to shake the enemy hunters, noting that his PR Spitfire seemed "about 40 mph [64 kph] faster" than the German fighter.

Those who didn't get away were often never heard from again. The recon pilot, flying alone on his prescribed photo route, simply never returned home.

DESIGNATION

The RAF began identifying their recon Spitfires initially with letters. The first aircraft drafted to PR work was a Type A. The lettering system caused confusion because it was similar to the lettering system for Spitfire wing types, leading to a mark system. The Type A became the PR Mk I, the Type B the PR Mk II, and so on. The lettering system was dropped after Type F (PR Mk VI).

It should be noted that the early PR designation system operated independently of the Spitfire aircraft mark system. For example, the PR Mk X aircraft was an equivalent machine not to the standard Mk X Spitfire fighter, but to a Spitfire Mk VII aircraft. After Mk X, both the PR version of the aircraft and the standard fighter version had the same mark number.

The final version of the PR Spitfire was the PR Mk XIX, a Griffon-engine Spitfire that stayed in RAF recon service through 1954.

SUPERMARINE SPITFIRE PR MK XI

CREW:	1
ENGINE:	1x Rolls-Royce Merlin 61, 63, 63A, or 70; 1,655 hp
WEIGHTS:	Empty: 6,100 lb (2,766 kg) Maximum: 8,040 lb (3,647 kg)
LENGTH:	30 ft (9.1 m)
WINGSPAN:	36 ft 10 in (11.2 m)
HEIGHT:	12 ft 7 in (3.8 m)
SPEED:	Maximum: 422 mph (679 kph)
CEILING:	40,000 ft (12,192 m)
RANGE:	1,360 mi (2,188 km)
ARMAMENT:	None

Retired. First flown in 1939, PR Spitfires operated in RAF military service from World War II through 1954 and flew meteorological missions up to 1957.

Besides the UK and US, Germany captured one or more PR Spitfires, re-marked them, and flew the planes on test flights and for training purposes. In 1947, both Norway and Denmark acquired a trio of PR Mk XI aircraft that flew in military service until 1954 and 1955 respectively. The Swedish Air Force used some of its PR Mk XIX Spitfires (designated S 31s) for photo reconnaissance duties from the late 1940s until the mid-1950s. ■

—Cory Graff

DE HAVILLAND PR MOSQUITO

The Royal Air Force's "fast bomber" first flew in November 1940. De Havilland's Mosquito was unique in that, in order to keep weight down, the plane was built primarily of wood composite structures. This construction had the added bonus of preserving war-critical duralumin and steel for other aircraft projects. The plane was powered by two Rolls-Royce Merlin V-12 engines, similar to those seen in the RAF's Spitfire and Hurricane.

Initial tests brought impressive results and the RAF almost immediately began to consider the plane for tasks beyond delivering high explosives. The initial aircraft was built as a bomber, but the second prototype took the form of a fighter aircraft, its nose packed with guns. The third plane, W4051, was fitted for testing photo reconnaissance work. The aircraft flew for the first time on 10 June 1941.

US Army Air Forces de Havilland Mosquito B. *NASA photo*

DESIGN

W4051 was outfitted with a large F.52 day camera, a K.17 mapping and survey camera, and one or two F.24s. The aircraft is notable as the first Mosquito to go into combat service, serving with the No. 1 PRU based at RAF Benson. The RAF's initial Mosquito order was 50 bombers, 176 fighters, and 19 PR Mosquitos.

Though the role of the PR Spitfire was clearly established, the new PR Mosquito offered advantages. The plane was almost as fast as the Spitfire under many conditions, but the twin-engine plane was much larger. Size allowed the Mosquito to carry more fuel, thus fly longer distances than the Spitfire, reaching faraway military bases and ports.

Its big, bomber-sized body meant the PR Mosquito could carry more cameras than the diminutive Spitfire, and its sizable fuselage allowed crewmen to reload

DE HAVILLAND MOSQUITO PR MK XVI

CREW:	2
ENGINES:	2x Rolls-Royce Merlin 72 V-12; 1,710 hp each
WEIGHT:	Maximum: 25,917 lb (11,756 kg)
LENGTH:	41 ft 6 in (12.6 m)
WINGSPAN:	54 ft 2 in (16.5 m)
HEIGHT:	12 ft 6 in (3.8 m)
SPEED:	Maximum: 408 mph (657 kph)
CEILING:	42,000 ft (12,802 m)
RANGE:	1,995 mi (3,211 km)
ARMAMENT:	None

some of the photographic equipment while in flight, thus allowing for more photos per sortie. The two-man Mosquito crew added another advantage: recon planes were most vulnerable as they were flying a prescribed path to capture their shots. With a crew of two, one could fly (and watch for threats) while the other man concentrated on shooting the images needed to make the mission a success. Plus, as crewmen related, flying a Mosquito meant you were far less lonely.

The RAF identified PR Mosquitos with a mark system. This system worked independent of the overall aircraft type mark system. For example, the PR Mk I was derived from the B Mk IV bomber airframe. The PR Mk 32 and beyond received numeric designations in the place of Roman numerals. The last recon type was the PR Mk 34A.

OPERATIONS

The RAF took advantage of the PR Mosquito's range almost immediately. The UK-based planes sniffed out sites as far away as Norway in late 1941 and reached Danzig on the Baltic Sea (today Gdańsk, Poland) in January 1942.

The planes were ideal for capturing before and after photographs of heavy bomber targets because they could reach nearly any place the big bombers could. In 1943, a PR Mosquito discovered the famous rocket-testing facility at Pennemünde while returning from a photo mission over Stettin (Szczecin, Poland). PR Mosquitos also had the fuel capacity to shuttle from place to place, exploring and exposing likely V-1 and V-2 rocket staging spots over large operational areas.

Commonly, the PR Mosquitos could fly high and fast enough that they could not be cornered, allowing them to roam over enemy-held territory with impunity. Only after mid-1944 did PR pilots have to be wary of an encounter with an occasional Me 163 rocket plane or Me 262 jet fighter.

Outside the UK, additional PR units flew Mosquitos northward into "Europe's underbelly" from bases in the Mediterranean, while others launched from India to explore Japanese operations in Burma, Thailand, and Malaysia, though the Mosquito's wood-and-glue construction caused worries among air crews in the hot, humid climate of the Far East.

The US acquired some 40 Canadian-built Mosquitos, which they designated F-8 reconnaissance aircraft. The planes, however, did not have the performance capabilities of the British aircraft. Later, some 100 or more English-built PR Mk XVIs came to US squadrons. While some completed standard PR missions, others were used for meteorology flights, chaff dispersion, radar reconnaissance, and secret communication with agents in enemy territory.

After the end of World War II, PR Mosquitos soldiered on in service of the RAF, the last one flying an operational sortie in 1955. Foreign users took on Mosquitos after the war, including some PR types. The French operated PR aircraft in French Indochina while Israel used them in the Middle East. Some civilian operators flew purpose-built and converted PR Mosquitos for aerial mapping and survey work in Canada, Australia, and Libya through the 1950s.

STATUS

Retired. First flown in 1941, PR Mosquitos operated in RAF frontline military service through 1955. Foreign nations and civilian users used the planes slightly longer. A handful of PR Mosquitos today reside in museum collections in Australia, Canada, and South Africa. ∎

—Cory Graff

ENGLISH ELECTRIC CANBERRA

The Canberra was the first jet-propelled bomber to enter British service and the nominal successor to the versatile Mosquito aircraft of World War II. In the early 1950s, the Canberra overflew the Soviet Union for intelligence collection on behalf of both the United States and Great Britain.

An effective bomber aircraft, British- and American-built Canberras also were configured for tactical and high-altitude strategic reconnaissance, the former to replace the de Havilland Mosquito and the latter to supplement U-2 operations. Both bomber and photorecon variants were unarmed, relying on speed, altitude, and maneuverability to escape enemy interceptors.

The aircraft was built in the United States by the Glenn L. Martin Company as the B-57 (see separate US Canberra entry on page 188) and in Australia.

DESIGN

The Canberra design featured a low-aspect-ratio, mid-fuselage wing that provided a high-altitude capability and outstanding maneuverability. Weapons were carried in an internal bomb bay.

The standard Canberra was flown by a crew of two or three: a pilot, a navigator, and, in the bomber variants, a bombardier. Most PR Canberras flew with a two-man crew, but on some missions a third crewmember assisted in navigation from a "rumble seat" in the cockpit.

RECON VARIANTS

The specialized photorecon aircraft, the PR.3 variant and its successors, were based on the B.2 bomber design with the addition of a 14 inch (35.6 cm) bay forward of the wing and increased fuel capacity. These aircraft could accommodate up to seven cameras.

The PR.7 and PR.9 variants followed. The PR.7 had more powerful engines and additional fuel tanks. The PR.9 featured improved engines (Rolls-Royce Avon 206 rated at 11,250 pounds static thrust each) and extended wingspan (67 feet, 10 inches; 20.68 meters) for high-altitude operations (that is, the "wide-wing" configuration).

OPERATIONS

On 8–9 October 1953, a PR.3 set a speed record from London to Christchurch, New Zealand, a distance of 12,270 miles (19,747 kilometers), in 23 hours, 51 minutes. On 4 May 1953, a modified Canberra established an official world altitude record of 63,668 feet (19,406 meters); on 29 August 1955, the same aircraft (and pilot) set an official altitude record of 65,876 feet (20,079 meters)—which was promptly and secretly broken by a U-2 aircraft.

In 1952, the CIA requested that the Royal Air Force use the new Canberra (bomber) to undertake a long-range photo mission over the Soviet missile test facility at Kapustan Yar on the Volga River. The British flew this

English Electric Canberra. *JohnnyOneSpeed, public domain*

ENGLISH ELECTRIC CANBERRA PR.7

CREW:	2 or 3
ENGINES:	2x Rolls-Royce Avon 109 turbojet; 7,500 lbst (3,402 kgst) each
WEIGHTS:	Empty: 49,000 lb (22,226 kg) Maximum: 55,000 lb (24,948 kg)
LENGTH:	66 ft 8 in (20.3 m)
WINGSPAN:	63 ft 11.5 in (19.5 m)
HEIGHT:	15 ft 7 in (4.8 m)
SPEED:	Maximum: 580 mph (933 kph) at 40,000 ft (12,195 m)
CEILING:	48,000 ft (14,634 m)
RANGE:	4,340 mi (6,984 km)
ARMAMENT:	None

mission (Project Robin), probably in 1952, and apparently a second in July 1953. The latter Canberra was damaged by antiaircraft gunfire over the Soviet Union, but it was able to land safely in Iran. (British sources are vague about these flights, but RAF officials briefed US officials on the overflights in February 1954.)

Subsequently, Canberra PR aircraft flew tactical and strategic reconnaissance missions over Europe, the Middle East, Africa, and Asia, and monitored Soviet naval activities in the Mediterranean

STATUS

Retired. The prototype Canberra bomber first flew on 13 May 1949, with the first production B.2 bomber becoming operational in May 1951.

The prototype recon variant—the PR.3—first flew on 19 March 1950, followed by the first of 35 production PR.3 aircraft being delivered to RAF No. 540 Squadron beginning in December 1952 (converting from the Mosquito PR.34). First PR.7 flight took place on 28 October 1953; 74 were built. The prototype PR.9 (a converted PR.7) first flew on 8 July 1957, followed by 23 production wide-wing aircraft.

By the mid-1950s, the RAF had five strategic reconnaissance squadrons with Canberras, in addition to Canberra bomber formations.

British firms built 1,376 Canberras of all types—including 133 PR variants—with another 57 bomber aircraft built in Australia. British-built Canberra PR aircraft were flown by the RAF until 2006. Thirteen other countries flew refurbished ex-RAF Canberras. ■

—*Norman Polmar and John F. Bessette*

DE HAVILLAND COMET 2R

Great Britain's prominent role in the development of the jet engine, pioneered by Royal Air Force engineer Maj. Frank Whittle, resulted in the production of two British turbine-powered World War II fighter aircraft: the Gloster Meteor and the de Havilland Vampire. De Havilland followed up its success with ambitious plans for the world's first commercial jetliner. The de Havilland Comet 1 went into service in 1952, and with it, Britain seemed to have gained a big lead in postwar commercial aviation. The Comet made the American propeller-driven Constellation and Boeing DC-7 seem archaic. It carried 28,000 passengers an aggregate of 104 million miles (167 million kilometers).

Then a cascade of catastrophes struck starting in 1953. In May of that year, and again in January and April 1954, three fatal crashes occurred, after which the British Overseas Aircraft Corporation (BOAC) shut down Comet service. Years of investigation followed, with the finding that 1) structural failures resulted from intense flexing of the Comet's airframe and wings and that 2) de Havilland's initial test program failed to account for the stresses arising from the faster climb rate of jet-powered aircraft. By 1958, when the Comet finally got clearance to resume service, the Boeing 707 jetliner had begun to dominate the international market for passenger aircraft. Even though de Havilland revamped the Comet with a Model 2 in 1953, Model 3 in 1954, and the significantly improved Model 4 in 1958, it fell into decline as an airliner. In all, de Havilland delivered 76 of the planes to customers from 1958 to 1964.

DESIGN

The basic Comet design remained fundamentally the same throughout its production run. The fuselage had a circular cross-section of 10 feet in diameter running the length of the cabin. The cantilevered low wings had moderate sweepback. All Comets flew with four Rolls-Royce Avon engines faired into the wings and featured cantilever tail planes with a single fin and rudder. With the development of the line, though, some distinctions appeared between early and late models. Comet 2 measured 96 feet long (3 feet more than Comet 1, for increased range); Comets 3 and 4 each added 15.5 feet to the Comet 2 airframe. Comet 2 accommodated 44 passengers; Comet 4 could hold 58 to 76, depending on the configuration. Comet 2's engines each developed 7,350 pounds of thrust; Comet 4's produced 10,500 pounds.

OPERATIONS

Although the Comet ultimately saw diminished success in its commercial career, at the height of the Cold War it served effectively in several military versions. Two Comet T. Mark 2s did crew training duties for RAF Transport Command and eight Comet C. Mark 2s served as 44-seat troop and freight transports.

De Havilland Comet 2. *TSRL, CC Attribution-Share Alike 3.0*

Despite its uneven history, the Comet's most enduring contribution may have been its role in reconnaissance, embodied by the Comet 2R. Beginning in 1958, RAF Squadrons 51 and 192 employed converted Comet 2 transports and troop carriers for gathering intelligence. The cabins of these aircraft underwent complete retrofits, transformed by special radio and surveillance equipment and operating stations. They carried a large human complement as well: a flight crew of 6 and up to 26 avionics technicians/operators. On the exterior, many antennae and two ventral (underbody) radomes hinted at its new role. By 1963, seven of these aircraft served with the squadron at RAF Watton, and later at RAF Wyton. The Comet 2Rs flew regular ELINT missions at the borders of the Warsaw Pact countries, recording radar signals and listening in to Eastern Bloc military communications.

STATUS

Retired. The last documented Comet flight occurred in 1997. ∎

—*Michael Gorn*

DE HAVILLAND COMET 2R

CREW:	32
ENGINES:	4x Rolls-Royce Avon 503 turbojets; 7,350 lbst (3,336 kgst) each
WEIGHTS:	Empty: 75,400 lb (34,200 kg)
	Maximum: 120,000 lb (54,431 kg)
LENGTH:	96 ft (29.3 m)
WINGSPAN:	115 ft (35.0 m)
HEIGHT:	29 ft 6 in (9 m)
SPEEDS:	Maximum: 500 mph (805 kph)
	Cruise: 490 mph (789 kph)
CEILING:	40,000 ft (12,192 m)
RANGE:	2,100 mi (3,380 km)
ARMAMENT:	None
RADAR:	Surveillance radar; EKCO E160 (Comet 4)

Avro 730 concept rendering. *Bzuk, public domain*

AVRO 730

The Avro 730 was conceived as a Mach 3 reconnaissance platform for the RAF. In addition to the reconnaissance role, the Avro 730 was to replace the RAF's fleet of Vickers Valiant, Handley Page Victor, and Avro Vulcan nuclear bombers.

DESIGN

Avro, originally A.V. Roe and Company, was one of the world's first aircraft builders, founded in 1910 in Manchester, England, by Alliott Verdon Roe and his brother Humphrey. Best known for the Lancaster and Vulcan bombers, Avro produced scores of aircraft for both the civilian and military markets until their absorption by Hawker Siddeley in 1963.

In May 1955, Avro responded to the RAF's Operational Requirement OR.330, which called for a supersonic reconnaissance aircraft to be placed into service as early as 1960. OR.330 was superseded shortly thereafter by an update that added bombing capability to the requirement; the service date was revised to 1963. Avro's submission, the 730, was accepted, and the firm was awarded a contract.

The Avro 730 was a highly streamlined and tailless delta-wing design with an elongated fuselage and a small canard located at the nose. It was projected to cruise at Mach 2.5, with a maximum speed of Mach 3 at altitudes in excess of 66,000 feet (20,000 meters). Originally designed with four Armstrong-Siddeley P.159 engines, the planned powerplants were upgraded to eight Armstrong-Siddeley P.176s in order to meet the bombing

AVRO 730

CREW:	3
ENGINES:	8x Armstrong-Siddeley P.176s; 9,700 lbst (4,400 kgst) each
WEIGHT:	Maximum: 220,000 lb (99,790 kg)
LENGTH:	159 ft (48.5 m)
WINGSPAN:	65 ft 7 in (20.0 m)
SPEEDS:	Maximum: Mach 3 (2,010 mph; 3,235 kph) at 60,000 ft (18,300 m) Cruise: Mach 2.5 (1,675 mph; 2,696 kph) at 60,000 ft (18,300 m)
CEILING:	66,400 ft (20,000 m)
RANGE:	5,750 mi (9,254 km)
ARMAMENT:	1x Blue Rosette standoff missile with 1-megaton nuclear warhead
RADAR:	Red Drover SLAR

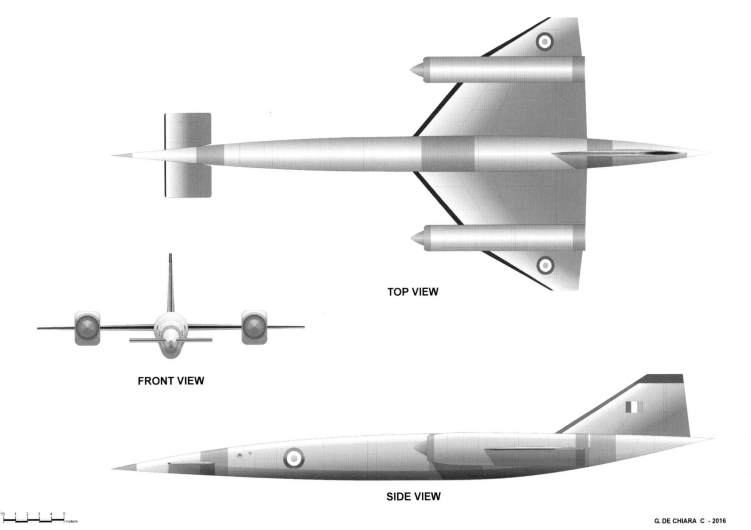

TOP VIEW

FRONT VIEW

SIDE VIEW

G. DE CHIARA C - 2016

Avro 730 concept rendering. *Giuseppe de Chiara*

capabilities added to the operational requirement; each engine produced 9,700 pounds of thrust (4,400 kilograms static thrust). The 730 didn't have a traditional canopy, since that would have reduced streamlining; instead, two windows were set above the pilots, in addition to a small, forward-looking periscope. Originally planned for a crew of three, the 730 was expected to employ a sophisticated autopilot, enabling one person to serve both as pilot and flight engineer, while the other two positions would be occupied by observer-navigators.

Just a single test fuselage had been built by 1957, when Defence Minister Duncan Sandys issued his famous *White Paper on Defence*, calling for widespread mergers among British aerospace firms and the cancellation of multiple manned aircraft projects—including the Avro 730—in favor of investments in guided missiles.

STATUS

No Avro 730s were ever built, though three Bristol Type 188s were built and two were flown as supersonic testbeds for the 730 project. ■

—*Hal Bryan*

HAWKER SIDDELEY NIMROD

If the Comet 2R reconnaissance aircraft helped salvage the reputation of the ill-fated Comet airliner, its ultimate vindication occurred with the long career of the Hawker Siddeley (de Havilland) Nimrod. Bearing the name of the biblical prophet Noah's great-grandson, famed as a hunter, the Nimrod aircraft lived up to its namesake.

Although the Nimrod did not supplant the Comet for reconnaissance—it actually replaced the Avro

Hawker Siddeley Nimrod. *National Archives and Records Administration*

Shackleton MR Mark 3 in the RAF inventory—its engineers used the Comet 4 airframe as the basis for its design; not modifying existing Comets (except for two prototypes), but fabricating Nimrods specifically for maritime surveillance.

The Nimrod specialized in anti-submarine warfare, a natural concern for the British Ministry of Defense for historical reasons. During both world wars, Great Britain lost enormous amounts of military and civil tonnage to enemy submarines. As a consequence, patrolling the North Sea and more distant points in the Atlantic Ocean became the focus of modern UK naval policy.

DESIGN

The Royal Air Force contracted with Hawker Siddeley for the development and production of the initial Nimrod (MR Mark 1) in June 1964. Using two unsold Comet 4s as prototypes, the manufacturer made the first flight in June 1967—a short development timeline aided by using off-the-shelf avionics. In June of the following year, the first of 38 MR Mark 1s flew to their initial assignments.

Although it relied on the Comet 4 for its basic structure, the Nimrod departed from the historic airliner in a number of ways. Designers accommodated a weapons bay and radar scanner in an unpressurized lower fuselage (that gave the aircraft a "double-bubble" cross-section). Pods on the top of the fin and at the tail boom housed electronic support measures (ESM) equipment and a magnetic anomaly detector (MAD) magnetometer, respectively. The Nimrod also had Rolls-Royce Spey turbofan engines, rather than the Comet's Avons, and wider air intakes.

In order to achieve the three main roles of the Nimrod—antisubmarine warfare, surveillance, and strike (against shipping)—designers produced an aircraft capable of fast transit speed and high-altitude flying, in addition to good maneuverability at low speeds. Moreover, it could climb and cruise on only one of its four engines and hold an array of weapons in its long cargo bay.

During their extensive service life, three Nimrod variants served the RAF. Strike Command took delivery of 38 MR Mark 1s between October 1969 and August 1972, and of eight more beginning in 1975. In 1971, three MR Mark 1s went to the RAF's 51st Squadron at Wyton as replacements for the Comet 2Rs. They assumed the roles of electronic reconnaissance, while also eavesdropping on hostile radar and radio transmissions. The Nimrod MR Mark 2 represented a retrofitted variant of the original MR Mark 1s, involving mostly updated avionics. Beginning in 1979, Hawker Siddeley delivered the first of 31 of these improved aircraft, with new communications equipment, advanced search radar, an increased data-processing rate, and upgrades in tactical sensors, the ESM system, and navigation.

The Ministry of Defense followed these incremental improvements with an ambitious and costly airborne early-warning Nimrod called the AEW Mark 3. It promised cutting-edge radar that would not only serve the UK maritime surveillance mission, but also the air defense requirements of central Europe. In its announcement of the program in 1977, the RAF proposed buying 11 of these aircraft; they retained the Nimrod profile, except for their long, bulbous noses and tails that concealed new antennae. In 1986, however, government officials concluded after cost overruns and uncertain results with the radar that the AEW should be cancelled.

Following it, work began on the Nimrod MRA4, a craft intended to replace the Mark 2. Like the AEW, however, it fell prey to vast cost increases and a nine-year delay in delivery. Development of the MRA4 ended in 2010, when it was replaced in part by unmanned drones for maritime surveillance.

OPERATIONS

The most important role of the Nimrods involved the detection of Soviet submarine movements. Once observations had been made, Nimrod crews shared the data with Royal Navy and NATO vessels, which then offered pursuit of the Russian submarines. An equally important role involved the protection of the UK's *Resolution*-class ballistic missile submarines, which carried Great Britain's nuclear deterrent.

HAWKER SIDDELEY NIMROD R.1

CREW:	12
ENGINES:	4x Rolls-Royce RB.168-20 Spey Mk 250 turbofans; 12,140 lbst (5,507 kgst) each
WEIGHTS:	Empty: 86,000 lb (39,009 kg)
	Maximum: 192,000 lb (8,709 kg)
LENGTH:	126 ft 9 in (38.6 m)
WINGSPAN:	114 ft 10 in (35.0 m)
HEIGHT:	29 ft 8.5 in (9.1 m)
SPEEDS:	Maximum: 576 mph (927 kph)
	Cruise: 489 mph (787 kph)
CEILING:	42,000 ft (12,800 m)
RANGE:	5,750 mi (9,254 km)
ARMAMENT:	Wide variety of anti-submarine weapons in the weapons bay, in addition to torpedoes and bombs used by the RAF; provision on board for sonobuoys and launchers, as well as for mines, gun or rocket pods, and air-to-surface missiles
RADAR:	Search radar in the nose: ASV.21D by EMI

In addition to regular sea duty involving reconnaissance and search and rescue, the Nimrods served in a number of conflicts and hotspots. During the Falklands War in 1982, Nimrods flew 111 missions as escort to the British fleet and on patrols around Ascension Island. During the Gulf War in 1990, Nimrods surveilled the Gulf of Oman and shadowed Iraqi shipping during the naval blockade of oil tankers in the Persian Gulf. Finally, at the start of the twenty-first century, Nimrods flew long overland missions to gather intelligence during the invasion of Afghanistan; after the beginning of the Iraq War in 2003, the aircraft directed attacks by coalition forces and used its sensors to spot enemy positions.

STATUS

Retired. The Royal Air Force retired the last flying Nimrods (R.1s) in 2011 from RAF Waddington. ∎

—Michael Gorn

Panavia GR4 Tornado. *UK Defence Imagery, Open Government License 3.0*

PANAVIA GR1A/GR4A TORNADO

Most nations pursue the development of reconnaissance technology as an issue of state sovereignty and self-defense. The Panavia Tornado differed radically from this pattern in that three countries combined resources to conceive and fabricate a multipurpose fighter aircraft, one of whose main roles involved reconnaissance.

Economy motivated the inception of the Tornado, at least in part. Faced with enormous costs to build modern fighters, the defense ministries of the United Kingdom, Germany, and Italy collaborated on an aircraft that would serve a number of military purposes, including close air support and battlefield interdiction; interdiction and counter-airstrike; air superiority; interception and air defense; naval strike; and reconnaissance (RAF Tornados also carried nuclear weapons up to 1998). The final agreement among the parties did not come easily, but the flexibility of

modern avionics helped, enabling many different weapons to be accommodated on one basic airframe. Still, despite the objective of savings, the Tornado represented the largest European aerospace program undertaken up to its time.

The project originated with an agreement in 1969 between British Aerospace Defence, Deutsche Aerospace Military Aircraft Division, and Alenia Aeronautica to form a consortium called Panavia. After the first flight in 1974, the three governments signed a Memorandum of Understanding in 1976 to produce 809 (later increased to 923) Tornados.

DESIGN

Much of the Tornado's multimission capabilities stemmed from its shoulder-mounted wings whose variable geometry enabled them to swing from 25 degrees in the fully forward position to 67 degrees swept all the way back, lending it exceptional versatility in a variety of flight regimes. Like the wings, the short, thick fuselage with its short nose cone consisted mainly of aluminum alloy, fabricated in three sections. Its swept tail section featured an unusually large two-spar fin and rudder and all-moving horizontal surfaces.

The reconnaissance variant, designated the GR1A, first flew in July 1985. Engineers removed the two Mauser cannons on the original interdictor/strike design and replaced them with the sideways-looking, horizon-to-horizon, Tornado Infra-Red Reconnaissance System (TIRRS). The Royal Air Force's Tactical Reconnaissance Wing took possession of 30 GR1As, 25 of which underwent major improvements starting in 1996 to enable medium- and high-altitude reconnaissance, as opposed to the low-level operations suited to the TIRRS system. Redesignated as GR4As, upgrades included precision-guided weapons (like the Air Launched Anti-Radiation Missile), an updated sensor package known as the Reconnaissance Airborne Pod for Tornado (RAPTOR), and the LITENING III Advanced Targeting Pod. RAPTOR represented a significant step forward in recon technology, enabling pilots to transmit real-time long-range oblique photography to commanders and to view the images themselves, in the cockpit. Because RAPTOR's sensors worked from long distances, data could be gathered with lower risk to the GR4As and their crews.

Germany, meanwhile, fielded 35 Electronic Combat Reconnaissance (ECR) Tornados starting in 1988, equipped with Forward-Looking Infrared (FLIR) that produced a television image and Infrared Linescan (IRLS) that recorded still optical images in high resolution.

OPERATIONS

Tornados have served in many war zones during their four decades of service. During the Gulf War in 1990–1991, GR1s flown by the RAF and the Italian Air Force saw some of the earliest and most sustained combat, and GR1As flew many recon missions with no losses. German and Italian pilots flew Tornados in the Kosovo War in 1999, and German Tornados took part in the Bosnian War, as well as in operations over Afghanistan in 2007 to support NATO troops. British

PANAVIA TORNADO INTERDICTOR STRIKE VERSION

CREW:	2
ENGINES:	2x Turbo-Union Rolls-Royce .199-34R-04 turbofan engines; each 16,000 lbst with afterburning, 9,000 lbst without (7,257 and 4,082 kgst, respectively)
WEIGHTS:	Empty: 22,000–23,000 lb (9,980-10,430 kg) Maximum: 58,400 lb (26,490 kg)
LENGTH:	54 ft 10 in (16.7 m)
WINGSPAN:	45 ft 7 in (13.9 m)
HEIGHT:	18 ft 9 in (5.7 m)
SPEEDS:	Maximum: 1,452 mph (2,337 kph) Cruise: 691 mph (1,112 kph)
CEILING:	50,000 ft (15,240 m)
RANGE:	2,420 mi (3,890 km)
ARMAMENT:	2x 27mm cannons; three attachments on the fuselage underside; 4x swiveling hard points under the outer wings provide mountings for a wide array of weapons, depending on the missions.
RADAR:	Multimode forward-looking radar, Doppler radar, "smart" radar altimeter

GR4 Tornados saw heavy use during the opening salvos of the invasion of Iraq in 2003.

The Tornado also played a prominent role during the enforcement of the United Nation's no-fly zone over Libya in 2011. And from 2009 to 2014 the RAF logged over 33,500 hours flying Tornados from Kandahar airfield in support of the Afghan government. During 2014 and 2015 RAF Tornados attacked Islamic State forces inside Iraq.

STATUS

The Tornado remains in service in the UK, Germany, Italy, and Saudi Arabia. ∎

—*Michael Gorn*

RUSSIA/SOVIET UNION

Sikorsky Ilya Muromets. *Library of Congress*

SIKORSKY ILYA MUROMETS

Just nine years after the Wright Brothers flew the first powered flying machine, Russian Igor Sikorsky conceived of an aircraft of almost unimaginable power and size. Still in his early twenties, Sikorsky was already the chief aircraft designer at the Russo-Baltic Carriage Factory. While serving in this role, Sikorsky got the idea in 1912 for a long-range bomber and the first aircraft with photo-reconnaissance capability. Prototypes flew the following year, and on a test flight in February 1914, his Ilya Muromets four-engine biplane flew at 6,500 feet (1,981 meters) over Moscow at 62 miles per hour (100 kilometers per hour) for *five hours*. At a time when other countries fielded aircraft that transported a few passengers at most, Sikorsky's aircraft on this day accommodated 16 people and a dog.

DESIGN

Sikorsky's plane (named for a mythological Russian folk hero) featured cabin windows, berths outfitted with lavatories, a long access corridor, and reasonably comfortable wicker chairs. By the outbreak of World War I in August 1914, modifications were made to adapt to weaponry and cargo needs, but the basic design remained the same.

Next to its overall size, the Ilya Muromets's wings caught the most attention. The upper wingspan exceeded the length of the 57-foot (17.4-meter) fuselage by 40 feet (12 meters), and the bottom wingspan by 30 feet (9 meters). A person standing by the tires on the runway needed to look up two stories to see the top wing. Vertical struts and heavy cables held the wings in place, and between them, the four engines faced forward, mounted close to the cabin. Each engine featured two-bladed propellers. The wings fitted over and under the central fuselage, a long, narrow structure characterized by straight surfaces and not much taper. Its tail structure consisted of a standard horizontal surface with three vertical fins above it. Attached to its belly were two main landing gears and a tail skid.

Between 1913 and 1918, the Imperial Air Force fielded about 80 aircraft in 11 variants that reflected advances in technology and evolving missions. The massive bombers that rolled off the assembly lines bristled with defensive cannon and machine guns, the former passenger cabin now held bomb racks, and armor as thick as 5 millimeters (0.2 inches) protected the engines. Pilots also had bomb sights at their disposal.

OPERATIONS

The Russian Air Force ordered the militarized Ilya Muromets the same month that World War I began.

ILYA MUROMETS V NO. 167

CREW:	4 to 12
ENGINES:	4x RBVZ-6 (Russo-Baltic Railway Factory) engines; 150 hp each
WEIGHTS:	Empty: 7,716 lb (3,500 kg) Maximum: 11,023 lb (5,000 kg)
LENGTH:	57 ft 5 in (17.5 m)
WINGSPAN:	97 ft 9 in (29.8 m) top wing; 68 ft 11 in (21.0 m) bottom wing
HEIGHT:	13 ft 2 in (4.0 m)
SPEEDS:	Maximum: 75 mph (120 kph) Cruise: 60 mph (97 kph)
CEILING:	9,843 ft (3,000 m)
RANGE:	311 mi (500 km)
ARMAMENT:	12.7mm and 15.3mm guns; 3-in and 37mm cannon; rocket and bomb load up to 1,100 lb (500 kg)
RADAR:	None

By the end of 1914, the service had organized the world's first bomber squadron, consisting of 10 aircraft (gradually increased to 20 in 1916). In its role as a bomber, the Ilya Muromets proved effective and hard to counteract. Its defensive weapons made it a fearsome adversary, and only a few fell to enemy fire. It also unleashed significant and accurate bomb loads (a total of 65 tons/59,000 kilograms), especially on railroad targets, transportation routes, and bridges.

On all of their wartime missions—bombing as well as reconnaissance—each plane carried a camera that provided the Russian Army with some 7,000 aerial photographs with photographic reconnaissance still in its budding stages across the war zones. Not only did this unique aircraft enable the Russian armed forces to initiate the use of heavy bombers, group bomber operations on enemy targets, and night bombing—its size, endurance, and high-altitude capability made it the perfect intelligence-gathering platform. On its missions, it commonly carried just two crew members, forced to make themselves vulnerable to attack by flying straight and level so that the onboard photographer could take overlapping images. In part, the Imperial Air Force deployed it for aerial photography geared specifically to assess bomb damage from the giant bomber's own sorties.

In addition to this purpose, the Ilya Muromets also served as long-range battlefield recon aircraft, capable of flying far behind enemy lines. This role developed during preparation against Germany for the Battle of Tannenburg, when Gen. Alexander Samsonov ignored intelligence warnings from his pilots about ground activities by opposing forces, resulting in the rout of his entire army. As a consequence, beginning in 1915, the Ilya Muromets began to fly wide-ranging reconnaissance missions (up to ten hours per flight). The intelligence value of these flights paid off notably in the Brusilov Offensive of 1916, during which aerial surveillance proved pivotal, giving Russian commanders the precise locations of enemy targets.

STATUS

Retired. The Ilya Muromets flew for the last time in 1922 at a training school in Serpukhov, USSR. ■

—*Michael Gorn*

Petlyakov Pe-2. *Public domain, via www.asisbiz.com*

PETLYAKOV PE-2 "BUCK"

The Petlyakov Pe-2 Peshka was a multirole, three-seat aircraft developed and mass-produced during the Soviet Union's Great Patriotic War with Nazi Germany. Production began in 1940 and ended in early 1945, with 11,427 units consisting of 1 prototype and 17 variants and subvariants. The Pe-2 served as a light bomber, dive-bomber, interceptor, night fighter, and recon aircraft. It was also one of the Soviets' most successful ground-attack planes of World War II.

DESIGN

Vladimir Petlyakov began work on the Pe-2 light bomber while imprisoned in the Sharashka (Experimental Design Bureau) gulag near Moscow on false charges of sabotaging the Tupolev ANT-42 heavy bomber project in 1937. The initial Pe-2 design was for a high-altitude escort fighter (design VI-100) for the ANT-42. The first prototype flew in December 1939. With the Luftwaffe's using tactical combat aircraft, such as the Ju 87 Stuka dive-bomber, during the blitzkrieg of Poland and France, the Soviets decided to change the VI-100 in development to a dive-/light bomber. Stalin gave Petlyakov 45 days to complete the transition to the new design, designated PB-100.

The Pe-2 was an all-metal, low-wing, twin-tail aircraft with primary armament comprising machine guns and/or cannon with up to 2,205 pounds (1,000 kilograms) internal and external bomb load. In addition to the internal bomb bay, the plane included an original design for an internal bomb rack in each engine nacelle capable of carrying one bomb of up to 220 pounds (100 kilograms). Initially powered by two Klimov VK-M107A inline V-12, liquid-cooled engines of 1,450 horsepower each, the aircraft was switched to the Klimov VK-M105PF inline V-12 (1,260 horsepower each), providing a maximum speed of 360 miles per hour (580 kilometers per hour). The cockpit with a navigator/bombardier seated behind the pilot, featured a raised canopy, while the radio operator/gunner operated in a separate compartment aft of the wing. A top hatch, two side windows, and a ventral gun position were major features of the aft compartment. The first production series included a glazed nose for the bombardier station but was changed to a hard nose on subsequent variants and fitted with machine guns.

Production of a reconnaissance version began in August 1941; ultimately, three variants were fielded: the Pe-2R, Pe-3R, and the upgraded Pe-2R. The first Pe-2R featured additional armor and lower nose glazing. It carried three to four cameras and three 12.7mm machine guns. Engines were either the 1,110 horsepower VK-M105RA or, as in the later version introduced in 1944, the 1,450 horsepower VK-M107A. The second series Pe-2R was armed with three 20mm cannons and powered by VK-107A engines. The typical camera package for daytime photo intelligence reconnaissance consisted of the AFA-B (standard in all aircraft), two AFA-1s, and one AFA-27T stationed in the radio operator's compartment. The AFA-B was replaced by the NAFA-19 and up to eight FOTAB-50-35 photo flash bombs for night photo intelligence.

The Pe-3R was the photorecon variant of the Pe-3 bomber interceptor, with slightly different armament than the standard version. Bow armament consisted of either one 20mm cannon and two BK 12.7mm machine guns, or two 12.7mm machine guns and two 7.62 machine guns. A 12.7mm machine gun and one remote-controlled 7.62mm machine gun were located in the aft compartment. Additional fuel tanks attached to motorized gondolas and installed in the bomb bay gave the aircraft greater range. A pair of vertical/oblique cameras installed in the tail section fulfilled the aircraft's recon role. Some Pe-2s powered by Schvetsov M-82 engines with a maximum speed of 338 miles per hour (545 kilometers per hour) were sent to the 11th and 99th Special Reconnaissance Air Regiments.

OPERATIONS

Red Army Air Force (Voenno-Vozdushnye Sily, VVS) Long Range Aviation Reconnaissance Regiments, comprising four squadrons each, received PE-2Rs. The 15th Separate Reserve Reconnaissance Regiment formed in November 1941 was equipped with the PE-2. This regiment trained two sister regiments and six individual squadrons. The 742nd Reconnaissance Regiment conducted operations during the Caucuses Campaign of 1942–1943. Units assigned to the Continuation War against Finland were the 15th Reconnaissance Regiment, 13th Separate Reconnaissance Aviation Regiment, and 47th Long Range Reconnaissance Aviation Regiment.

STATUS

Retired.

Production of the Pe-2 ceased in early 1945, but the aircraft remained in service with the Soviets until replaced primarily by the Tupolov Tu-2. The Soviets exported the Pe-2 during the postwar years, with customers that included the Czechoslovakia Air Force's 715th Independent Reconnaissance Squadron. Yugoslavia was the last nation to operate the model, retiring its remaining inventory in 1954. ∎

—*Alan C. Carey*

PETLYAKOV PE-2

CREW:	3
ENGINES:	2x Klimov M-105PF liquid-cooled V-12s, 1,210 hp each; or 2x Klimov M-105RA liquid-cooled V-12s, 1,100 hp each
WEIGHTS:	Empty: 24,412 lb (5,630 kg) Maximum: 17,014 lb (7,718 kg)
LENGTH:	41 ft 10 in (12.8 m)
WINGSPAN:	56 ft 3 in (17.2 m)
HEIGHT:	11 ft 6 in (3.5 m)
SPEEDS:	Maximum: 323 mph (520 kph) Cruise: 255 mph (410 kph)
CEILING:	26,247 ft (8,000 m)
RANGE:	876 mi (1,410 km); 1,056 mi (1,700 km) with external drop tanks
ARMAMENT:	2x 20mm cannon; 2x UBK 12.7mm machine guns; 2x 7.62 machine guns; 2,205 lb (1,000 kg) bomb load

Stamp celebrating the Pe-2. *Voyageur Press collection*

Tupolev Tu-16. *US Department of Defense photo*

TUPOLEV TU-16 "BADGER"

The Badger was one of the most capable and versatile—and longest serving—aircraft of its type. Designed as a "medium" bomber to deliver a single nuclear bomb, the Badger has served conventional bomber, missile carrier, torpedo bomber, minelayer, anti-submarine, tanker, maritime reconnaissance, electronic reconnaissance, and electronic countermeasures roles.

The Badger was developed as a replacement for the Tu-4 Bull, the Soviet copy of the US B-29 Superfortress and the first Soviet nuclear-capable aircraft. The Badger was the nominal equivalent of the US Boeing B-47 Stratojet and served in the markings of several air forces in addition to the Soviet Union and Russia.

A Badger released the first Soviet air-drop of a hydrogen bomb (RDS-37) on 22 November 1955, at the Semipalatinsk test site in present-day Kazakhstan. (The RDS-6 test on 12 August 1953 was of an enhanced fission bomb.)

The Tupolev bureau's design designation for the Badger was Tu-88. Additionally, the Tu-98 Backfin was a Badger airframe flown in 1955 in a research role.

DESIGN

The Badger had a swept-wing configuration with two large turbojet engines housed in nacelles faired into the fuselage at the wing roots. The inner one-third of the leading wing edges was swept back 42 degrees and the outer portion 35 degrees; all tail surfaces were swept back 42 degrees. The engines were updated during

Tupolev Tu-16. *US Air Force photo*

the aircraft's long production run. Some aircraft had a glazed nose position for the bombardier, while other variants had solid nose structures.

Most aircraft had two 23mm cannon in dorsal, ventral, and tail turrets controlled from remote gunner positions in the after end of the aircraft (two sighting blisters and a tail gunner position). Those bombers without a large radome could mount a seventh cannon on the starboard side of the nose.

The bomber variants could carry up to 19,800 pounds (8,981 kilograms) of conventional bombs.

RECON VARIANTS

The Tu-16Ye Badger-D was a navy ELINT recon aircraft with Puff Ball and Short Horn (NATO designations) radars. Some were modified Badger-C aircraft and had a solid-nose configuration.

The Tu-16R/Tu-16RM BadgerE were air force and navy photo recon aircraft with a large camera fitted just behind the nosewheel bay and a glazed nose. The naval (RM) aircraft could also provide midcourse guidance and targeting for submarine-launched cruise missiles.

The Tu-16RR Badger-L comprised eight Tu-16Rs converted in the early 1970s to monitor Soviet (underground) and Chinese nuclear tests.

The Tu-16P Badger-F was a navy ELINT and photo recon aircraft with two large ELINT pods under wings. They were rebuilt Tu-16A and Tu-16KS aircraft and had the glazed nose configuration. (Other Badger-F aircraft served in the ECM/jamming role.)

The Tu104 (NATO designation Camel) was a civilian airliner derived from the Badger.

OPERATIONS

Soviet Badgers were employed in conventional bombing attacks again the Mujahideen (insurgent groups) in Afghanistan from 1979 to 1989. This was the only use of the Soviet aircraft in combat. Iraqi Badgers attacked Iranian positions in the two nations' 1980–1988 conflict.

An Egyptian force of some 20 Badgers was destroyed on the ground by Israeli air attacks in the opening hours of their 1967 conflict. Twenty replacement Badgers launched a reported 25 Kelt air-to-surface missiles against Israeli targets in the Sinai Peninsula in the 1973 Yom Kippur War. No Egyptian Tu-16s are believed to have been destroyed in the latter conflict.

Soviet Badgers with Egyptian markings flew from bases in Egypt to monitor the US Sixth Fleet during much of the Cold War. Badgers also conducted surveillance flights against US and other western warships in other maritime areas.

Soviet Badgers flew from the former US air base at Camranh Bay in Vietnam from the late 1970s to 1991.

STATUS

Retired. The Badger's first flight was on 27 April 1952; production began the following year, with squadron delivery to the Soviet Air Force from early 1954, and deliveries to the navy beginning in the late 1950s (with many air force aircraft transferred to naval aviation).

Soviet production totaled 1,507 Badgers of about 50 major variants and many modifications, with deliveries from 1953 to 1963. Seventy Tu-16R specialized recon variants were delivered in 1957 and 1958. Badgers were also employed in a variety of research and test roles, adding additional (mostly unique) configurations.

Two Badgers were transferred to China in 1958, along with a third in "knocked-down kit" form for assembly in China. Subsequent Badger production probably continues in China as the H-6 series *Hongzhaji* bomber. The first production H-6 entered service in 1968, some ten years after the Soviet Union supplied Tu-16s to China. Some 150 Chinese Badgers of several variants have been produced and continue in service. (An H-6 dropped an atomic bomb in the third Chinese nuclear weapons test on 14 May 1966.)

Badgers have been transferred to Egypt, Indonesia, Iraq, and Libya. Iraq was the last nation to fly these aircraft, with all but one being destroyed by US forces in Operation Desert Storm in 1991. The surviving aircraft was destroyed in Operation Iraqi Freedom in 2003. After the dissolution of the Soviet Union in December 1991, the Badgers remaining in four republics—Armenia, Azerbaijan, Georgia, and Ukraine—were flown for a limited period. All of these aircraft were retired by the late 1990s. ∎

—*Norman Polmar and John F. Bessette*

TUPOLEV TU-16 BADGER-F

CREW:	6 or 7 (pilot, copilot, navigator, weapons systems officer, gunner, radio operator, systems operator)
ENGINES:	2x Mikulin RD-3M turbojet; 19,285 lbst (8,748 kgst) each
WEIGHTS:	Empty: 82,000 lb (37,195 kg) Maximum: 165,350 lb (75,003 kg)
LENGTH:	118 ft 11.25 in (36.3 m)
WINGSPAN:	108 ft 0.5 in (32.9 m)
HEIGHT:	45 ft 11.25 in (14.0 m)
SPEED:	Maximum: 616 mph (992 kph)
CEILING:	45,350 ft (13,822 m)
RANGE:	2,000 mi (3,219 km)
ARMAMENT:	7x 23mm MR-23 cannon (no internal bomb load)
RADAR:	Varied (see text); gunfire control (NATO designation Bee Hind)

Tupolev Tu-95. *US Air Force photo*

TUPOLEV TU-95 "BEAR"

The Bear originally was developed as a long-range strategic bomber. It has served the Soviet and Russian air forces in various roles for more than 60 years as a bomber, cruise missile carrier, and anti-submarine aircraft with several reconnaissance variants having been developed. Later variants remained in service when this volume went to press (see Bear-F entry).

The Bear-D was a specialized maritime patrol/missile-targeting aircraft. A CIA description noted:

> The Bear-D represents an efficient combination of performance capabilities (large search area, long endurance, and rapid reaction), available sensors (radar, electronic intercept equipment, cameras, and the significant human element), and operational flexibility which is unique among Soviet reconnaissance platforms.
>
> The Bear-D is a highly adaptable multimission aircraft configured to perform peacetime missions of ocean surveillance, intelligence collection, aid in search and rescue, and support of the Soviet manned space flight program.[102]

A Bear carried the largest nuclear weapon ever detonated: the AN602 hydrogen bomb (called the "Tsar Bomba" in the West). It was delivered by the Tu-95V, a modified Bear with bomb bay doors and fuselage fuel tanks removed to accommodate the bomb, which weighed 27 metric tons. The test—estimated to have an explosive force of 50 megatons—was conducted in the Arctic's Novaya Zemlya archipelago at Sukhoy Nos on 30 October 1961. (The "normal" yield of the weapon, de-rated for the test, was estimated to be 100 megatons.

DESIGN

The Bear design evolved from the Tupolev Tu-4 (NATO designation Bull), which was a virtual copy of the Boeing B-29 Superfortress. The Tu-4 was developed into the Tu-80 and, in turn, Tu-85 designs, neither of which entered Soviet service. The Tu-95 was a further refinement of (and considerable improvement upon) the Tu-85.

The only turboprop-propelled strategic bomber to achieve operational service with any air force, the Bear is a large, swept-wing (35 degrees) aircraft with four contra-rotating turboprop engines with fourblade propellers. Defensive armament originally consisted of up to three 23mm twin gun turrets (dorsal, ventral, and tail), plus a fixed cannon in the nose. Only the tail-gun

turret, with two twin-barrel cannon, was retained in some later variants.

The aircraft has three pressurized compartments—large ones ahead of and behind the wings, linked by a tunnel, and a tail compartment; the last houses the tail gunner and two other gunner positions (with large blister positions).

Beyond conventional and nuclear bombs (up to 25,000 pounds; 11,340 kilograms) carried by early bomber aircraft, strike aircraft were subsequently armed with air-to-surface cruise missiles for land attack. The plane's long range can be further extended through in-flight refueling with a fixed receiving probe fitted in the nose.

The Tu-95 engines, wing, tail assembly, and other components were used for the Tu-114 Rossiya (NATO designation Cleat) civil airliner, the world's largest passenger aircraft prior to the Boeing 747. The Bear also was the basis for the Tu-114D (NATO designation Moss) Soviet Airborne Warning and Control Aircraft (AWACS).

Tupolev Tu-95. *National Archives and Records Administration*

RECON VARIANTS

The Tu-95RT Bear-D was a maritime reconnaissance/over-the-horizon missile-targeting aircraft in naval service from 1963. The aircraft detected surface ship targets for submarine-launched missiles and provided midcourse guidance. The aircraft was fitted with a massive J-band surface-search radar in place of the bomb bay, as well as datalinks to transmit targeting and guidance data to the surfaced launching submarine.

The aircraft became a familiar sight over international waters, tracking US warships beginning in 1963, although it was not declared fully operational until 1964. Fifty-three Bear-Ds were produced for Soviet Naval Aviation.

The Tu-95MR Bear-E was ordered by the Soviet Air Force in 1960 with four units produced. The Bear-E had both photo and electronic recon capabilities, and it developed into a maritime reconnaissance platform that became operational in 1964. Seven cameras were fitted in a detachable "pallet" in place of the bomb bay. The dorsal 20mm gun turret was deleted (retaining the ventral and tail guns).

DESIGNATION

Tu-95 was the Tupolev Design Bureau designation, which has become the universal identification for the aircraft. The original military designation was Tu-20.

According to *Air Power Journal*, "Never was a NATO reporting name more apt than that for the Tu-95/142 series. 'Bear' sums up the beast's attributes—strength, size and bad temper! Even its crews now call it by the NATO name."[103]

OPERATIONS

The first Tu-95 flight occurred 12 November 1952. The aircraft entered service with Soviet Strategic Aviation in 1955. The first Tu-95RT flight was in 1962.

Bear-D aircraft based in the Northern and Pacific Fleet areas monitored US and NATO naval activity throughout the Atlantic, western Pacific, and Indian oceans. During the 1970s and 1980s they often deployed to Da Nang and Cam Ranh Bay in Vietnam, as well as Cuba, Angola, Somalia, and Guinea. This extended their coverage to the central and south Atlantic, as exemplified by their monitoring the British deployments to the Falkland Islands during their conflict with Argentina in 1982.

The Bear-D remained active until late 1991, when the Soviet Union dissolved.

Operated by Naval Aviation, the Bear-E began shadowing US aircraft carriers in the Atlantic. A Tu-95KM missile carrier would usually detect the target ships by radar and then direct the Bear-E to overfly the ships to collect photography.

Bear-Es flew recon missions into the late 1980s.

STATUS

Retired. Approximately 300 Bear bombers were produced into the mid-1960s, with production of the naval Bear-D models following. By 1961, Soviet long-range aviation was believed to have peaked with some 200 Bear bombers in service. ■

—*Norman Polmar and John F. Bessette*

TUPOLEV TU-95 BEAR-D

CREW:	7 to 9
ENGINES:	4x Kuznetsov NK-12 turboprop; 15,000 shp each
WEIGHTS:	Empty: approx. 200,000 lb (90,720 kg) Maximum: 401,234 lb (182,000 kg)
LENGTH:	159 ft 1 in (48.5 m)
WINGSPAN:	164 ft 2 in (50.0 m)
HEIGHT:	47 ft 4.5 in (14.5 m)
SPEEDS:	Maximum: 550 mph (885 kph) Cruise: 422 mph (680 kph)
CEILING:	33,784 ft (10,500 m)
RANGE:	8,000+ mi (12,875+ km)
ARMAMENT:	Up to 7x 20mm AM-23 cannon
RADAR:	Bomb/nav (NATO designation Short Horn); surface surveillance (NATO designation Big Bulge); gunfire control (NATO designation Bee Hind)

Myasishchev M-4s. *National Archives and Records Administration*

MYASISHCHEV M-4 "BISON"

The Myasishchev M-4 was a Soviet-era Russian strategic bomber that served both the Soviet Air Force and Navy in a variety of roles throughout its nearly 40-year career. The M-4 (sometimes Mya-4) was known in the Soviet Union as the Molot, Russian for "Hammer," but it's best known in the West by its NATO codename, "Bison."

The M-4 was a product of the V. M. Myasishchev Experimental Design Bureau, led by Vladimir Myasishchev and formed for the express purpose of building a jet bomber that could strike targets in the United States.

The M-4 was the Soviets' first turbojet strategic bomber and the topic of rampant speculation after its first public appearance during the May Day flyover of Moscow in 1954. Because of the veil of secrecy that surrounded the Soviet Union, little was known about the airplane at the time; even contemporary volumes of the esteemed *Jane's All the World's Aircraft* referred to it as a Tupolev design—the Myasishchev Bureau remained unknown until later.

DESIGN

When Myasishchev designed the M-4, he was working at the Moscow Aviation Institute. Once his strategic bomber proposal was accepted by the Soviet government, he established his own design bureau. Originally designated VM-25, Myasishchev's bomber went through a number of design iterations, at varying stages sporting straight wings and a swept V-tail. Most of the designs had turbojet engines embedded in the wing roots like the final production models, but some used underwing nacelles and at least one—design number five—called for eight turboprops.

The final design employed four Mikulin AM-3 turbojets in the wing roots to give the airplane a superficially cleaner appearance than its Western counterparts. At the same time, the production M-4—with its swept wings and centerline bicycle landing gear—bore at least a passing resemblance to the Boeing B-47. Speaking of landing gear, the nose gear had a hydraulic ram system that would raise the nose to set a higher angle of attack during takeoff. At first this feature confused pilots, who would over-rotate out of instinct until breaking themselves of the habit.

The original M-4 was heavy and inefficient, lacking the 7,450-mile (12,000-kilometer) range to make the round trip to North America and back; only 35 were built. Around the same time, as the M-4 was starting

Myasishchev M-4. *Boris Vasiljev, CC Attribution-Share Alike 3.0*

MYASISHCHEV M-4

CREW:	7
ENGINES:	4x Dobrynin VD-7B turbojets; 20,940 lbst (9,500 kgst) each
WEIGHTS:	Empty: 158,290 lb (71,800 kg)
	Maximum: 400,800 lb (181,800 kg)
LENGTH:	169 ft 7 in (51.7 m)
WINGSPAN:	174 ft 4 in (53.1 m)
SPEEDS:	Maximum: 574 mph (924 kph)
	Cruise: 497 mph (800 kph)
CEILING:	36,000 ft (10,973 m)
RANGE:	6,800 mi (10,944 km)
ARMAMENT:	3x NR-23 or AM-23 23mm cannons; up to 4x cruise missiles carried externally; up to 52,900 lb (24,000 kg) bomb payload, conventional and nuclear

its service, Myasishchev began testing an updated version, known as the 3M. Named the "Bison-B" in the West, it featured an inflight refueling probe and more efficient engines—Dobrynin VD-7B turbojets replacing the AM-3s. The new engines meant redesigned wings that were longer and more aerodynamically efficient. A dihedral-free, variable-incidence tailplane was added as well.

Several additional versions were projected, including the 3M-R, which would have been fully dedicated to reconnaissance, and the 3M-A, also a reconnaissance platform but planned to be nuclear powered. A total of 93 Bisons were built by the time production ceased in 1963, representing more than a dozen variants.

OPERATIONS

The M-4 first flew in 1953 and went into production in time to be introduced in Soviet Air Force service in 1956, followed quickly by the 3M in 1958. The combination of the 3M's greater efficiency and inflight refueling capability made the Bison-B of particular interest to the Soviet Navy, which was eager to make use of the upgraded airplane in a maritime patrol and reconnaissance role. Other versions followed, notably the Bison-C, with its upgraded search radar.

The Bison was eventually outclassed by other Soviet designs and relegated to secondary roles. Many of the original M-4s, along with a number of the subsequent 3Ms, were converted for use as tankers. While the Bison saw some continued development as an aerial cruise missile launch platform, it spent most of its career refueling other, more capable aircraft. While some tankers were reportedly converted back into bombers for use during the Soviet invasion of Afghanistan in the 1980s, there appear to be no confirmed reports that the Bison ever dropped a bomb in combat. The last flying tankers flew their final missions and were retired in 1994.

STATUS

Retired. While most airframes were scrapped for compliance with various treaties, a handful of Bisons survive in Russian museums. ∎

—*Hal Bryan*

Ilyushin Il-18. *National Archives and Records Administration*

ILYUSHIN IL-18/IL-20 "COOT"
AND ILYUSHIN IL-38 "MAY"

The Il-20M Coot-A (alternative designation Il-18D-36 "Bizon") is the military recon version of the Il-18 passenger plane produced between 1957 and 1985 by the Ilyushin Design Bureau. The reconnaissance prototype first flew in March 1968. Twenty were produced by 1976, with some upgraded as the Il-20DSR and Il-20 Coot-N, and four converted to the Il-20-RT communication and communication-relay variant. The Il-38 is a maritime reconnaissance/ASW ("May") variant, also based on the Il-18 frame. Both variants are similar in appearance to the Lockheed P-3 Orion operated by the US Navy and allies as a maritime recon platform.

DESIGN

The aircraft features a long, cigar-shaped fuselage with a low-wing design, powered by four 2,450 horsepower Ivenko Al-20M turboprop engines giving the aircraft a top speed of 450 miles per hour (724 kilometers per hour). The ELINT variant is distinguishable by the side-scanning radar (SLAR) Igla-1 pod mounted underneath the forward fuselage, along with a pair of antenna fairings for the COMINT/ESM Vishnaya

system protruding from each side of the forward fuselage's top for locating, tracking, and analyzing communication transmissions. Additional electronic packages include the Kvadrat-2 for detecting and identifying electromagnetic emitters; the ROMB SRS-4B ELINT/ESM, which was more precise than the Kvadrat-2; and photo intel capability with two A-87P LORAP oblique cameras mounted on the lateral fairings of the forward fuselage. The prototype conducted its maiden flight in March 1968 with production beginning in 1970 and ending in 1976; at total of 20 aircraft entered service. The crew of 13 included 8 technical specialists.

The Il-38 prototype's maiden flight occurred on 27 September 1961, with production beginning in 1967. As with the Coot-A, the Il-38 utilized the Il-18's airframe, engines, wings, and tail. It took nine years before the Soviet Navy accepted the aircraft; approximately 55 to 65 units were produced until 1972. Major design differences included the wings moved forward nearly 4 feet (1.2 meters), a long tail boom housing APM-73 MAD gear for ASW, and a forward-looking infrared FLIR turret under the forward fuselage to house the Berkut STS (NATO "Wet Eye") search-and-targeting

Ilyushin Il-20. *UK Defence Imagery, Open Government License 3.0*

ILYUSHIN IL-20

CREW:	13
ENGINES:	4x Ivchenko AI-20M turboprops; 4,250 hp each
WEIGHTS:	Empty: 77,162 lb (35,000 kg) Maximum: 141,096 lb (64,000 kg)
LENGTH:	117 ft 9 in (35.9 m)
WINGSPAN:	122 ft 8 in (37.4 m)
HEIGHT:	33 ft 4 in (10.2 m)
SPEEDS:	Maximum: 410 mph (660 kph) Cruise: 388 mph (531 kph)
CEILING:	32,800 ft (9,997 m)
RANGE:	4,030 mi (6,486 km)
ARMAMENT:	None
RADAR:	Igla-1

radar. Subsequent modifications have occurred over the years in efforts to enhance recon and ASW capability. During the 1970s and 1980s, the aircraft were fitted with Vishnaya communications system and antenna array for COMINT. Some carried the improved Izumrud (Emerald) STS radar system.

An upgraded variant, designated Il-38N with ELINT capability, appeared in 2005. It was equipped with a multisensor Novella electronics package that can track up to 32 air, surface, and submerged targets simultaneously. This package consists of a radar system with a detection range of 200 miles (320 kilometers) for surface vessels and 56 miles (90 kilometers) for aircraft; a high-resolution thermal-imaging system; electro-optical scanners; 13-inch LCD television monitors; and other equipment. The ESM/ELINT system is housed in a large pod attached to the upper forward fuselage The Il-38 remains primarily an ASW platform and can carry torpedoes, depth charges, mines, and missiles such as the AS-20 and R-73RDM2 in two internal weapons bays on the forward and rear sides of the wings.

Between 2002 and 2005, Mir Company of Russia modernized five Il-38s, known as Il-38SDs due to the Sea Dragon electronics package. They vary little from the Il-38N except for the composition of the avionics gear and the support struts of the ESM/ELINT pod. The Indian variant could be armed with the supersonic (Mach 2.8) BrahMos cruise missile.

OPERATIONS

The 390th ORAE operated the Coot-A during the Afghan-Soviet War to locate, record, and identify Afghan rebel communications. The Coot-A currently conducts routine long-range recon missions over the Baltic Sea and the VVS had at least one operating in support of Russian forces in Syria in 2015. Coot-A flight crews have been notorious for flying in international airspace with the aircraft's transponder turned off; over the years, this has resulted in near collisions with civilian airliners.

Coot-As were sold to India in 1977 for service with Indian Navy Squadron 315. Five were upgraded to the Il-38 configuration between 2002 and 2005. Two Indian Il-38s of that squadron were involved in a midair collision on 1 October 2002, killing both crews. In 2007, India suspended the Il-38DS contract

STATUS

Operational. An unknown number of upgraded Coot-As remain in VVS inventory, reportedly based at Chkalovskaya near Moscow with the 8th Special Purpose Aviation Division (ADON). The Russian Navy received the first Il-38N in March 2012 with a total of 28 scheduled to join the service by 2020. ∎

—*Alan C. Carey*

ANTONOV AN-12 "CUB"

The Antonov Design Bureau modified several models of transports as recon platforms during the Cold War, including the An-12 Cub, AN-24 Coke, and An-26 Curl. Antonov produced 27 variants of the An-12 medium-range transport between 1957 and 1973, and it became the Soviets' most important transport during that period. Six known ECM and ELINT versions were produced: the An-12B-I, An-12BK-IS, An-12-BK-PPS (Cub-D), An-12PP/An-12BKPP (Cub-C), An-12R, and An-12RR (Cub-B).

DESIGN

The An-12 is a high-wing aircraft resembling the Lockheed C-130 Hercules, with a rounded fuselage, glazed nose, upward tail section, and rear cargo door. It is powered by four AI-20D-6 turboprop engines. Military transport versions featured a tail-gunner position armed with a pair of 23mm NR-23 cannons. The ECM and ELINT variants were fitted with an array of antennae, pods, pylons, tail cone, and an undernose radome housing the Toad Stool RBP-2 weather and navigation radar. The ECM variants were the An-12B-I, An-12BK-IS, An-12-BK-PPS, and An-12PP (Cub-C), also known as An-12BK-PP. The An-12R served as an ELINT platform. Two AN-12RRs operated as nuclear, biological, and chemical (NBC) collecting platforms.

Forty An-12s modified as the An-12BI/BKS (Cub-C) series were equipped with the SPS-5 Fasol noise jammer and SPS22/33/44/55 Buket active jammers, a Sirena-3 radar warning system housed in four pylons on either side of the forward fuselage, and a tail cone.

The Cub-D An-12PP/BKPP ECM platform was developed in 1970 from the An-12-BK with significantly better jamming capabilities, including an upgraded Buket and Sirena systems housed within three blisters under the fuselage, and an ASO-24 chaff dispenser in a tail cone. Twenty seven were produced. The An-12-PP developed into the An-12BK-PPS with four ECM pods mounted on each side of the forward fuselage and tail section with the Buket located in the tail cone and the chaff dispenser moved to the side cargo door. Nineteen were produced and remained operational with the Russian Air Force until around 2006–2007.

Antonov produced the An-12R Cub-B ELINT variant in small quantities, which the Soviet Air Force began operating in 1970. Dialectic fairings are located on both sides of the fuselage's midsection, while a pair of blade aerials were mounted on the forward fuselage's top and under the nose section. It appears that some aircraft retained the rear observer/gunner position while others featured a nose cone. At least three An-12RRs, equipped with RR8311-100 air-sampling pods mounted on each side of the forward fuselage, were operated by the Soviet Air Force.

OPERATION

Antonov produced a total of 1,243 An-12s in Irkutsk, Voronezh, and Tashkent. More than 200 remained active as of 2016 as civilian and military transports. The aircraft is known for having a short takeoff distance of approximately 2,300 feet (700 meters) and the ability

Antonov An-12. *US Navy photo*

ANTONOV AN-12

CREW:	5 to 6
ENGINES:	4x Ivchenko AI-20M turboprops; 4,250 hp each
WEIGHTS:	Empty: 67,240 lb (30,500 kg)
	Maximum: 119,050 lb (54,000 kg)
LENGTH:	108 ft 3 in (33.0 m)
WINGSPAN:	125 ft (38.0 m)
HEIGHT:	33 ft 6 in (10.2 m)
SPEEDS:	Maximum: 398 mph (640 kph)
	Cruise: 373 mph (600 kph)
CEILING:	33,465 ft (10,200 m)
RANGE:	3,418 mi (5,500 km)
ARMAMENT:	Two NR 23mm cannon
RADAR:	Toad Stool RBP-2

to operate from unimproved airstrips. The first prototype performed its maiden flight in December 1957. During the Cold War, the Soviet 226th OSAP operated the An-12PP along with the An-26 Curl-B and Il-20 Coot-A out of Sperenberg, Germany, near East Berlin. The primary transport version was widely utilized in Afghanistan between 1979 and 1989.

STATUS

Operational. As of 2015, the VVS had approximately 60 An-12s to be replaced by the Il-76 "Candid." The Russian Navy may have three An-12 recon aircraft, possibly the An-12BKPPS. The Chinese Xian Aircraft Industrial Corporation obtained a license in 1983 from Antonov to develop the Y-8 version of the An-12 for military and civilian applications. The Y-8X/Y-8MPA maritime reconnaissance platform went into operation with the PLA Naval Aviation Corps in late 1984. It is similar in design to the An-12R, with the exception that a mission equipment window has replaced the rear cargo door; it is powered by Zhuzhou Aero WJ6 Turbo engines. Eight People's Republic of China PLA military recon variants are known to have been produced: the Y-8Q/Y-8X-6 ASW, Y-8XZ ECM, Y-8CB COMINT, Y-8JB/KZ-800 ELINT, Y-8G SIGINT, and Y-8H ISR. ∎

—*Alan C. Carey*

Yakovlev Yak-28I ("Brewer C"). *US Navy photo*

YAKOVLEV YAK-28 "BREWER"

The Yak-28 was a supersonic, multiuse tactical aircraft based on the Yak-25 and -27; it was operational from 1960 to 1992. Initial work on the prototype Yak-129 began in 1956, and the first flight test took place in March 1958. Approximately 1,100 units were produced beginning in 1960 and ending in 1970, with multiple modifications and variants, including the Yak-28R, Yak-28RR, and Yak-28SR recon versions. The United States and NATO allies became aware of the aircraft when it appeared at the Tushino Airshow in 1961.

Production and modifications took place at the Irktusk Aviation Plant, with the Yak-28B tactical bomber (Brewer A) as the first full production model. Modified versions of the B variant followed with the Yak-28L (Brewer B) and Yak-28I (Brewer C). Other variants included the Yak-28P (NATO "Firebar"); a long-range interceptor with additional fuel tanks and

Oriol-D intercept radar; a dual-control trainer Yak-28U ("Maestro"); and the Yak-28PP (Brewer E), the Soviets' first dedicated ECM platform, introduced in 1970.

DESIGN

The Yak-28 featured a high, 45-degree swept wing and a swept tail. Tricycle landing gear with outrigger wheels near the wingtips was similar to that found on the American Boeing B-47 Stratojet. Bomber and recon variants featured a glazed nose for the bombardier/radar operator station. Two wing-mounted Tumanski R-11AF-300 afterburning turbojets with a maximum thrust of 13,670 pounds (6,200 kilograms) gave the aircraft a maximum speed of over 1,100 miles per hour (1,770 kilometers per hour). Its rated top speed made it the fastest tactical aircraft of the period.

The main reconnaissance variant was the unarmed Yak-28R (Brewer-D), utilizing the Yak-28I airframe but powered by two R-11AF2-300 turbojets. The prototype rolled out in 1963, and 183 were eventually produced. Structural changes included a larger cockpit, an underbelly blister radome, modified nose glazing, and a slight bulge forward of the cockpit to provide additional headspace for the radar operator. Reconnaissance equipment housed in the bay consisted of the Initsiava-2R radar system, three pallets of three to four cameras (comprising one 190mm panoramic housed in a bay, two side cameras, and a long-focus camera mounted in the fuselage's center), and a SIGNET system. The bomb bay could carry photo flash bombs and flares for night recon. Later production models designated Yak-28SR carried ECM SPS-141 or SPS-143 Gvozdika radar/radio jammer sets. Several Yak-28Rs were modified to carry TARK-1 television with a datalink system, which replaced the Initsiava-2R. Yak-28Rs modified to conduct radiation monitoring during the late 1960s were designated Yak-28RR; Yak-28Ls

similarly modified were designated Yak-28LRs. Other recon versions included one Yak-28I, modified as the Yak-28BI and fitted with a side-looking SLAR radar with the antenna housed in the bomb bay and lowered for operation.

OPERATION

The Yak-28R entered service in 1966, with reconnaissance units operating the Yak-28R from bases inside the Soviet Union and Eastern Bloc nations. The 11th Reconnaissance Aviation Regiment (RAP) flew from East Germany over Czechoslovakia prior to the invasion in August 1968 (Operation Danube) and saw combat service during border clashes with the Red Chinese in 1969. The 39th Independent Reconnaissance Unit (OARP), operating the Yak-28R and MiG-25R, flew ELINT and PHOTINT missions over Afghanistan during the Soviet-Afghan War of 1979–1989.

STATUS

Retired. Voyenno-Vozdushnye Sily (VVS, or Soviet Air Force and voyska protivovozdushnoy oborony (PVO, or National Air Defense) units operated the Yak-28 bomber and interceptor variants until the early 1980s, when the MiG-25 became available; the recon and ECM versions remained in active service until replaced by the SU-24MR/MP Fencer. It has been reported that some Yak-28PP ECM platforms remained on active duty with the Russians through 1993.

The 931st RAP, based in East Germany, began transitioning from the Yak-28R to the MiG-25R in 1988, completing the change a year later. The newly formed Russian Air Force retired the Yak-28 in 1992, replacing it with the Sukhoi SU-24MR "Fencer." After the Soviet Union's collapse, the Ukrainian Air Force took possession of 35 Yak-28s, operated primarily by the 118th Independent ECM Regiment (OAPREB), while the Turkmen Air Force of Turkmenistan acquired at least eight, which went to the 31st Separate Aviation Squadron (CAE). Ukrainian Yak-28s were replaced by the SU-24MR in 1995. The Turkmen Air Force reported three nonoperational Yak-28s in its inventory in 2003. ■

—*Alan C. Carey*

YAKOVLEV YAK-28

CREW:	2
ENGINES:	2x R-11AF2-300 turbojets; 13,670 lbst (6,200 kgst) each
WEIGHTS:	Empty: 21,980 lb (9,970 kg) Maximum: 44,092 lb (20,000 kg)
LENGTH:	75 ft (22.9 m)
WINGSPAN:	41 ft (12.5 m)
HEIGHT:	12 ft 11 in (3.9 m)
SPEEDS:	Maximum: 1,142 mph (1,838 kph) Cruise: 497 mph (800 kph)
CEILING:	54,954 ft (16,750 m)
RANGE:	1,550 miles (2,500 km)
ARMAMENT:	None
RADAR:	Initsiava-2R radar

Mikoyan-Gurevich MiG-25. *Richard Dann collection*

MIKOYAN-GUREVICH MIG-25 "FOXBAT"

The Foxbat MiG-25 served with the Soviet Air Defense as supersonic, high-altitude interceptor and recon variants from 1970 to 1991. The Foxbat MiG-25R is one of the reconnaissance variants produced by the Mikoyan Gurevich Group.

The MiG-25's development was the Soviet Union's response to American high-altitude recon aircraft (the Lockheed U-2 and the later A-12) and supersonic, nuclear-capable, strategic bombers (Convair B-58, North American A-5 Vigilante, and North American XB-70 Valkyrie) in service or under development. MiG-25 development began in 1959 and the first prototype, the Ye-155R-1, a recon variant, first flew on 6 March 1964. A second reconnaissance prototype, Ye-155R-2, was followed by two interceptors, Ye-155P-1 and Ye-155P-2. The Ye-155 series performed several

record-breaking speed and altitude flights between 1965 and 1977.

Production of the MiG-25 series began in 1969 with the MiG-25R (Foxbat-B), a high-altitude reconnaissance aircraft; the MiG-25P, an all-weather interceptor appeared two years later. Soviet air and defense forces operated 22 variants, including 10 recon/recon bomber versions (the R, RR, RB, RBF RBK RBN, RBS, RBT, RBV, and RBsh), for a total of 220 units manufactured between 1969 and 1982.

DESIGN

The Foxbat has rectangular air intakes blended into a slender fuselage. Its cantilevered high-wing design with twin vertical stabilizers is reminiscent of the McDonnell Douglas F-15. The MiG-25 is constructed primarily of nickel-steel alloy steel with titanium along the leading edges and engine exhaust areas. Most of the electronics used vacuum-tube technology, not the solid-state electronics seen in NATO aircraft of the period. The use of such outdated technology at first confounded the analysts who dismantled a MiG-25P flown to Japan by a Soviet defector in 1976. Careful examination, however, showed the tubes to be more resistant to temperature extremes and electromagnetic pulse; they also created a powerful 600 watt RP-25 Smerch radar system enclosed in the nose.

The MiG-25R recon version carried two 317-gallon (1,200-liter) fuel tanks integrated in the tail fins for extended flight time, and the radar was removed to house surveillance equipment. Photo intelligence reconnaissance equipment consisted of four oblique, general-purpose AFA-70M cameras and one AE-10 topographical camera located in detachable hatches with clear windows under the fuselage's nose.

Production MiG-25Rs were sent to the Lipetsk pilot training center while the Moscow military district received the rest. The Israeli victory in the Six Day War of 1967—and subsequent targeting of Egyptian

military facilities and industrial areas such as electrical stations—forced the Egyptian government to seek Soviet military assistance. The Soviet response in late 1969 was the modification of the 25R as a dual-use recon and bomber platform with the designator MiG-25RB ("Foxbat-B").

First flown on 29 January 1970, and entering service in 1972, the RB had four underwing bomb mounts for 500-pound (227-kilogram) bombs; later, it was fitted with additional underbelly mounts. For bombing accuracy, the aircraft carried the Peleng-D or Peleng-DR, and later the Peleng-DM navigation/bombing system. For photo intelligence flights, the original surveillance camera package remained, but two A-72 or one A-87 cameras were added as alternatives. ELINT equipment consisted of the SRS-4A/B or SRS-4V for detecting radar emissions. The RB carried the SPS-141 ECM pack for defense.

Production ended in 1982 when more sophisticated variants became available, and the MiG-25RB airframe was used to develop other variants between 1972 and 1982.

The ability to locate enemy radio transmitters and identify those exact systems became possible with the development of the MiG-25RBK, using the RB fitted with the Kub-3M (KOOB-3) ELINT package. This gear weighed several hundred pounds, which required lengthening the nose, removing camera equipment, and adding a fairing over the camera ports. Production began in 1972 and ended in 1980. The variant was upgraded in 1981 with the testing of the MiG-25RBF featuring a Shar-25 (Ball/Balloon) short-range ELINT system. It carried flare/chaff dispensers and could carry panoramic cameras.

The all-weather MiG-25RBS had Sablya-E SLAR; the first preproduction model flight tested between 1972 and 1973. Dielectric panels were installed on each side of the fuselage's nose. Full production began in 1973 and continued until approximately 1977. Beginning in 1978, the MiG-25RBS underwent additional modifications and was redesignated MiG-25RBV, with the SRS-9 Virazh-1 ELINT system replacing the SRS-3A and SRS-3B along with interchangeable camera equipment. This system was carried internally.

Late-production RBSs carried the SPS-151 Lyutik ECM set instead of the SPS-141 Siren. Slight modifications to the MiG-25RV occurred during 1978, with the RBT that carried the lighter SRS-13 Tangazh ELINT

MIKOYAN-GUREVICH MIG-25RB

CREW:	1
ENGINES:	2x Tumanskie R-15B-300 turbojets; approx. 22,500 lbst (10,206 kgst) each
WEIGHTS:	Empty: 44,000 lb (19,958 kg) Maximum: 79,800 lb (36,197 kg)
LENGTH:	64 ft 2 in (19.6 m)
WINGSPAN:	43 ft 8 in (13.3 m)
HEIGHT:	21 ft 4 in (6.5 m)
SPEED:	Maximum: 1,875 mph (3,018 kph)
CEILING:	75,460 ft (23,000 m)
RANGE:	900 mi (1,148 km)
ARMAMENT:	None (external mounts for bombs)
RADAR:	Sabre-E SLAR (MiG-25RBS)

package offering a wider range to detect and locate enemy radar. Production lasted from 1979 to 1982. Eight RBVs designated RR were fitted with equipment to detect radioactivity from nuclear testing. The RBS was again upgraded when the Sablya side-screening radar system was replaced with the Shompol SLAR, which had better resolution and could operate up to approximately 75,500 feet (23,000 meters). This variant was designated the MiG-25RBsh.

A high-altitude night reconnaissance variant went into production in 1972, designated the MiG-25RBN, which featured NAFA-75 night-vision cameras. It could carry four to ten underwing-mounted FOTAB-100 or FOTAB-140 flash bombs. A few RBs became weather reconnaissance aircraft designated MiG-25MRs.

The training version was the two-seat MiG-25RU, manufactured between 1971 and 1982, with the first taking flight in March 1971. Fifty units were built, with some exported to countries operating the MiG-25.

The RBF was the final ELINT reconnaissance variant with dialectic panels on each side of the nose. It was equipped with the Shar-25 system.

OPERATION

Four MiG-205Rs and RBs were sent to Egypt during 1971–1972 to fly recon missions over Israel. In the course of these missions, Israeli McDonnell F-4 Phantoms failed to intercept any of the 20 flyovers. The Foxbats were withdrawn and returned to the Soviet Union in July 1972. Egypt's launch in October 1973 of the Yom Kippur War saw the return of Soviet RB-25RBs at the request of President Anwar Sadat. However, only one was flying by the time of the truce.

The Iraqi Air Force operated eight MiG-25RBs in bombing runs on Iranian oil rigs in the Persian Gulf during the Iran-Iraq War.

The Soviet Union exported approximately 30 MiG-25RBs during the 1980s and 1990s to Algeria, Bulgaria, India, Iran, Iraq, and Syria. Former Soviet territories Armenia, Belarus, Georgia, Kazakhstan, Turkmenistan, and Ukraine inherited aircraft after the collapse of the Soviet Union.

STATUS

Operational. Most exported MiG-25s were taken out of active inventories beginning in the late 1990s. By 2014, Libya and Syria kept several airframes but it is unclear which variants, with Syria reportedly having two airworthy examples. An incomplete Iraqi MiG-25RB was found by American forces in 2003 buried in the sand near Baghdad. It was delivered to the National Museum of the United States Air Force for eventual restoration. The Indian Air Force has a MiG-25R on display and the Indian Air Force base at Kalaikunda has two MiG-25U trainers on outdoor exhibit. ∎

—*Alan C. Carey*

SUKHOI SU-24 "FENCER"

With a crew of two (pilot and weapons officer), the Su-24 is an all-weather attack aircraft produced by Sukhoi between 1971 and 1993. The aircraft is strikingly similar in design to the American General Dynamics F-111 Aardvark introduced three years earlier in 1968. Six variants of the Su-24 were produced: the Su-24, Su-24M ("Fencer-D," upgraded to the Su-24M2 in 2000), and an export version of the Su-24M with downgraded electronics and weapons capacity. The Su-24MR ("Fencer-E") and Su-24MP ("Fencer-F") are the recon and ELINT variants of the Su-24M.

Development of the aircraft began with the Soviet government's demand in 1961 for an all-weather tactical aircraft produced in conjunction with its acceptance of the Sukhoi's Su-7B ("Fitter-A") fighter-bomber. The intent was to counteract the Su-7B's shortcomings, which included poor cockpit visibility and a high landing speed, requiring a longer runway.

DESIGN

The Su-24 features high-level, variable-sweep wings and is powered by two Lyulka AL-21F-3A afterburning turbojets that allow the aircraft to reach Mach 1.08 or 815 miles per hour (1,312 kilometers per hour). Design to production took ten years, beginning in 1961, and included a feasibility study to see if the Su-7B could be modified as an all-weather aircraft. This approach was rejected, though, as the bomber lacked enough space to house the required equipment. The program halted until 1964, when the first prototype of the Su-15, designated T-58M, became a flying testbed for a supersonic,

Sukhoi Su-24. *Public domain*

SUKHOI SU-24MR

CREW:	2
ENGINES:	2x Saturn/Lyulka AL-21F-3A afterburning turbojets; 24,675 lbst (11,192 kgst) each
WEIGHTS:	Empty: 49,163 lb (22,300 kg) Maximum: 87,524 lb (39,700 kg)
LENGTH:	73 ft 11 in (22.5 m)
WINGSPAN:	57 ft 10 in (17.6 m) extended; 34 ft (10.4 m) swept
HEIGHT:	20 ft 4 in (6.2 m)
SPEED:	870 mph (1,400 kph)
CEILING:	36,090 ft (11,000 m)
ARMAMENT:	Two R-60/AA-8 missiles
RADAR:	MR-1 SLAR

low-level, all-weather aircraft. The official designation for the aircraft changed to T-6 in late 1965, with two prototypes built and tested during 1967. Continued redesign and testing continued with the T-62I, fitted with sweep wings, which was flight-tested for the first time in November 1969. Series production began in 1971, with the first Soviet Air Force unit receiving the aircraft in 1973. The designator was changed from T-6 to Su-24 in 1975.

Development and production of a recon prototype (TM-58R) and ECM variant (TM-58MP) were completed in 1973, but apparently further work did not resume until 1976. The program, upon restarting, changed the designators to T-6MR and T-6MP. Successful flight tests of both variants occurred during the summer of 1980 and concluded that November. Sukhoi produced only ten SU-24MP ECM aircraft, with the first taking flight in April 1983; the initial test of the TM-58MR occurred a week later. The aircraft were given the designations of Su-24P and Su-24MR.

The Su-24MP retained the standard cannon for self-defense and could carry four R-60 (AA-8) missiles on wing racks. The exact nature of the Su-24MP electronic suite is unknown, but it can carry various ECM and SIGNIT pods under the centerline.

The Su-24MR kept the original Relyek navigational system, but the cannon and Orion-A "Puma" attack radar were removed for the SLAR RDS-BO/BKR-1 Bortovoy Kompleks Razvedki package with the Shtik (Bayonet) Mr-1 SLAR and Zima (Winter) infrared system in the nose. The Aist-M Stork television package is housed under the forward fuselage. Photo intelligence is handled by the AFA AP-402 panoramic camera in the center fuselage and an A-100 oblique camera under the left air intake. A pod mounted on the right wing pylon carries Efir-1M for radiation monitoring. A pod containing SIGNIT or laser imaging equipment can be mounted under the fuselage. Approximately 100 were produced between 1983 and 1993.

OPERATION

The Su-24MR replaced the Yak-27R and Yak-28R as the Soviet supersonic recon aircraft during the summer of 1983. The first reconnaissance aviation detachment to test the aircraft was the 47th SGRAR based at Shatalovo during 1987 and 1988. Libya received one Su-24MR from the Soviets in 1989, and this aircraft may have been transferred to the Syrian Air Force. One Russian Su-24MR may have been shot down during the 2008 war with Georgia.

STATUS

Operational. As of 2016, operators of the recon variant were Russia, Algeria, and Ukraine. Russian Air Force Su-24MRs number approximately 80, operated by the 11th, 47th, 98th, 313th, and 779th RAPs. ■

—Alan C. Carey

TUPOLEV TU-142 "BEAR F/J"

The Tu-142M series was developed to provide Soviet naval aviation with an advanced reconnaissance/anti-submarine aircraft. While resembling the Tu-20/Tu-95, the Tu-142 incorporates advances in aerodynamics, structures, and systems. Performance is enhanced over the earlier Bear design, with an unrefueled endurance of some thirty hours.

In the 1960s, designation Tu-142 was applied to later aircraft (NATO designations Bear-F/J). The Tu-142 designation also is applied to the Bear-G, an extensive rebuild of earlier Bear aircraft as cruise missile carriers, and the new-build Bear-H missile carrier.

DESIGN

Compared with its predecessors, the Tu-142 features increased wing camber, more powerful engines, and, due to its greater weight, redesigned landing gear. The aircraft is longer than the Tu-20/95, with a 70-inch (177.8-centimeter) plug fitted forward of the wings. An in-flight refueling probe is fitted in the nose.

Like the Bear-D, the -F has a massive surface-search radar in place of a bomb bay; the smaller, undernose navigation radar of the earlier aircraft has been deleted. The aircraft also has magnetic anomaly detection (MAD) sensors (fitted in pod fairings) and SIGINT

Tupolev Tu-142. *US Department of Defense photo*

TUPOLEV TU-142 BEAR-F

CREW:	7 to 9
ENGINES:	4x Kuznetsov NK12MV turboprops; 15,000 shp each
WEIGHTS:	Empty: 198,000 lb (90,000 kg)
	Maximum: 407,848 lb (185,000 kg)
LENGTH:	174 ft 6 in (53.2 m)
WINGSPAN:	164 ft 2 in (50.0 m)
HEIGHT:	47 ft 4.5 in (14.5 m)
SPEEDS:	Maximum: 531 mph (855 kph)
	Cruise: 456 mph (735 kph)
CEILING:	approx. 40,000 ft (12,195 m)
RANGE:	7,000+ mi (11,265+ km)
ARMAMENT:	2x AM-23/GSh-23 23mm cannon
RADAR:	Korshun-K surface search; gunfire control (NATO designation Bee Hind)

collection systems. Some mods have the MAD pod mounted atop the tailfin.

Unlike the Bear-D, this aircraft can carry ordnance: depth charges (possibly nuclear as well as conventional) and torpedoes. The aircraft also can release sonobuoys. Twin 20mm cannon are fitted in the tail position.

OPERATIONS

The Bear-F aircraft augmented and then supplanted Bear-Ds on overwater surveillance missions, beginning with deployments to Cuba in 1983, followed by operations from bases in Angola and Guinea.

STATUS

Operational. Its first flight occurred 18 June 1968, and it entered service with Naval Aviation in May 1970.

Russian Naval Aviation had more than two dozen Tu-142M Bear-Fs, as well as a few Bear-J communication relay aircraft in inventory in 2015. (At the time, the Russian Strategic Aviation was estimated to have about 30 Bear-G and 30 Bear-H aircraft in service.)

Six Tu-142M Bear-F aircraft were transferred to the Indian naval air arm. ■

—*Norman Polmar and John F. Bessette*

ANTONOV AN-26 "CURL"

The Curl is a Soviet twin-turboprop, multiuse tactical transport produced between 1969 and 1986 by the Antonov Design Bureau. Approximately 1,400 were produced with over three dozen variants and subvariants, including several reconnaissance versions. It was developed from the An-24 "Coke," another twin-engine turboprop tactical transport. The first production example An-26A took flight in May 1969.

DESIGN

The aircraft features a high-wing design with tricycle landing gear configuration, and is equipped with a rear ramp. It is powered by two Ivchenko/ZMKB Progress AI-24VT turboprops and one Tumansky Ru-19-A300 turbojet housed in the left nacelle for increased climb rate and high-altitude cruising. ELINT, SIG-NIT, and ECM variants have been produced: the An-26REP, An-26LL-PLO, An-26RR, An-26RT, and An-26RTR. One An-26A was modified and tested for anti-submarine warfare (ASW) as the An-26LL-PO, while another, designated An-26REP, was tested as an ECM platform. Neither entered production. Approximately 40 to 50 An-26RR/RT/RTR ELINT recon variants were produced and operated, primarily by the VVS. There is some confusion regarding the designation of the initial Curl-B An-26RT, as that designator was used for both the ELINT and a battlefield communication relay variant, along with An-26RR and An-26RTR. The Curl-B has a distinctive array of swept-back antennae above and below the forward fuselage.

OPERATION

The 226th OSAP operated the Curl-B from Sperenberg in East Germany during the Cold War, and the Soviets are known to have utilized at least one An-26-RT reconnaissance aircraft during the Afghan-Soviet War to track and record communications of mujahideen rebels. The post–Cold War German Air Force retained

Antonov An-26. *UK Defence Imagery, Open Government License 3.0*

one Curl-B, designated An-26ST, and the Czech Air Force operated one as the An-26M. The Pakistan Air Force claims to have shot down several Afghan and Soviet An-26s on separate occasions when the aircraft penetrated Pakistan airspace. However, the Soviets and their Afghan ally claimed the An-26s were all transports carrying supplies and passengers. The only recorded loss of a Soviet An-26RT (whether it was a recon or communications variant is unknown) occurred 29 December 1986 when one was destroyed by a rebel missile.

STATUS

Operational. The An-26 continues to operate in over 40 countries in military and civilian applications. China produced the Xian Y-14/Y-7 under a licensing agreement with Antonov. The number of recon variants still active as of 2016 was unclear, though the Russian Air Force reportedly had 150 in inventory. ∎

—*Alan C. Carey*

ANTONOV AN-26

CREW:	3 to 5
ENGINES:	2x Ivchenko AI-24VT turboprops, 2,820 hp each; 1x Tumansky Ru-19-A300 turbojet thruster, 1,795 lbst (814 kgst)
WEIGHTS:	Empty: 33,100 lb (15,014 kg)
	Maximum: 53,000 lb (24,040 kg) transport
LENGTH:	78 ft 1 in (23.8 m)
WINGSPAN:	95 ft 9.5 in (29.2 m)
HEIGHT:	28 ft 1.5 in (8.6 m)
SPEEDS:	Maximum: 336 mph (540 kph)
	Cruise: 273 mph (440 kph)
CEILING:	24,606 ft (7,500 m)
RANGE:	1,585 mi (2,550 km)
ARMAMENT:	None
RADAR:	Groza-26

UNITED STATES

Lockheed F-5. *US Air Force photo*

LOCKHEED F-4/F-5 LIGHTNING

Of all the World War II-era fighter aircraft designs, the Lockheed's P-38 Lightning was perhaps the most radical. The plane had a distinctively unconventional twin-boom arrangement with a pilot's central "pod" mounted between a pair of Allison V-12 engines. The pod's rounded nose contained four heavy-hitting .50-caliber machine guns and a 20mm cannon.

The P-38 was big, but it was also fast. It was the first fighter to fly at over 400 miles per hour (644 kilometers per hour). The prototype took to the skies on its initial flight on 27 January 1939.

The first combat-ready version made in large numbers was the P-38E. The initial recon aircraft developed from the Lightning platform were based on the P-38E fighter variant.

DESIGN

Designated F-4, the first recon Lightnings substituted cameras in place of their guns. The ample nose compartment carried up to four K-17 aerial cameras (producing up to 250 individual 9x9-inch negatives per camera) aimed vertically and obliquely. Versions of the plane were also fitted with a drift sight and autopilot system. Some 99 F-4s were built, along with 20 F-4A aircraft with slightly improved (P-38F type) engines and additional camera stations. The F-4 was the first high-performance photoreconnaissance plane ever mass-produced by the USAAF. Depending on the number of cameras carried, in rare cases the F-4 could fly with a pair of .50-caliber machine guns squeezed back into their noses for protection.

Improved F-5A aircraft were based on the P-38G version of the Lightning, with 181 produced. Beyond the factory-built aircraft, many additional P-38s were converted to F-model photo planes in the combat theaters of Europe and the Pacific.

Additionally, blocks of new army P-38 fighters were modified to fill the role of F-planes stateside. Some 128

Lockheed F-5. *US Marine Corps photo*

LOCKHEED F-5B

CREW:	1
ENGINES:	2x Allison V-1710-89/91; 1,425 hp each
WEIGHT:	Maximum: 20,600 lb (9,344 kg)
LENGTH:	37 ft 10 in (11.5 m)
WINGSPAN:	52 ft (15.2 m)
HEIGHT:	9 ft 10 in (3.0 m)
SPEED:	Maximum: 424 mph (682 kph)
CEILING:	44,000 ft (13,411 m)
RANGE:	863 mi (1,389 km)
ARMAMENT:	None
RADAR:	None

F-5C types were converted P-38H aircraft, while 905 P-38J and P-38L aircraft became F-5B, F-5E, F-5F, and F-5G aircraft, built with varying camera arrangements and engine types.

OPERATIONS

Like the P-38 fighter, F-model Lightning reconnaissance aircraft served in nearly every theater of war. The planes were commonly assigned to small, specialized reconnaissance units, often operating a mixture of aircraft types to complete various photography missions. In Europe, the American recon units worked in a similar fashion as their UK counterparts, and they immediately possessed baseline imagery created by the Royal Air Force's photo "recce" squadrons. In the Pacific and China-Burma-India theaters, information was hard to find.

In order to gain knowledge about Japanese operations in the Pacific, much of Lockheed's production run in January 1942 was F-model photo aircraft. That month, 84 recon machines left the factory. while only 32 P-38 fighter planes were built.

An unarmed F-4 flown by Capt. Karl (Pop) Polifka of the 8th Photo Reconnaissance Squadron became the first Lightning to see action in the Pacific in April and May. The "combat" was one-sided—with Captain Polifka carefully recording the actions of the Japanese ships massing near Rabaul while avoiding being cornered by scores of defending Zero fighters. His intelligence data led, in part, to the Battle of the Coral Sea in May 1942.

In the years after, reconnaissance Lightnings scouted island after island in the months before American troops stormed ashore. Meanwhile, in Europe, scores of Lightnings scoured enemy territory in the endless search for information. Sometimes the targets were large—such as ports, cities, or airfields—while other missions meant gathering information on individual canals, bridges, highways, or rail yards. As Allied armies pushed in from all sides in 1944, an F-5C Lightning of the 7th Photo Reconnaissance Group named *Dot+Dash* became the first combat aircraft to fly on a "shuttle mission" from England to Soviet-held territory on the Eastern Front.

A Lightning recon pilot's bag of tricks included all the old standbys, such as accelerating out of trouble, climbing away from a fight, or ducking into the clouds. However, Lightning pilots developed another effective tactic: bluffing.

While it only took a moment to figure out that a plane in the distance was an American Lightning, an enemy flyer had to be much closer to know if it was armed or not. The heavily gunned and stable-flying P-38 fighter was notoriously deadly in head-on attacks. By acting like a fighter, aggressively turning to face a threat head-on, more than one F-5 flyer bluffed his way into making enough room for a quick escape.

STATUS

Retired. The first Lockheed F-4 was produced in December 1941. F-4 and F-5 types served the USAAF throughout World War II in both Europe and the Pacific. The Free French employed a number of recon Lightnings as well.

The first Lockheed Lightning sold to a civilian was an F-5C model, turned over to Leo Childs in March 1945. A handful of other F-planes followed, used for mapping or converted to racers. A few of the airframes, usually rebuilt to fighter specifications, survive today. ∎

—Cory Graff

NORTH AMERICAN F-6 MUSTANG

Perhaps the best all-around fighter aircraft of World War II, the P-51 Mustang started as a fighter built for the British. First versions of the plane's exceptionally aerodynamic airframe were fitted with an Allison V-1710 engine.

But the plane became a real success when it was mated to a Packard-built copy of Rolls-Royce's Merlin engine. With the Merlin, Mustangs could fly far and reasonably fast, as well as cruise at very high altitude. The P-51 became the "escort of choice" to shepherd heavy bombers to and from their targets over Germany, keeping Luftwaffe fighters at bay.

Mustangs, too, made their mark in the Pacific, particularly in the last year of combat, when the United States held islands that were within striking distance of Japan.

At the end of the war, fighting Mustangs were valued enough to be brought home in great numbers. The planes again flew in combat over Korea in the early 1950s. Today they are among the most sought-after museum pieces from the World War II era.

DESIGN

Early Mustangs were at their best at altitudes of 15,000 feet (4,572 meters) or less. As a result, many of the RAF's first Allison-equipped Mustang I aircraft were intentionally assigned to missions that kept them close to ground. Army Cooperation Command fighters flew tactical reconnaissance missions, with an F.24 camera mounted obliquely behind the pilot. The Mustang's big airframe allowed for the camera plane to fly with its normal compliment of guns in the wings. As one London newspaper put it, "One day it shoots pictures, the next day it shoots German troops."

The Americans eventually followed suit, with F-6 Mustangs modified to carry two K-24 cameras, one obliquely behind the pilot and the other located behind

North American F-6. *Elden Williams collection*

North American F-6. *National Archives and Records Administration*

the plane's radiator, facing downward. The first "Photo Joe" planes served with units in North Africa.

The first Packard Merlin–powered aircraft built in California and Texas were designated F-6C aircraft and kept the same camera locations with options to change out the pair of K-24 cameras for K-17 or K-22 types as needed. With the redesign of the fuselage to allow bubble-canopied versions, the location of the oblique camera position had to change. On F-6D and F-6K models, the side-facing camera was moved directly above the vertically oriented camera, its lens facing out of a viewport cut into the side of the plane's fuselage.

F-6As were built from P-51 airframes and F-6Bs were made from P-51A fighters. F-6C aircraft were the designation for P-51Bs (built in California) and similar P-51Cs (built in Texas).

F-6D aircraft were P-51Ds, and F-6K aircraft were P-51Ks. After the US Air Force was created, these aircraft became RF-51D and RF-51Ks, with RF indicating "reconnaissance, fighter."

OPERATIONS

The first Mustang victory was scored by a recon machine flown by an American pilot serving in a Canadian squadron of Britain's Royal Air Force. Hollis Hills was shooting up a German armored column near Dieppe on 19 August 1942, when he and his wingman were attacked by Focke-Wulf Fw 190 fighters. After losing his wingman, Hills got the German flyer.

The fact that the camera-equipped Mustangs remained fully armed brought a grin to many a recon pilot's face. Captain Clyde East of the 10th Tactical Reconnaissance Group was snapping photos of German troops on D-Day when he got his first chance to take on an enemy fighter. Over the next year, a total of 13 German aircraft fell to the guns of his F-6 photo Mustang while he snooped behind enemy lines. Captain East would go on to fly 130 combat recon missions over Korea and complete four "verification flights" in an RF-101 over Soviet missiles in Cuba during the Cuban Missile Crisis in 1962.

In the Pacific in January 1945, Capt. William Shomo and his wingman were monitoring Japanese airfields in the Philippines with their F-6D Mustangs. Nearby, they observed a Betty bomber being escorted by 12 fighters. Though outnumbered 13 to 2, Shomo and his wingman instantly maneuvered to attack the formation. In the ensuing battle, Shomo's wingman shot down three aircraft. Shomo was credited with seven victories for the day and earned the Medal of Honor. Soon after, he changed the name on the side of his F-6 from *Snooks* to *The Flying Undertaker*.

After World War II, versions of the F-6D and F-6K continued flying with army and then air force units. Redesignated RF-51Ds and RF-51Ks, served during the first years of the Korean War before being replaced

NORTH AMERICAN F-6D

CREW:	1
ENGINE:	1x Packard Merlin V-1650-7; 1,490 hp
WEIGHT:	Maximum: 10,600 lb (4,808 kg)
LENGTH:	32 ft 3 in (9.8 m)
WINGSPAN:	37 ft (11.2 m)
HEIGHT:	12 ft 2 in (3.7 m)
SPEED:	Maximum: 440 mph (708 kph)
CEILING:	42,000 ft (12,802 m)
RANGE:	1,766 mi (2,842 km)
ARMAMENT:	6x .50-caliber machine guns
RADAR:	None

with jet aircraft. The recon Mustangs photographed before and after bombing assessments, reconnoitered enemy positions, and flew weather missions.

STATUS

Retired. The first Mustangs were equipped with cameras were assigned to Squadron 26 in the UK in January 1942. They went into combat some months later.

Mustangs primarily served with the USAAF throughout World War II, with camera-modified aircraft of every major P-51 fighter type.

After the war, a handful of F-6 aircraft were acquired by civilian owners. The most famous were the two F-6 (P-51C) Mustangs owned by Hollywood stunt pilot and racer Paul Mantz. The planes won the Bendix Trophy (Burbank, California, to Cleveland, Ohio) in 1946, 1947, and 1948, as well as a number of distance records, including a run from Fairbanks, Alaska, to New York City (3,450 miles; 5,552 kilometers) in 9 hours and 31 minutes. ■

—*Cory Graff*

Transport version of Douglas C-47 Skytrain, basis for the RC-47. *Library of Congress, Office of War Information, LC-USE6- D-008559*

DOUGLAS RC-47 SKYTRAIN/DAKOTA

Among the many platforms used for air reconnaissance, the C-47 Skytrain (Dakota in the United Kingdom) does not seem a prime candidate for this role. Slow, with a cruising speed of just 175 miles per hour (281 kilometers per hour), and steady rather than agile in the skies, it nonetheless proved to be of high value under the right circumstances. The C-47 Skytrain had its direct origins in the DC-3 ("Douglas Commercial") airliner, one of the first truly viable aircraft of its kind (perhaps sharing the honor with the Boeing 247).

In 1934, American airlines ordered a bigger version of Douglas's DC-2, and the manufacturer delivered the 24-passenger DC-3 the following year. During the six years that followed, leading up to World War II, the DC-3 swept the skies, vastly increasing civil air travel and attracting the interest of the armed forces due to its reliable, rugged construction. For military purposes, the Army Air Force asked Douglas for more powerful engines, a stronger rear fuselage and cabin floor, and enlargement of the loading doors; the manufacturer complied and C-47s began rolling off factory floors by the thousands.

The C-47s flew many different roles in every theater of World War II and long afterward. They served as glider tugs at Normandy and Sicily, contributed (as Dakotas) to D-Day operations under Lend-Lease to Great Britain, and they saw service during the Berlin Airlift, the Korean War, and as gunships in Vietnam.

DESIGN

True to its reputation for durability, the C-47 looked tough. Broad-winged with a thick fuselage, it actually represented one of the most modern aircraft designs of its day, enhanced by extensive wind tunnel research at the California Institute of Technology. It featured a low-wing, cantilever configuration and a multi-spar wing construction that contributed much to its strength. Its fuselage had an almost circular cross-section and a cantilever tail. Inside, the C-47 had six compartments: a pilot and operator's cockpit, two baggage holds, a radio section, a cargo bay, and a lavatory. Down the sides of the cabin, the C-47 had folding seats that accommodated 28 fully armed combat troops.

DOUGLAS RC-47D

CREW:	3
ENGINES:	2x Pratt & Whitney R-1830-90 Wasp engines; 1,200 hp each
WEIGHTS:	Empty: 16,970 lb (7,705 kg) Maximum: 33,000 lb (14,965 kg)
LENGTH:	64 ft 5 in (19.6 m)
WINGSPAN:	95 ft (28.9 m)
HEIGHT:	16 ft 11 in (5.1 m)
SPEEDS:	Maximum: 232 mph (373 kph) Cruise: 175 mph (281 kph)
CEILING:	24,450 ft (7,452 m)
RANGE:	1,513 mi (2,436 km)
ARMAMENT:	None
RADAR:	ALR-34 or ALR-35

Transport version of Douglas C-47 Dakota. *Adrian Pingstone photo, public domain*

OPERATIONS

Project Blue Sky during the Korean War gave the C-47 its first taste of recon. In an almost accidental wartime adaptation, the Skytrain's new career started when a junior officer in the USAF's 6920th Security Group suggested outfitting C-47s with COMINT equipment. He persuaded officials at higher headquarters to make three aircraft available and in late 1952 they arrived at the 6053rd Radio Flight Mobile. Once airborne, they flew with significant success as RC-47s to targets well inside North Korea and China. To distribute the results, the aircraft's crew put tape recordings of the eavesdropped data on parachutes and dropped them on Cho Do Island, Korea, where waiting air force personnel collected them and disseminated the intelligence to US combat forces.

The concept of the RC-47 saw its full expression during the Vietnam War. First, though, its designation changed during the early 1960s. Because they now carried ELINT gear consisting of signal intercept and emitter location equipment, the aircraft became known as EC-47s, designed to intercept hostile radio transmissions, locate the enemy, and call in airstrikes. They relied, in part, on ALR-34 and -35 radar systems to detect the low-power, high-frequency signals typical of North Vietnamese Army transmissions. Depending on their electronic warfare suites, the aircraft—assigned to the 460th Tactical Reconnaissance Wing—bore the designations EC-47N, P, or Q.

When US Army officials learned about the air force's new eye in the sky, they expressed an urgent need for it, and the USAF responded with a crash program to retrofit C-47s as EC-47s. The first 68 of these converted planes took the battlefield in spring 1966. Although successful in its role, the EC-47 posed a serious danger to her crews. She cruised at only 175 miles per hour, typically flew around 10,000 feet (3,050 meters), had no cabin pressurization, and could be hit, especially by 37-millimeter antiaircraft artillery.

STATUS

Retired. The USAF transferred most of the EC-47s produced for the Vietnam War to the South Vietnam government, but, with the fall of the South, many pilots flew them to the Philippines or Thailand, where they survived for a time in the air forces of those countries. ■

—*Michael Gorn*

BOEING F-13/RB-29 SUPERFORTRESS

The B-29 Superfortress was the most effective bomber flown by any nation in World War II and was the world's first nuclear-delivery-capable aircraft. It was in service from 1944 until 1954 as a long-range/very-heavy bomber in combat in World War II and the Korean War. The F-13/RB-29 variants served as long-range reconnaissance aircraft from 1944 to 1956.

By the end of World War II, the USAAF had almost 1,500 B-29s in the western Pacific area. B-29s dropped the only atomic bombs used in combat, on the Japanese cities of Hiroshima and Nagasaki, in August 1945.

DESIGN

The B-29 was developed for the USAAF as a long-range strategic bomber. It was a four-engine, streamlined aircraft with three pressurized compartments for the flight crew. The Norden bombsight and the AN/APQ-7 Eagle bomb-navigation radar were installed.

Standard defensive armament consisted of eight to ten .50-caliber machine guns in four remote-control turrets, the top forward turret often having four guns. The tail turret mounted two additional .50-caliber guns and an optional 20mm cannon. Photo aircraft generally had all guns removed except for the tail guns, though additional gun turrets were reinstalled in the Korean War era in response to the Soviet MiG-15 fighter threat. Subsequently, only the WB-29 weather recon variants were unarmed.

The standard recon configuration provided for six cameras mounted in the pressurized rear compartment. The first installation had a single vertical camera for general work; the second had two split-vertical cameras mounted to cover a strip of ground three miles wide, providing high-resolution stereo imagery for detailed interpretation; the third consisted of three cameras, one mounted vertically and the other two aimed obliquely, covering ground about 30 miles (48 kilometers) wide.

Boeing F-13. *National Archives and Records Administration*

OPERATIONS

On 1 November 1944, an F-13 (photo) variant became the first US aircraft to fly over the Japanese capital of Tokyo since the Doolittle bombing raid of April 1942. Taking off from Saipan, the F-13 flew over the Japanese capital at 32,000 feet (9,754 meters) in clear weather, without opposition. That total mission was almost 14 hours.

A typical photo mission had an F-13 remaining over a Japanese city for an hour, flying a 3,000-mile (4,828-kilometer) round trip from Saipan. At that altitude, the recon aircraft were virtually immune to Japanese fighters and antiaircraft guns.

Heightened tensions in 1945 and 1946 led the AAF's newly created Strategic Air Command (SAC) to plan Arctic routes for air strikes against the Soviet Union. The 46th Reconnaissance Squadron deployed to Alaska

in March 1946 with a mix of B-29s and F-13s to map the vast, little-known Arctic basin. By 1947, the unit—redesignated the 72nd Reconnaissance Squadron—began flying peripheral photographic missions off Siberia's Chukotka Peninsula, the closest Soviet territory to Alaska. The first priority of these missions was seeking out possible Soviet bomber bases. Flying as high as possible in good visibility, the F-13s could photograph coastal facilities.

SAC also deployed the RB-29-equipped 31st Strategic Reconnaissance Squadron to Okinawa in the late 1940s. After the Korean War began in June 1950, the 31st moved to Japan to fly photo missions over North Korea.

Early in the post–World War II era, both ELINT and COMINT versions of the RB-29 were developed. The

BOEING F-13/RB-29

CREW:	Up to 13 (including 5 or 6 recon specialists)
ENGINES:	4x Wright radial R-3350-57 or -57A; 2,200 hp each
WEIGHTS:	Empty: 68,821 lb (31,217 kg) Maximum: 137,000 lb (62,143 kg)
LENGTH:	99 ft (30.2 m)
WINGSPAN:	141 ft 3 in (43.1 m)
HEIGHT:	7 ft 10 in (8.5 m)
SPEEDS:	Maximum: 407 mph at 35,000 ft (10,666 m) Cruise: 24 mph (409 kph)
CEILING:	41,500 ft (12,650 m)
RANGE:	3,500 mi (5,633 km)
ARMAMENT:	Varied (see text); minimum 2x .50-caliber machine guns (1,000 rounds)
RADAR:	AN/APG-15 tail fire control (in some aircraft); AN/APQ-7 Eagle bomb/nav

46th Reconnaissance Squadron jury-rigged a photo aircraft with rudimentary ELINT gear, which first flew missions off the western Siberian coast in late 1946.

The first dedicated ELINT "ferret" aircraft—with a crew of 13, including 6 electronic warfare officers—began flying missions the next summer out of Alaska. On those missions, the aircraft detected a hitherto unknown string of Soviet early-warning radars. Later in 1947, this RB-29 deployed to West Germany, from which base it flew several missions along the East German border as well as one mission in the Berlin corridors over East Germany. Upon their return to the United States, the crew and aircraft formed the nucleus of the first permanent ELINT reconnaissance organization, the 324th Radio Countermeasures Squadron. In 1948, more ELINT-modified RB-29s were deployed, flying missions out of Okinawa and Alaska as well as West Germany, complementing the RB-29 photo effort.

In 1950, the Air Force Security Service (AFSS)—whose mission was collecting and processing COMINT—began testing aerial COMINT collection on an RB-29 flying ELINT missions. The following year, AFSS began full testing using a dedicated RB-29, with a crew that included five COMINT operator positions. Testing continued in the United States, followed in June 1952 by intensive flight tests from Japan.

Operational missions were then flown over the Sea of Japan along the Soviet Far East and Arctic coasts as well as off the North Korean coast. In 1952, the aircraft deployed to Europe, where it spent six months evaluating COMINT collection flying from British, West German, and Libyan bases. The prototype aircraft returned to the Far East, where it flew operational missions until 1956. No other RB-29s were fitted as COMINT collectors; that role in the air force went to specially modified Boeing RB-50s, which became operational in 1956.

The 31st and 91st Strategic Reconnaissance Squadrons' RB-29 photo aircraft flew missions throughout the Korean conflict from bases in Japan. They identified targets and provided damage assessments primarily for the SAC B-29 bombing effort. Some photo RB-29s were modified to include ELINT capability and collected against Soviet and Chinese radars on the Manchurian side of the border with North Korea (the aircraft remaining in Korean airspace). Several aircraft were attacked by MiG-15 fighters; three RB-29s were shot down, while others were damaged.

These losses resulted in the introduction of the turbojet RB-45C Tornado for this role. In addition, the Soviets shot down three RB-29s (photographic and electronic) over international waters, well away from the combat area, between 1950 and 1954. (The more heavily armed B-29 bombers were also attacked by MiG-15s and, on 27 October 1951, B-29 gunners downed six MiG-15s—the highest number of enemy aircraft downed on any day of the war.)

In 1946, the AAF Air Weather Service (AWS) was created to provide information to support US military operations. The command began with 46 RB-29 aircraft with specialized equipment. These aircraft would be designated WB-29 in the early 1950s. A weather officer's position was created, and a newly developed dropsonde ejection chamber was installed with a table and seat for the dropsonde operator in the starboard scanner location. Additionally, a 640-gallon (2,423-liter) fuel tank was placed in each bomb bay, and the atmospheric sampling "bug catcher" was installed where the aft-lower turret had been, along with an access panel so that sampling filters could be retrieved in flight. Other modifications included new radar, a radar altimeter, and improved radios.

The 59th Weather Reconnaissance Squadron flew almost daily missions between Eielson AFB, Alaska, and Yokota AB, Japan, beginning in May 1949, seeking evidence of a Soviet nuclear detonation. The effort was rewarded when one of its RB-29s, flying this route on 3 September 1949, obtained evidence that the Soviet Union had exploded its first atomic weapon on 29 August. AWS RB-29s followed the nuclear cloud as it crossed over Canada, the Atlantic, and into British airspace. An AWS WB-29 detected the first Soviet hydrogen bomb test on 12 August 1953.

The WB-29s were phased out in the mid-1950s, replaced by WB-50s.

In the early 1950s, the United States supplied 87 B-29s to the British—named "Washington"—as interim strategic bombers pending delivery of British-built aircraft. Three of these were SIGINT reconnaissance variants, entering service with the RAF No. 192 Squadron and flying missions from 1953 to 1957 along the Soviet periphery from the Barents Sea in the north to the Caspian Sea in the south. These aircraft were unarmed and usually carried four ELINT and two COMINT collection specialists. Occasionally the Washingtons were tasked to collect intelligence on high-interest Soviet naval ships at sea. In 1956, a Washington flying missions in the Mediterranean collected ELINT on the Egyptian air defense system prior to the Anglo-French-Israeli seizure of the Suez Canal. In late 1957, these aircraft were withdrawn from service, replaced in this role by the reconnaissance variant of the de Havilland Comet.

In 1944 and 1945, three US B-29s made emergency landings in Soviet Siberia after strikes on Manchuria and Japan. These planes were carefully copied to produce the Tupolev Tu-4, given the NATO codename "Bull." Approximately 1,200 Tu-4s were built with production ending in 1952. A few of these aircraft were transferred to China. Several Soviet Bulls were converted into photorecon variants with the designation Tu-4R. Some of these were additionally fitted with ELINT collection gear, and a few with a rudimentary ECM capability.

One Soviet Tu-4 reportedly was modified to a "radiation reconnaissance" aircraft and flew missions out of southern Chinese bases in the 1950s, collecting against American nuclear tests in the Pacific.

STATUS

Retired. The prototype XB-29 flew on 21 September 1942, with the first delivery to an AAF unit in July 1943. The Boeing, Bell, and Martin companies produced 3,628 aircraft, with all but 230 delivered by August 1945. The last aircraft was delivered in June 1946 (another 200 B-29 and 5,000 B-29C aircraft were cancelled at the end of the war). The much-improved B-29D model was produced as the B-50 Superfortress.

The F-13 reconnaissance variant was in service from 1944 to 1956 (redesignated RB-29 in 1948). The first purpose-built F-13 was delivered in October 1944. A total of 118 specialized F-13/RB-29 variants were produced. Additional B-29s were field modified in the western Pacific for reconnaissance missions. ■

—*Norman Polmar and John F. Bessette*

CONSOLIDATED PB4Y-2/P4Y-2 PRIVATEER

A highly successful maritime patrol aircraft, the Privateer carried out electronic surveillance missions for the US Navy along Soviet-controlled coasts after World War II. The aircraft was derived from the famed four-engine B-24 Liberator heavy bomber, which was produced in larger numbers than any other US combat aircraft. It flew in every World War II theater with the USAAF and RAF, as well as with the US Navy and Marine Corps as the PB4Y-1.

In 1951, the navy changed the designation of patrol bombers to patrol aircraft, with the PB4Y-2 becoming the P4Y-2. Still another designation change came in 1962, but the only type of Privateer flying at that time was the P4Y-2K radio-controlled drone, which became the QP-4B.

DESIGN

The Privateer was a high-wing aircraft with distinctive gun turret "blisters" on the aft fuselage. It was distinguished by a tall tailfin that replaced the familiar twin-tail configuration of the B-24. The PB4Y-2 also had a seven-foot fuselage

Consolidated PB4Y-2. *US Air Force photo*

extension forward of the wing to carry additional electronic gear and operators. Other major changes included the fitting of Pratt & Whitney R-1830-94 engines (without turbo-superchargers) for low-altitude operations. The PB4Y-2 was normally flown by a crew of 11.

The aircraft normally was armed with 12 machine guns in twin mounts (blisters) and twin turrets (nose, two dorsal, and tail). The internal weapons bay could hold 8,000 pounds (3,629 kilograms) of bombs. From April 1944, some Privateers carried the ASM-N-2 Bat radar-guided glide bomb, used mainly against Japanese merchant and coastal shipping. The Bat, mounted on wings, was retired in 1953.

OPERATIONS

The aircraft completed before the end of the war were employed exclusively in the western Pacific. In the final stages of the Pacific War, patrol squadron VP-24 used Privateers as carriers for Bat guided bombs.

After the war, the Privateer was flown by active and reserve patrol bomber squadrons—the PB4Y-2B as a

Bat missile carrier, the PB4Y-2S as an anti-submarine aircraft, and the PB4Y-2M for meteorological missions.

As the Cold War heated up, several Privateers were configured for ELINT, ferreting out Soviet electronic signals by flying along the periphery of the Soviet Empire. Soviet fighters attacked one of these unarmed PB4Y-2s, which had taken off from Wiesbaden, West Germany, on an ELINT flight over the Baltic Sea on 8 April 1950. It was the first US spyplane known to be shot down by the Soviets. None among the crew of ten survived, although there were unsubstantiated reports of some men being captured by the Soviets.

Few Privateers were in service when the Korean War erupted in June 1950; many in mothballs were recalled, and both active and reserve squadrons flew offshore patrols with the plane during that conflict. Some aircraft were used over land to drop flares in support of marine night operations; those Privateers generally carried 250 high-intensity parachute flares.

The Nationalist Chinese on Taiwan received several Privateers for bombing missions and covert operations over China. Seeing signs that the Chinese were building a sophisticated air defense system, one PB4Y-2 was modified for electronic intelligence collection, with 14 ELINT missions flown in 1955 and 1956, confirming increased early-warning radar coverage. Privateers continued on other covert operations through 1961, when one was lost in the Burma-Thai-Chinese border area after being attacked by Burmese fighters.

STATUS

Retired. In May 1943, the Consolidated Aircraft Company was directed to convert three B-24D bombers—on order for the navy as PB4Y-1 aircraft—to the XPB4Y-2 configuration. The first of these prototypes flew on 20 September 1943, and, in the following month, the navy ordered production of the new aircraft. Privateer deliveries to the fleet began in March 1944 and continued through October 1945, with 740 Privateers procured by the navy, a few of which went to the Marine Corps.

The Privateer served in navy squadrons until June 1954, with a few individual aircraft remaining in service for several more years.

Beginning in 1945, the US Coast Guard flew nine PB4Y-2G aircraft in search-and-rescue and weather-reconnaissance roles. The coast guard used the PB4Y-2G until 1960.

CONSOLIDATED PB4Y-2/P4Y-2

CREW:	11
ENGINES:	4x Pratt & Whitney R-1830-94 Twin Wasp radial; 1,350 hp each
WEIGHTS:	Empty: 39,400 lb (17,872 kg) Maximum: 64,000 lb (29,030 kg)
LENGTH:	110 ft (33.5 m)
WINGSPAN:	95 ft 9.5 in (29.2 m)
HEIGHT:	29 ft 2 in (8.9 m)
SPEED:	Maximum: 237 mph (381 kph) at sea level: 247 mph (398 kph) at 12,800 ft (3,901 m) Cruise: 160 mph (257 kph)
CEILING:	18,300 ft (5,578 m)
RANGE:	1,886 mi (3,035 km)
ARMAMENT:	12x .50-caliber M2 machine guns (4x twin turrets and 4x twin waist mounts); some unarmed after World War II
RADAR:	APS-15B search

A transport version also was produced, of which 33 went to the US Navy and Marine Corps as the RY-3; another 26 were supplied to the RAF as the Liberator IX. One of the latter was used by the Royal Canadian Air Force for ice research flights until 1948.

Privateers were also flown by British and Commonwealth air forces, and, beginning in 1951, several Privateers were transferred to the French Navy. Based at Tan Son Nhut (near Saigon) in Indochina, these planes flew bombing missions in support of the French troops at Dien Bien Phu and elsewhere. These were the largest aircraft flown by the French in Indochina. Some of the 24 Privateers flown by France were used as bombers in Tunisia, and a few flew missions against the Egyptians during the Anglo-French Suez campaign of 1956. The last five Privateers were retired from Aéronavale (the French Air Force) in 1961, replaced by Lockheed P2V-6 Neptunes.

The Honduran Air Force flew three Privateers as transports into the 1970s. ■

—*Norman Polmar and John F. Bessette*

Lockheed RF-80. *National Archives and Records Administration*

LOCKHEED RF-80 SHOOTING STAR

After experiencing disappointment with the performance of the first American jet aircraft—the underpowered Bell P-59 Airacomet, which never saw combat—the US Army Air Forces made an urgent request to Lockheed in June 1943 to develop another prototype turbine engine fighter. Kelly Johnson and his Skunk Works team had a candidate, designated the XP-80, ready for flight testing just 178 days later in January 1944. This miraculous feat was due in part to Johnson and his engineers using an off-the-shelf British Halford H1.B engine, soon succeeded by a General Electric I-40 turbojet.

Lockheed geared up the P-80 production line in 1944 and made its first deliveries the following year. At first, the Shooting Star suffered a high accident rate as pilots adjusted to the powerful turbine engine. The solution: a two-seat version known as the T-33—a ubiquitous trainer that would successfully transition newcomers to jets until the air force withdrew it from service in 1987.

DESIGN

The Shooting Star distinguished itself by its clean, low-drag silhouette. Skunk Works engineers designed it with a semi-monocoque fuselage, cantilever, low-mounted, non-swept wings, and a tail plane with a single fin. Its GE powerplant, located in the center section of the fuselage, received air from two inlets on either side of the fuselage, forward of the wing leading edge. The P-80's armament consisted of six half-inch forward-firing machine guns with 297 rounds each, mounted in the lower portion of the nose. The aircraft could be modified to carry two 1,000-pound (454-kilogram) or four 260-pound (118-kilogram) bombs. Its cockpit accommodated one pilot.

Some P-80s carried no weapons at all. During World War II, the value of tactical fighter recon became well recognized and, by the Korean War, the P-80 seemed a good candidate for the role. An aircraft designated the XFP-80A served as a testbed for the concept. Mechanics mounted a set of cameras by removing the nose guns, elongating the nose, and hinging it upwards. The air force ordered 51 P-80s with this special configuration and asked Lockheed to modify an additional 66 production aircraft, installing in each a K-17 camera with a 6-inch lens and two K-22 split vertical cameras with 24-inch lenses. These RF-80A aircraft (upgraded later to RF-80C) served in the 8th Tactical Reconnaissance Squadron from June 1950 until after the armistice, flying from Itazuke, Japan, and from Taegu and Kimpo, Korea.

OPERATIONS

The F-80C flew in four USAF wings and groups during the Korean War: the 8th Fighter-Bomber Wing, the 51st Fighter-Interceptor Wing, the 49th Fighter-Bomber Group, and the 35th Fighter-Interceptor Group.

The F-80 experienced mixed results during the Korean War. While an F-80 recorded a victory in the world's first jet-on-jet aerial combat, its main antagonist, the swept-wing MiG-15, proved faster and more maneuverable. Moreover, because it had to fly to Korea from distant Japanese air bases, the Shooting Star lacked enough fuel to linger over the battlefield. It also needed long, smooth runways, which were uncommon in the rough combat conditions of Korea. As a consequence, F-80s were relegated to ground-attack assignments, leaving air-to-air combat to the newer and more nimble F-86.

If the F-80 had its ups and downs, the work of the reconnaissance RF-80A and C proved to be of unquestioned value. They provided invaluable intelligence for UN forces through overflights of North Korea, and their pilots took photographs above the border between China and North Korea, along the Yalu River.

LOCKHEED F-80

CREW:	1
ENGINE:	1x Allison J33-A-35-turbojet; 5,400 lbst (2,449 kgst)
WEIGHTS:	Empty: 8,420 lb (3,819 kg)
	Maximum: 16,856 lb (7,646 kg)
LENGTH:	34 ft 5 in (10.5 m)
WINGSPAN:	38 ft 9 in (11.8 m)
HEIGHT:	11 ft 3 in (3.4 m)
SPEEDS:	Maximum: 594 mph (966 kph) at sea level
	Cruise: 410 mph (660 kph)
CEILING:	46,800 ft (14,265 m)
RANGE:	825 mi (1,328 km)
ARMAMENT:	6x 0.5 in (12.7mm) machine guns; 2x 1,000-lb (454-kg) bombs; 8x rockets
RADAR:	All-weather

In fact, as they flew over the Yalu, RF-80 pilots aimed their cameras obliquely into China to photograph airfields filled with MiG-15s. Recon missions to the Kuril and Sakhalin Islands and the closed Russian city of Vladivostok also took place during this period.

STATUS

Retired. The last Shooting Star—a T-33 variant—was retired from service in April 1997. ■

—*Michael Gorn*

BOEING C-97 STRATOFREIGHTER

An outgrowth of the B-29 Stratofortress bomber, the C-97 series was intended for military use as well as a civilian passenger/cargo aircraft. The civil version—the Boeing Model 377 Stratocruiser series—took advantage of the aircraft's pressurized cabin and long range to attract airline customers for the postwar passenger market.

One C-97A and 12 KC-97G aircraft became US Air Force covert aerial reconnaissance platforms, and two others performed that role for the Israeli Air Force.

These recon variants included specialized photoreconnaissance and ELINT aircraft.

DESIGN

In the initial C-97 version, the aircraft's wings, tail, undercarriage, and engines were the same as the B-29's, with the fuselage expanded in cross section to allow for a large passenger/cargo capacity.

The military C-97 configuration was designed to accommodate 134 troops plus three 1.5-ton trucks or two light tanks. Clamshell rear doors, built-in ramps, and a ceiling hoist were provided to facilitate loading vehicles and bulk cargo. The C-97, flown by the USAF in the cargo role, was the basis for the large-scale production of the KC-97 aerial tanker.

When C-97G aircraft were assigned to the Air National Guard (ANG) in 1964, 82 were modified to the C-97L configuration with J47-GE-25A jet pods; 28 were converted to HC-97G air-sea rescue aircraft. As KC-97 tankers were retired from that role, some were converted to "straight" C-97 cargo aircraft.

BOEING KC-97G

CREW:	Up to 13 (including up to 8 recon specialists)
ENGINES:	4x Wright radial R-4360-59B; 3,000 hp each
WEIGHTS:	Empty: 82,500 lb (37,500 kg)
	Combat: 120,000 lb (54,431 kg)
	Maximum: 175,000 lb (79,545 kg)
LENGTH:	110 ft 5 in (33.7 m)
WINGSPAN:	141 ft 3 in (43.0 m)
HEIGHT:	38 ft 3 in (11.7 m)
SPEED:	Maximum: 375 mph (604 kph) at 25,000 ft (7,622 m)
	Cruise: 300 mph (483 kph)
CEILING:	30,200 ft (9,207 m)
RANGE:	4,300 mi (7,167 km)
ARMAMENT:	None
RADAR:	AN/APS-23 navigation (recon variants)

OPERATIONS

The KC-97 served the SAC as its principal aerial refueling aircraft from 1952 to 1965, reaching peak strength of 780 tankers in 1958. (The KC-97 was succeeded by the all-jet KC-135 Stratotanker.)

RECON VARIANTS

In 1952, US Air Force Europe (USAFE) had a major need for a photorecon aircraft capable of operating above 30,000 feet (9,144 m) and covertly configured for possible use in the Berlin corridors. The solution was to establish a special projects office—Big Safari—to undertake such high-priority projects.

The project oversaw the modification of a C-97A Stratofreighter with the world's largest aerial camera, a 240-inch focal-length monstrosity mounted in the forward part of the cargo compartment. The aircraft was delivered to USAFE's 7499th Support Squadron in 1953 and became fully operational in 1955 after solving many camera problems.

The aircraft, codename Pie Face, flew numerous missions on routes from West Germany into Berlin, and along the borders of northern Norway, Greece, Turkey, and Iran. It proved less able to use its oblique capability to great effect in the Berlin corridors because of the 10,000-foot (3,048-meter) altitude limitation. The photography from Pie Face was highly prized because of the high resolution of the film, resulting in unprecedented details. The Pie Face aircraft was retired in late 1962 after the Cuban Missile Crisis, where it performed several high-altitude sorties around the island in October and November.

Twelve KC-97G aircraft were modified under Big Safari to fill various recon and support roles. These aircraft were shared by the 7405th Support Squadron in USAFE and the 6091st Support Squadron in the Pacific Air Force, both commands having similar missions, albeit in different theaters. Five of these C-97s were equipped for photography with the cameras hidden under the cargo deck, thus permitting the aircraft to fly "routine cargo" missions to locations like West Berlin and Bangkok without raising undue suspicions. Two of the five aircraft had two ELINT collection positions, also hidden.

Two other C-97Gs were outfitted with very noticeable ELINT antennae, including a long canoe-shaped

A 7405th Support Squadron C-97G 52-2688 takes off from Tempelhof Airfield, West Berlin, for a photo collection mission in the Berlin corridors. Camera ports are all secured. *Ralf Manteufel via John F. Bessette*

tub under the fuselage housing several collection systems. These aircraft were overt collectors, and thus confined to long-endurance missions along hostile borders.

Another C-97G was covertly configured for ELINT, one of several aircraft that the CIA modified in the 1960s to collect so-called "fine-grain ELINT" on hostile air defenses, initially the Soviet SA-2 Guideline system. This aircraft flew numerous missions in the Berlin corridors from 1963 through 1975, directly overflying Soviet missile and radar sites. This operation became important in helping to develop countermeasures against SA-2 missile systems in North Vietnam during that conflict.

In 1962, Israel improved its airlift capability by acquiring five ex–Pan American Airways Model 377 Stratocruisers, which they modified to carry cargo and/or passengers. Later, nine ex-USAF KC-97Gs supplemented these aircraft for the same role. After the June 1967 Six Day War resulted in the Israeli occupation of the Sinai Peninsula, the Soviets provided major military assistance to Egypt, including a modern air defense system along the Suez Canal that included the SA-2 missile system.

Israel's response was to refit one of the ex-USAF KC-97s with a long-range, oblique camera system.

While this aircraft was flying a mission along the canal on 17 September 1971, it was struck by two SA-2s and brought down. Seven of the eight crewmen in the aircraft were killed, while one parachuted to safety.

Israel acquired one more C-97, equipped for airborne ELINT collection. This was a former 7405th Support Squadron C-97G, a veteran of many ELINT missions in Europe during the 1960s. It was modified by Big Safari in 1970 and delivered to Israel in early 1971. The aircraft flew many collection missions before it was retired when Israel acquired a Boeing 707 turbojet airliner modified for this role.

STATUS

Retired. The first of three XC-97 prototypes flew on 15 November 1944. These were followed by six YC-97s, three YC-97As, and one YC-97B aircraft, some flying operational missions beginning in late 1947 for the newly established USAF Air Transport Command.

Of the 875 C-97s that followed, 811 were KC-97E/F/G tanker variants, initially serving SAC's bomber force. The last was delivered in July 1956.

Many of the KC-97Gs later were converted for other roles, such as passenger, cargo, air rescue, VIP transport, and as flying testbeds. ■

—*Norman Polmar and John F. Bessette*

LOCKHEED P2V/P-2 NEPTUNE

The Neptune was the only US aircraft designed from the outset for the land-based maritime patrol role, and the first US Navy aircraft that could carry a nuclear weapon. All previous US land-based maritime patrol aircraft were adapted from bomber or transport designs. Beyond being produced in greater numbers than any other land-based maritime aircraft in history, the Neptune gained fame as an intelligence collection aircraft, especially in peripheral fights in the Far East.

The aircraft was flown by ten other nations as well as by the US Army and CIA. The aircraft was also produced in Japan. The aircraft's designation was changed from the P2V series to the P-2 on 1 October 1962.

DESIGN

The Neptune was a conventional, straight-wing aircraft with a tall tailfin and was powered by twin radial engines. Most Neptune variants were fitted with 400-gallon (1,514-liter) wingtip tanks. Early variants had a solid nose, subsequently replaced in different variants with a glazed bombardier nose, a solid structure with six fixed 20mm cannon, or with two 20mm cannon in a powered nose turret. Other armament modifications included a twin 20mm dorsal turret and a tail turret with twin .50-caliber machine guns or 20mm cannon (with six 20mm guns in twin turrets being the maximum armament).

The final Neptune production aircraft, the P2V-7/P-2H, was built with a dorsal turret fitted with two .50-caliber machine guns.

The Neptune had an internal weapons bay that could accommodate anti-submarine torpedoes, depth charges, and mines. In later aircraft, rockets and torpedoes could be carried on eight wing pylons. Maximum weapons payload—internal and external—was 12,000 pounds (5,443 kilograms).

The Neptune received a steady progression of improvements. The ultimate variant to enter service was the P2V-7, which was additionally fitted with two turbojet engines mounted in wing pods for "burst speed" when closing with submarine contacts as well as for increased takeoff power. In addition to the standard anti-submarine sensors of surface search radar and droppable sonobuoys, the P2V-7 introduced the AN/ASQ-8 magnetic anomaly detection (MAD) antenna fitted in a large tailcone "stinger" (replacing the tail-gun turret). Subsequently, MAD as well as the jet pods were refitted to earlier P2V-5 and P2V-6 aircraft.

The P2V-6M (later MP-2F) fitted to carry the Petrel air-to-surface missile. The P2V-3W and later aircraft had the large AN/APS-20 search radar intended primarily for detecting submarine snorkel breathing tubes. The P2V-3Z was an armored VIP transport. Small numbers of P2V-7LP (LP-2J) aircraft were fitted with skis and other specialized gear for Arctic/Antarctic photorecon and mapping.

VARIANTS

The Neptune's outstanding design led to the modification of 1 P2V-2 and 11 P2V-3 aircraft to the P2V-3C

Lockheed P2V. *National Archives and Records Administration*

configuration for carrier takeoff carrying a nuclear weapon. This provided a limited, interim nuclear strike capability. The Neptunes were to be flown to overseas bases and lifted by crane aboard *Midway*-class carriers, loaded with Mark 8 atomic bombs, and launched against targets in the Soviet Union. In preparation for such operations, on 28 April 1948, two P2V-2 Neptunes, with JATO rocket assistance, took off from the carrier *Coral Sea* (CVB 43) off the Virginia coast after scores of practice takeoffs from airfields ashore. More carrier launches followed, establishing the feasibility of such ad hoc operations. (Although Neptune landings aboard *Midway* CVBs were proposed, and practiced ashore, no such trials were undertaken.)

Several Neptunes that had been extensively modified for special attack operations in the Vietnam War were designated the OP-2E, with the US Army flying the AP-2H variant.

RECON VARIANTS

Several Neptunes were fitted with additional electronic intercept equipment to fly spy missions along the coasts of Soviet Siberia, North Korea, and China. Some of these flights were made under the aegis of the CIA by seven P2V-7U aircraft—designated RB-69A (see separate entry)—and flown by Taiwanese crews.

OPERATIONS

On 29 September 1946, with Cmdr. Thomas D. Davies at the controls, the first production P2V—named *Truculent Turtle*—took off from Perth, Australia, to fly

LOCKHEED P2V-7/P-2H

CREW:	10 to 14
ENGINES:	2x Wright R3350-32WA 3,400 hp each; and 2x Westinghouse J34-WE-36 turbojets, 3,400 lbst (1,542 kgst) each
WEIGHTS:	Empty: 49,256 lb (22,343 kg) Maximum takeoff: 80,000 lb (36,288 kg)
LENGTH:	91 ft 8 in (28.0 m) over MAD boom
WINGSPAN:	101 ft 4 in (30.9 m)
HEIGHT:	29 ft 4 in (8.9 m)
SPEEDS:	Maximum: 402 mph (647 kph) at 19,200 ft (5,854 m) Cruise: 200 mph (322 kph)
CEILING:	29,700 ft (9,055 m)
RANGE:	2,970 mi (4,780 km)
ARMAMENT:	2x .50-caliber machine guns (dorsal turret) in some aircraft (400 rounds per barrel); 8,000 lb (3,628 kg) bombs, mines, torpedoes
RADAR:	AN/APS-20E

antiaircraft fire. Others were damaged by Chinese and Soviet fighters, with Neptune gunners fighting off several attackers. In addition, three P2V-7U/RB-69A aircraft were lost over China.

STATUS

Retired. The first of the two XP2V-1 prototypes flew on 17 May 1945. The P2V-1 entered the fleet in March 1947.

Lockheed produced a total of 1,099 P2Vs from 1945 through 1962. Kawasaki in Japan produced an additional 89 through 1979 (designated P-2J). This effort marks one of the longest aircraft production runs in history:

2	XP2V-1
15	P2V-1
81	2V-2
83	P2V-3
52	P2V-4 (later P-2D)
424	P2V-5 (later P-2E)
83	P2V-6 (later P-2F)
359	P2V-7 (later P-2H)

The Neptune remained in active US Navy patrol squadrons until 1970; the last flight by an active anti-submarine Neptune, in February 1970, was piloted by then–Rear Adm. Tom Davies. The aircraft continued in service with the Naval Air Reserve until 1979, with specialized EP-2H electronic and DP-2H Firebee drone variants flown until 1980.

Lockheed proposed a lighter variant of the Neptune, designated P2V-8, but it was not pursued because of the introduction of the firm's P-3 Orion.

Ten other nations flew Neptunes. The 25 P2V-7 aircraft flown by Canada could carry US B57 nuclear depth bombs, as could the 12 P2V-5 aircraft flown by the Netherlands. The latter aircraft were replaced by 15 improved P2V-7/SP-2H aircraft in 1962. The 52 P2V-5 Neptunes provided to the RAF for maritime patrol did not have a nuclear capability.

Japan was the last nation to operate Neptunes, which were flown by the Maritime Self-Defense Force until 1994. ∎

—Norman Polmar and John F. Bessette

11,235.6 nautical miles (20,808.3 kilometers), landing in Columbus, Ohio, after a flight of 55 hours, 17 minutes. The aircraft was overloaded with an estimated 8,592 gallons (32,524 liters) of fuel plus a crew of three and a kangaroo. At takeoff, aided by four JATO rockets, the aircraft at 85,575 pounds (38,816 kilograms) was the heaviest twin-engine aircraft to take off up to that time. Still, the flight established an unrefueled distance record that stood until 16 years later, when it was bested by an air force B-52H Stratofortress. (Neptunes were not configured for in-flight refueling.)

Far Eastern spy flights by Neptunes became the target of Soviet and Chinese fighter aircraft. Soviet fighters shot down three Neptunes over international waters, while another Neptune fell to Chinese ground

Republic RF-84F. *US Air Force photo*

REPUBLIC RF-84 THUNDERSTREAK THUNDERFLASH

Unlike many military recon aircraft fielded before and after it, the RF-84F Thunderflash came into being not as a modified fighter retrofitted for overflight assignments, but as a purpose-built intelligence-gathering prototype. It performed its reconnaissance duties effectively, but it also suffered from the same performance woes as the other F-84s.

Republic Aircraft planned the F-84 Thunderjet as the successor to its renowned World War II fighter, the P-47 Thunderbolt, designing it to supplant the P-47 as a frontline day fighter. The Army Air Forces awarded a contract to Republic Aircraft in 1945 for three straight-winged YF-84 prototypes, followed by a production contract for 221 F-84Bs. By 1953, Republic had fabricated an immense run of 4,450 aircraft across four variants. Despite that number, the early F-84s suffered from chronic deficiencies such as excessive weight, inadequate engine thrust, and weak wing spars. In 1948, the air force considered cancelling the F-84B and C, and the Thunderjets started the operational phase with just the F-84D. Still, they played a variety of important roles in the Korean War, escorting B-29 bombers, providing

close air support and daytime interdiction strikes, and serving as fighter-bombers (including the air force's first tactical nuclear bomber).

DESIGN

Republic decided that to compete with the highly successful F-86 Sabre, the F-84 needed to be retooled with swept wings. So the manufacturer modified an F-84E with a sweep of 40 degrees both for the wings and tail; it was flight tested in 1950. Even though the prototype performed only marginally better than the standard F-84E, Republic geared up for production and designated the new aircraft: the F-84F Thunderstreak. Like the earlier F-84s, however, the F-84F experienced serious issues with stability and control that caused stall pitch-up and unsatisfactory maneuvering at combat speeds.

Republic's engineers struggled to correct these deficiencies until 1954, when they reached a partial solution for the stability and control dilemma with a one-piece stabilator that replaced the conventional tail. By that time, the sweptwing F-84F diverged

REPUBLIC RF-84F

CREW:	1
ENGINES:	1x Wright J65-W-3 turbojet; 7,220 lbst (3,270 kgst)
WEIGHTS:	Empty: 13,830 lb (6,273 kg) Maximum: 28,000 lb (12,701 kg)
LENGTH:	43 ft 5 in (13.2 m)
WINGSPAN:	33 ft 7 in (10.2 m)
HEIGHT:	14 ft 5 in (4.4 m)
SPEEDS:	Maximum: 695 mph (1,118 kph) at sea level Cruise: 535 mph (861 kph)
CEILING:	46,000 ft (14,020 m)
RANGE:	1,900 mi (3,058 km) Combat radius 810 mi (1,304 km) with drop tanks
ARMAMENT:	6x 0.5 in (12.7mm) Browning M3 machine guns
RADAR:	APG-30 or MK-18 ranging

almost completely from the original F-84E, in part the result of a new powerplant. Designers replaced the Thunderstreak's initial engine—an Allison J35 with 5,200 pounds (2,360 kilograms) of thrust—with a much bigger Wright J65 rated at 7,200 pounds (3,266 kilograms), causing major modifications. Despite all of these changes, the Thunderstreak and the straight-winged Thunderjet shared basic flight characteristics: good handling at cruise speed (within the performance envelope); poor takeoff, requiring 7,500 feet (2,286 meters) of rollout on a hot day; and unpredictable stall pitch-up, with the potential for wing failure.

In its design and performance, the reconnaissance RF-84F behaved just like its stablemate, the Thunderstreak. Yet the RF-84F—designated the Thunderflash—did not simply constitute a modified Thunderstreak, but rather an all-new, factory-inspired prototype: the YRF-84F. As such, it represented a genuine reconnaissance trailblazer. The prototype appeared in 1952 but, because it suffered, like the Thunderstreak, from engine flameouts in snow and heavy rain, it did not enter the operational force until 1954.

Otherwise the same structurally, the Thunderflash and the Thunderstreak differed in one respect. Unlike the F-84F, with an air intake at its nose, the RF-84F had wing-root intakes so that its nose section could be elongated and filled with photographic equipment. The F-84F carried 15 cameras: six conventional forward facing; eight in oblique and vertical positions for targeted photos; and one advanced horizon-to-horizon TriMetrogen camera. It also featured a computer control system that adjusted camera settings, taking into account lighting conditions, aircraft speed, and altitude. Republic engineers also included a wire sound recorder so that the pilot could narrate ground movements associated with the photographs.

OPERATIONS

Ultimately, Tactical Air Command and the Strategic Air Command's 71st Reconnaissance Wing maintained a total of 388 Thunderflashes in their inventories. In 1957–1958, though, both Majcoms transferred their entire fleets to the air national guard (ANG). With the Berlin Crisis in 1961, the RF-84Fs came out of retirement and served with the ANG's 117th Tactical Reconnaissance Wing. Then, during the Vietnam War, a depleted Tactical Air Command called up six of seven RF-84F squadrons to high combat readiness status. At first the USAF wanted to keep the Thunderflash until 1976, but, as newer equipment like the RF-4Cs came along, the ANG disposed of its older aircraft.

Under the Military Assistance Program, 327 Thunderflashes joined the air forces of Taiwan, Germany, France, Greece, Turkey, Italy, Belgium, Denmark, and Norway.

STATUS

Retired. In January 1972, the ANG's 155th Tactical Reconnaissance Group sent the last RF-84F to a storage depot. ■

—Michael Gorn

Republic XF-12. *National Archives and Records Administration*

REPUBLIC XF-12 RAINBOW

During World War II, the army worked to develop a purpose-built reconnaissance airplane that could fly high and fast enough to avoid conventional enemy anti-aircraft and fighters. Two distinctly different aircraft were brought to the prototype stage to meet the army's requirements. Hughes Aircraft Company offered the twin-engine XF-11, while Republic Aviation chose a bigger, and ultimately faster, four-engine platform.

The Republic XF-12 program was initiated in mid-1943 as Allied commanders began to plan bombing attacks on the home islands of Japan. The new photorecon airplane was required to cruise at over 400 miles per hour (644 kilometers per hour), operate at 40,000 feet (12,192 meters), and fly over 4,000 miles (6,437 kilometers). Both the XF-11 and XF-12 would take advantage of the development of the new large and powerful Pratt & Whitney R-4360 engine, generating over 3,200 horsepower, to attain these lofty requirements.

The Army Air Forces assigned Republic's photo aircraft the XF-12. The *X* stood for "experimental" and reconnaissance projects received an F mission designator (for "photo," or "foto"). As the USAAF became

Republic XF-11. *US Air Force photo*

the US Air Force, and the pursuit designation gave way to F for "fighter," the plane was re-coded XR-12, the *R* standing for "reconnaissance."

The plane's company and official military nickname was Rainbow. *Aviation Magazine* dubbed the aircraft the "Flying Photo Laboratory" in their December 1945 issue.

DESIGN

The primary concern of Republic engineers was uncompromising aerodynamic design for their new aircraft. The plane's bullet-shaped fuselage, tightly cowled engine nacelles, and thin, straight-tapered wings helped keep performance projections high. Even the plane's exhausts

were deliberately routed directly aft, allowing escaping gases to add a small amount of thrust.

The plane's sleek, clean design made it look like a swift-swimming shark or a graceful bird of prey. Along with the Lockheed Constellation, many judge the XF-12 to be one of the best-looking aircraft of the era.

The XF-12's pilots sat in a long, pointed Plexiglas nose. Behind, the plane's slender 10 foot, 3 inch (3.1 meter) fuselage could hold a plethora of photographic equipment. Electrically heated cameras, both standard and stereographic, could be mounted in arrays in three bays equipped with aerodynamically clean retractable doors. For night missions, the bays could accommodate flash photo bombs to illuminate a photo target.

Perhaps most unusual, the big XF-12 carried a fully equipped photo lab, allowing crewmen to develop film while still in flight and have the data ready for analysis immediately upon return to base.

The plane's four large R-4360 engines were nearly completely covered by sizable propeller spinners and tapered nacelles. Impeller fans pulled cooling air into the cowlings and then released it directly aft, along with the engine exhaust.

The XF-12 was designed to operate unarmed. Theoretically, the plane's speed and high ceiling would allow it to complete missions without any threat of interference from hostile forces.

OPERATIONS

Two prototype aircraft were initiated at Republic's Farmingdale, New York, facility as the war progressed. At the cessation of hostilities, the future of most military aircraft projects was in doubt, but the army informed Republic that they would like to continue with the XF-12.

The first example took to the skies on its maiden flight on 4 February 1946. Both Republic and the army were pleased with the plane's performance. The sleek XF-12 was one of the fastest large-sized piston-engine aircraft ever built. With speeds of over 400 miles per hour, ceiling beyond 40,000 feet, and a range of 4,000 miles or more, Republic ads touted that the new plane could fly "On All Fours."

The post–World War II era brought another consideration into play: examples of the plane could be sold to civilian airlines as passenger-carrying aircraft. With upcoming military production keeping the price per plane low, Republic offered a 46-passenger aircraft based on a stretched version of the army aircraft. The airliner could make the flight from New York to London two hours faster than the competition. American Airlines and Pan American Airways signed contracts to buy civil versions, designated RC-2.

In 1947, as the new US Air Force, the military changed the designation of their airplanes too. The XF-12 became the XR-12.

In 1948, the second XR-12 completed Operation Bird's Eye. The aircraft and its crew began shooting film off the coast of Los Angeles and photographed a continuous picture (over 390 end-to-end photographs

REPUBLIC XF-12/XR-12

CREW:	7
ENGINES:	4x Pratt & Whitney R-4360-31; 3,250 hp each
WEIGHTS:	Empty: 68,000 lb (30,844 kg) Maximum: 101,400 lb (45,994 kg)
LENGTH:	93 ft 10 in (28.6 m)
WINGSPAN:	129 ft 2 in (39.4 m)
HEIGHT:	28 ft 4 in (8.6 m)
SPEED:	470 mph (756 kph)
CEILING:	45,000 ft (13,716 m)
RANGE:	4,500 mi (7,242 km)
ARMAMENT:	None
RADAR:	None

joined in a continuous strip) across the entire country to Long Island, New York.

The military eventually cancelled the program when it found that other, existing platforms (as well as new jet aircraft) could tackle their long-range reconnaissance mission needs. When the air force backed out, the cost of civilian versions of the aircraft skyrocketed, causing airlines to abandon the design as well. In the end, Republic built only two aircraft.

STATUS

Retired. The first of the two prototype aircraft, serial number 44-91002, was severely damaged during a landing test on 10 July 1947. The plane went back to Republic for extensive repairs and then was put back into service. The XR-12 was officially retired from air force testing and was turned over to the Aberdeen Proving Ground to be used as a gunnery target in 1952.

The second Rainbow aircraft, serial 44-91003, was lost after an in-flight engine explosion in 1948. Five of the seven air force crewmen were able to bail out. The plane crashed in the Choctawhatchee Bay near Eglin AFB, Florida. ∎

—*Cory Graff*

Hughes XF-11A-HU. *Nicholas A. Veronico collection*

HUGHES XF-11	
CREW:	2 (1 pilot, 1 navigator/camera operator)
ENGINES:	2x Pratt & Whitney R-4360-31 radials; 3,000 hp each
WEIGHTS:	Empty: 37,100 lb (16,828 kg) Maximum: 58,300 lb (26,444 kg)
LENGTH:	65 ft 5 in (19.9 m)
WINGSPAN:	101 ft 4 in (30.9 m)
HEIGHT:	23 ft 2 in (7.1 m)
SPEED:	450 mph (724 kph)
CEILING:	44,000 ft (13,411 m)
RANGE:	5,000 mi (8,047 km)
ARMAMENT:	None
RADAR:	None

HUGHES F-11

At the height of World War II, Hughes Aircraft sold a design for a long-range photo-reconnaissance aircraft to the US Army Air Forces. Because of the pressing need for intelligence, the AAF was using modified fighters and heavy bombers for aerial recon. Cameras replaced armament, and these aircraft flew as high as possible; the recon pilot's motto was: "Unarmed and unafraid." As enemy air defenses and fighter aircraft improved, and reconnaissance aircraft flew farther and farther into hostile territory, a dedicated camera platform was needed. The major fighter aircraft manufacturers—Curtiss, Lockheed, North American, and Republic—were swamped with wartime production and could offer only modified versions of existing designs to meet the AAF's aerial reconnaissance needs.

Pressure from Gen. Henry H. "Hap" Arnold helped secure the recon aircraft deal for Hughes. As the contract was let, the AAF Materiel Command objected, believing Hughes did not have the manufacturing capacity to deliver the order as contracted.

By May 1945, less than two years after the contract had been issued, Hughes had not delivered a single F-11. On May 29, shortly after the Allies proclaimed victory in Europe and with the Japanese Empire crumbling, the AAF terminated the contract. Hughes was given the opportunity to complete and deliver both prototypes; however, the maiden flight of the first prototype was still more than a year in the future.

Recognizing that Materiel Command's predictions about Hughes Aircraft's inability to deliver were coming true, the AAF awarded Northrop Aircraft a contract for a highly modified, photo-recon version of its P-61 Black Widow, known as the F-15 Reporter. The prototype Reporter first flew on July 3, 1945, two months before the end of World War II.

DESIGN

Designated XF-11 ("X" for eXperimental, "F" for photographic, design 11), the AAF ordered one hundred of the type in late 1943. The first was powered by a pair of 28-cylinder Pratt & Whitney R-4360-31 radial engines turning contra-rotating propellers. The second aircraft was designed XF-11A. These two aircraft were to be followed by 98 additional F-11s with deliveries slated to begin in 1944. The massive aircraft was nearly as large as a B-17 Flying Fortress, with a crew of just two and a payload of cameras. The XF-11 and XF-11A never saw operational service.

STATUS

Retired. The two prototypes were XF-11-HU serial number 44-70155 and XF-11A-HU serial number 44-70156. Ninety-eight additional aircraft were canceled at the end of World War II. The XF-11 was crashed by Howard Hughes on 7 July 1946, and the XF-11A (redesignated XR-11 after September 1947, when the air force became a separate service) ended its days when flown to the 3750th Technical Training Wing, Sheppard AFB, Texas, on 29 July 1949, where it served as a ground instruction airframe. ∎

—*Nicholas A. Veronico*

CONVAIR RB-36 PEACEMAKER

The B-36 was the largest combat aircraft flown by any nation. The maximum bomb load of the B-36J was 43 tons (39 metric tons), with a gross aircraft weight reaching 410,000 pounds (185,973 kilograms). While US Air Force documents credited the aircraft with a maximum altitude of over 40,000 feet (12,192 meters), there are reports that the aircraft could climb considerably higher, with 60,000 feet (18,288 meters) cited by some sources.

The B-36 was developed to bomb European targets from bases in the United States, as the US War Department in 1941 believed that the United States would likely be drawn into the war and that all of Europe—including Britain—could eventually fall under Axis control. In the spring of 1943, when it appeared that the Chinese government might collapse under Japanese attack, the B-36 was considered for long-range operations in the Pacific in the event of problems with the B-29 Superfortress and B-32 Dominator heavy-bomber programs. When the B-29 program achieved success, the B-36 continued, but with a lesser priority.

The size and cost of the B-36 made it the most publicized bomber of the immediate postwar era. During World War II, Army Air Force planners proposed a force of up to 3,740 B-36s (the name "Peacemaker" was rarely used; the aircraft was generally known as simply the B-36). The air force leadership in 1949 planned a B-36 force of four bomber groups—120 aircraft plus 39 spares—and two groups of the RB-36 long-range reconnaissance variant. Although the B-36 was relatively slow, it could fly an Arctic route and reach the Soviet Union from bases in the United States without in-flight refueling.

The B-36 was the centerpiece for the 1948–1949 debate between the navy and air force on the relative effectiveness of land-based and carrier-based bombers. There was also controversy over the aircraft within the air force: Gen. George C. Kenney, the first commander of SAC, declared, "The B36 is a night bomber. I would not use it in daytime," and noted that the plane might be suitable for the navy's anti-submarine mission. On 12 December 1946, he recommended the procurement of the B-36 only for test purposes, instead preferring the B-50 as a strategic bomber until jet-propelled bombers became available.

General Kenney's successor as head of SAC, the outspoken and innovative Gen. Curtis LeMay, supported the B-36, claiming, "We can get a B-36 over a target and not have the enemy know it is there until the bombs hit."

As Soviet air defenses improved in the 1950s, an effort was made to increase the altitude of the RB-36 through the "Featherweight" (FW) program, in which most of the aircraft guns and some other gear were removed to reduce weight. The lightened aircraft could reach an altitude of just over 45,000 feet (13,716 m), some 5,000 to 8,000 feet (1,524 to 2,438 m) more than a standard B-36.

The B-36 force peaked in October 1955 with ten heavy bombardment wings: six with B-36s and four with RB-36s. Each wing had a nominal assignment of ten planes in each of three squadrons for a total of 209 B-36 and 133 RB-36 aircraft. When the last B-36J was retired on 12 February 1959, SAC became an all-jet bomber force.

No B-36 ever dropped a bomb in anger.

DESIGN

With its long, cylindrical fuselage and wings swept at 15.5 degrees, the B-36 was propelled by six large piston-pusher engines. The B-36D and later models also had four turbojet engines in underwing pods to provide a burst of speed over the target or while under attack by fighters.

Two prototype, all-jet variants with swept wings designated YB-60 were produced in an unsuccessful attempt to compete with the B-52 Stratofortress.

The maximum bomb load was 72,000 pounds (32,659 kilograms), although the B-36D could carry two 42,000-pound (19,051-kilogram) Grand Slam bombs in the internal weapon bays. The B-36B was the first model configured to carry nuclear bombs. Eighteen B-36B aircraft were fitted to carry the VB-13 Tarzon guided bomb (two per aircraft); those aircraft had the AN/APG-24 bomb/nav radar. Later, one of these aircraft was fitted to carry the GAM-63 Rascal guided missile. One B-36H was fitted as an aerial tanker and one B-36H, redesignated NB-36H, served as an aerial testbed for a nuclear reactor in support of the nuclear aircraft program, making 47 test flights (the reactor did not propel the aircraft).

The aircraft had the heaviest defensive armament ever carried by an aircraft, with eight twin 20mm power turrets. Four dorsal and two ventral turrets were retractable to reduce drag, with additional two-gun turrets mounted in the nose and tail, all directed by a central control system (there was no gunner position in the tail). The Featherweight program reduced the

Convair RB-36. *National Archives and Records Administration*

Convair XB-36. *US Air Force photo*

number of guns until the modified B-36H (III) had only the tail turret with two guns. The B-36A aircraft were unarmed and initially were used primarily for training.

RECON VARIANTS

The RB-36 aircraft were fitted with up to 14 cameras (weighing 3,300 pounds, or 1,497 kilograms) in the forward bomb bay; 80 flash bombs could be carried in the second bomb bay; 3,000-gallon (11,356-liter) fuel tanks were provided in the third bomb bay; and electronic countermeasures (ECM) equipment was installed in the fourth bomb bay. The largest of the cameras had a 47-inch focal length.

The RB-36D endurance was 30 hours.

Most RB-36 recon variants retained a bombing capability. In June 1954, the RB-36s were given a primary bombing mission but retained a limited, secondary recon role.

OPERATIONS

On 12–13 March 1949, a B-36 demonstrated the aircraft's endurance, flying 43 hours, 37 minutes without refueling. The flight began and ended at Fort Worth, Texas, and covered 9,600 miles (15,450 kilometers). The aircraft had a crew of 12.

The primary mission of the RB-36 aircraft was to fly prestrike recon over Eastern Europe and the Soviet Union to confirm known targets and find new ones. They would then recover at forward bases to process film and await further orders.

Additional flights for bomb damage assessment would possibly follow.

All B-36s were based in the United States, although they periodically deployed to overseas bases on a temporary basis. The first flight by B-36 bombers beyond the continental United States occurred on 16 January 1951, when six B-36D bombers flew into the RAF base at Lakenheath, England. There are unconfirmed reports that three of the planes were fitted with a hidden camera battery. From Lakenheath, each of the three camera planes allegedly flew a recon mission over the Soviet base complex at Murmansk on the Kola Peninsula. The planes returned safely to Lakenheath, although two MiG fighters are said to have tried to intercept them. The six B-36D aircraft flew back to their continental US base on 20 January.

In August and September 1953, the first mass flight of B-36s to the Far East occurred as Operation Big Stick. Taking place shortly after the armistice in the Korean War, 23 of the bombers operated from bases in Japan, Okinawa, and Guam. There also are unconfirmed reports that there were two overflights of the Soviet base complex at Vladivostok by camera-equipped B-36D aircraft, flying from Kadena, Japan.

STATUS

Retired. The XB-36 first flew on 8 August 1946. SAC received the first (unarmed) B-36A on 26 June 1948; the first operational B-36B aircraft in November 1948; and the B-36D in August 1950. These aircraft were not

	CONVAIR RB-36D	CONVAIR RB-36H (FW 111)
CREW:	22	19*
ENGINES:	6x Pratt & Whitney R-4360-41; 3,250 hp each 4x General Electric J47-GE-19 turbojets; 5,200 lbst (2,359 kgst) each	6x Pratt & Whitney R-4360-53; 3,800 hp each 4x General Electric J47-GE-19 turbojets; 5,200 lbst (2,359 kgst) each
WEIGHTS:	Empty: 164,029 lb (74,404 kg) Maximum: 370,000 lb (167,832 kg)	Empty: 162,619 lb (73,764 kg) Maximum: 370,000 lb (167,832 kg)
LENGTH:	162 ft 2 in (49.4 m)	162 ft 2 in (49.4 m)
WINGSPAN:	230 ft (70.1 m)	230 ft (70.1 m)
HEIGHT:	46 ft 9 in (14.3 m)	46 ft 9 in (14.3 m)
SPEEDS:	Maximum: 400 mph (644 kph) at 36,500 ft (11,128 m) Cruise: 218.5 mph (352 kph) at 35,000 ft (10,670 m)	Maximum: 416 mph (669 kph) at 38,000 ft (11,585 m) Cruise: 239 mph (385 kph)
CEILING:	43,400 ft (13,232 m)	43,900 ft (13,384 m)
RANGE:	3,490 mi (5,615 m) at 2,410 lb (1,093 kg) payload	3,617 mi (5,820 m) at 3,664 lb (1,662 kg) payload
ARMAMENT:	16x 20mm M24A1 cannon (600 rounds per barrel)	2x 20mm M24A1 cannon (600 rounds per barrel)
RADAR:	AN/APQ-24 navigation; AN/APG-32 gun control	AN/APQ-24 navigation; AN/APG-41A gun control

* Aircraft commander, pilot, copilot, 2 flight engineers, 2 navigators, radar observer, weather observer, 2 radar operators, photographic technician, 4 ECM operators, 3 gunners.

considered fully operational until 1951 and were not free of significant mechanical problems until 1954.

The first recon aircraft, an RB-36D, made its first flight on 18 December 1949, and the first Featherweight III flew in June 1954. The first flight of an RB-36E occurred in July 1950, while the first flight of an RB-36F was in May 1951, and the first flight RB-36H was in January 1950.

The first RB-36s entered service in 1950. The last RB-36 was retired in 1958.

A total of 385 B-36 bombers were produced through 1954, with 136 built or converted to the recon role:

  1 XB-36
  1 YB-36 (modified to RB-36E)
 22 B-36A (21 modified to RB-36E)
 73 B-36B
  — B-36C (cancelled)
 22 B-36D
 17 RB-36D (7 modified to GRB-36D)
  — B-36E (cancelled)
 34 B-36F
 24 RB-36F (1 modified to GRB-36F)
  2 YB-36G (redesignated YB-60)
 83 B-36H (1 modified to NB-36H)
 73 RB-36H
 33 B-36J

The YB-36G/YB-60 was an all-jet, swept-wing aircraft. A single XC-99 cargo variant of the B-36 was built and had a 400-man troop capacity. ■

—*Norman Polmar and John F. Bessette*

MARTIN P4M-1Q MERCATOR

The Mercator was a navy land-based maritime reconnaissance/anti-submarine aircraft employed almost exclusively in the ELINT role. The aircraft, developed by the Glenn L. Martin Company, was one of several attempts in the late 1940s to combine reciprocating and jet engines in a single aircraft for maximum range and high speed.

While the P4M lost out to the P2V/P-2 Neptune for the maritime patrol mission, it was successively employed in the ELINT role from 1951 to 1960.

DESIGN

The Mercator had two piston engines and two jet engines housed in combination nacelles on each wing. The aircraft had a streamlined shape with a cantilevered, shoulder-level wing. The planes often encountered problems with their large reciprocating engines.

The XP4M-1 armament consisted of nose and dorsal turrets with twin .50-caliber machine guns, two flexible .50-caliber guns in the waist, and a tail turret with two 20mm guns. In production aircraft, the nose turret had twin 20mm guns and the waist guns were eliminated. The elongated internal weapons bay could accommodate 12,000 pounds (5,443 kilograms) of bombs, two large aerial torpedoes, or 12 Mark 26-1 mines.

At full load the aircraft were "sluggish" to maneuver.

In the ELINT role, no bombs or torpedoes were normally carried on ELINT missions.

Martin P4M-1. *National Archives and Records Administration*

MARTIN P4M-1Q

CREW:	14 (captain/pilot, pilot, copilot, navigator, electronics officer, 6 intercept operators, 3 gunners)
ENGINES:	2x Pratt & Whitney R-4360-20 radial, 3,250 hp each; 2x Allison J33-A-10 turbojet, 4,600 lbst (2,087 kgst) each
WEIGHTS:	Empty: 52,723 lb (23,915 kg) Combat: 76,600 lb (34,746 kg) Maximum: 92,500 lb (41,958 kg)
LENGTH:	86 ft 3 in (26.3 m)
WINGSPAN:	113 ft 10 in (34.7 m)
HEIGHT:	29 ft 2 in (8.9 m)
SPEEDS:	Maximum: 256.5 mph (412.8 kph) at 8,000 ft (2,439 m); 362 mph (582.6 kph) at sea level; 382 mph (614.75 kph) at 20,000 ft (6,098 m) Cruise: 191 mph (307.4 kph)
CEILING:	31,000 ft (9,451 m)
RANGE:	2,830 mi (4,554 km)
ARMAMENT:	2x 20mm cannon (nose turret; 800 rounds); 2x 20mm cannon (tail turret; 800 rounds); 2x .50-caliber machine guns (dorsal; 800 rounds); 12,000 lb (5,443 kg) bombs, torpedoes, or mines
RADAR:	AN/APA-5A bomb; AN/APS-33A search

OPERATIONS

The first four P4M-1s to reach the fleet were assigned to patrol squadron VP-21 in June 1950 and began modification to the P4M-1Q configuration in February 1953, with P2V-6 Neptunes replacing them in VP-21.

Four P4M-1Q aircraft became operational in October 1951, flying ELINT missions against China from Sangley Point in the Philippines. This detachment became part of airborne early-warning squadron VW-1 in 1953, and of VW-3 in 1954, although their mission was in no way related to those organizations. Subsequently, these aircraft became electronic countermeasures squadron VQ-1, established at Iwakuni, Japan, on 1 June 1955. Again, the aircraft were not engaged in the ECM role.

Similarly, a P4M-1Q detachment was established in 1950 at Port Lyautey (now Kenitra), Morocco, as a component of squadron VW-2. These aircraft became squadron VQ-2 on 1 September 1955, and were subsequently relocated to Rota, Spain.

During the Mercator's peripheral missions in the Pacific, Soviet, Chinese, and North Korean fighters buzzed the aircraft as they flew off those countries' coasts, just outside the 12-mile (19.3-kilometer) territorial limit, monitoring radar and communications transmissions. Chinese fighters shot down a Mercator on 22 August 1956, with all 16 American crewmen lost. Another Mercator was damaged by North Korean fighters with one crewman wounded.

Typical ELINT missions were 8 or 9 hours, with some taking up to 14 hours.

STATUS

Retired. The XP4M-1 first flew on 20 September 1946. Two prototypes were built, followed by four P4M-1s and 15 P4M-1Q production aircraft. The production aircraft were delivered in 1950. The P4M-1s subsequently were converted to the ELINT configuration.

The aircraft were withdrawn from service with VQ-1 and VQ-2 in 1960. They were replaced by A3D-1Q/2Q Skywarriors and VW-2Q Warning Stars and redesignated EA-3 and EC-121 in 1962. ■

—*Norman Polmar and John F. Bessette*

NORTH AMERICAN RF-86 SABRE

The designers of the F-86 Sabre and the team that made the F-84 Thunderjet regarded their first-generation jet aircraft as carryovers of two of the most famous American fighters of World War II: the P-51 Mustang and the P-47 Thunderbolt, respectively.

With this comparison in mind, engineers at North American Aviation responded in 1944 to a US Army Air Force's requirement for a day fighter that doubled as a dive bomber or escort. At first, they proposed a straight-wing prototype but, as Allied expeditions to a defeated Germany brought home plans for swept-wing aircraft, North American revised the design to include swept-wing and tail surfaces. The first production version flew in 1948 as the F-86A Sabre. Three air force fighter groups—the 1st, 4th, and 81st—took delivery of a total of 554 F-86As starting in February 1949.

DESIGN

Adaptable and reliable, the F-86A lent itself to many variants. The F-86D served as an all-weather interceptor whose air intakes, positioned under rather than through the nose, allowed for the placement of radar scanners. The F-86E featured power controls and the F-86F, a bigger engine. The TF-86A trainer, the F-86H fighter-bomber, and the F-86K for NATO delivery also rolled out of the North American plant.

The F-86 Sabre family featured an oval fuselage cross-section and cantilever, low-mounted wings with a 35-degree sweepback. The cantilever tail unit also had 35-degree sweepback and integrated elevator and tail plane movements controlled from the cockpit control column. A sliding bubble canopy enclosed the single-seat cockpit.

For all of its many uses, the Sabre became associated with reconnaissance missions only under wartime conditions, and almost accidentally. During the early phase of the Korean War, the 67th Tactical Reconnaissance Wing at Kimpo, Korea, flew a number of older aircraft for recon missions, mainly because frontline fighters like the F-86 could not be spared from combat. But the unit's commander persuaded headquarters to release two high-mileage F-86As for modification under Project Ashtray. In these aircraft, technicians mounted horizontally a high-speed K-25 camera in the right gun bay; this camera shot into an angular mirror through a camera port on the right ammunition bay. Designated RF-86As, their successful reconnaissance forays persuaded Far East Air Force (FEAF) officials to release ten more aging F-86As for conversion to RF-86As. By removing the gun sight radar in their noses and two lower guns, more extensive photographic equipment could be added: a 36-inch focal length forward oblique camera and, on the lower fuselage, a K-9 6-inch focal length vertical camera. Near the end of the war, three of the newer F-86Fs underwent modifications in Project Haymaker, by which a horizontal K-14 camera shot images through a series of mirrors aligned with a port on the belly of the fuselage.

NORTH AMERICAN F-86F

CREW:	1
ENGINE:	1x General Electric J47-GE-27 turbojet; 5,910 lbst (2708 kgst)
WEIGHTS:	Empty: 10,815 lb (4,906 kg)
	Maximum: 17,772 lb (8,061 kg)
LENGTH:	37 ft (11.3 m)
WINGSPAN:	39 ft 1 in (11.9 m)
HEIGHT:	14 ft (4.3 m)
SPEEDS:	Maximum: 688 mph (1,107 kph) at sea level
	Cruise: 513 mph (826 kph)
CEILING:	48,000 ft (14,630 m)
RANGE:	1,317 mi (2,120 kph)
ARMAMENT:	6x .50 cal M-3 machine guns; 2,000 lb (907 kg) bombs; reconnaissance variants usually unarmed
RADAR:	AN/APG-30

Two other K-14s pointed downward from the underside of the fuselage.

Finally, recognizing the value of these makeshift reconnaissance platforms, North American fabricated eight purpose-built F-86 reconnaissance aircraft, designated the RF-86F. Unarmed to make space for bigger photo equipment, the RF-86F had room for enlarged film magazines and three ports (one for each camera)

RF-86F over Korea. *US Air Force photo*

beneath the fuselage: two for the vertically mounted K-22s and one for a K-17.

OPERATIONS

During the Korean War, the Ashtray and Haymaker aircraft flew together on recon missions, arriving at the 15th Tactical Reconnaissance Squadron at Kimpo in 1953. Commanders concealed the true mission of the RF-86s by joining them with the 4th Fighter Tactical Group (FTG), where they flew amid combat F-86s and bore the same markings, even to the extent of adding painted-on gun ports. During operations, the RF-86As and RF-86Fs took off as lead aircraft with four flights of FTG F-86s; as they approached their objectives—often in the vicinity of the Yalu River—the recon planes broke from the pack and flew at high speed over targets while the other aircraft loitered nearby.

Both Ashtray and Haymaker RF-86s enjoyed much success during the war. Meanwhile, North American's far more capable RF-86F production models began arriving in Korea in June 1953, too late to serve in the conflict, but used later by the US Air Force in acknowledged and clandestine reconnaissance missions over Soviet and Chinese airspace.

STATUS

Retired. Japan, South Korea, and Taiwan continued to fly them until the 1980s. The last American RF-86s served as target drones at the China Lake Naval Air Station. ∎

—Michael Gorn

BOEING RB-50 SUPERFORTRESS

The Boeing B-50 bomber/RB-50 reconnaissance variant represented the Cold War embodiment of the bomber-reconnaissance relationship. It originated with a US Army Air Forces decision in 1944 to update the B-29A Superfortress and redesignate it as the B-29D. In the end, the improvements turned out to be substantial: they added engines 60 percent more powerful than before; a lighter yet stronger wing; a taller fin and rudder; and landing gear able to withstand 20 percent more weight than the B-29A.

As World War II ended, the magnitude of these changes persuaded the USAAF to end the B-29 line and to rename the B-29D the B-50A.

DESIGN

After taking delivery of 79 B-50As (many converted to other roles), the air force ordered the B-50B, which differed only in being about 2,000 pounds (907 kilograms) heavier and destined for use as an atomic bomb carrier. But as air force officials grasped the even greater need for Cold War intelligence-gathering, SAC asked Boeing to reconfigure all 45 of its new B-50Bs for this purpose and, in January 1949, the planes began arriving at the Wichita factory for modification.

The remodeled B-50Bs ultimately rolled out of the Boeing plant in 1950 and 1951 as RB-50Es, Fs, and Gs. To enable reconnaissance and meteorological observations for the RB-50Es, Boeing technicians added four camera stations and nine cameras, weather-recording instruments, photo flash bombs for night photography, and two optional 700 gallon (2,650 liter) wingtip fuel tanks. They also converted the left-side gunner's space for weather reporting and built 31 pressurized compartments for the other nine crew members. The RB-50F differed only marginally from the E, but it featured the Shoran32 radar system to facilitate mapping, charting, and geodetic surveys. In this configuration, the aircraft had no defensive equipment, but the Shoran came in removable kits that, when taken out, enabled machine guns to be installed. Finally, the RB-50G contrasted sharply with the architecture of the E and F in that it specialized in electronic countermeasures, for which purpose Boeing added six stations and modified the antennae and radomes to accommodate the corresponding radar. And, unlike the RB-50F, the G's big crew of 16 did not need to switch out radar to activate the defensive equipment—they could operate the electronics and radar and the 12.7 millimeter firepower all at the same time.

OPERATIONS

The RB-50s served Cold War reconnaissance for a relatively short period, with mixed results. They suffered from the same deficiencies that plagued many of the B models: leaks from fuel cells, fuel tank overflows,

Boeing RB-50F. *US Air Force photo*

engine turbocharger failures, and, like the B-50A, trailing wing cracks (seen also in the B-29s).

Despite these defects, the RB-50s served a valuable purpose. Flown by SAC's 55th and 91st Strategic Reconnaissance Wings, they patrolled and penetrated the immense northern boundaries of the Soviet Union, where poor radar coverage prevailed. Even if detected, the RB-50s flew at higher altitudes than World War II–era Soviet aircraft could reach. With the eventual deployment of the MiG-15 fighter over the vast Russian airspace, the RB-50s faced much higher risks; at least four went down during six encounters between 1953 and 1955. With the increasing threat, the RB-50s left SAC service in 1955, replaced by B-47 Stratojets that flew higher and at near supersonic speeds.

STATUS

Retired. The last operational B-50 (a WB-50) left service in 1965. An Air Force System Command B-50 test aircraft flew its last flight in March 1968. ■

—*Michael Gorn*

BOEING B-50A

CREW:	8 to 10
ENGINES:	4x Pratt & Whitney R-4360-35 Wasp Major turbocharged radial piston; 3,500 hp each
WEIGHTS:	Empty: 81,050 lb (36,764 kg)
	Combat: 121,850 lb (55,270 kg) (D model)
	Maximum: 168,408 lb (76,389 kg)
LENGTH:	99 ft (30.2 m)
WINGSPAN:	141 ft 3 in (43.0 m)
HEIGHT:	32 ft 8 in (10.0 m
SPEEDS:	Maximum: 385 mph (620 kph)
	Cruise: 235 mph (378 kph)
CEILING:	37,000 ft (11,280 m)
RANGE:	4,650 mi (7,483 km)
ARMAMENT:	12x 12.7mm M2 Browning machine guns; 1x 20mm cannon; 20,000 lb (9,072 kg) bombs internal; 8,000 lb (3,600 kg) external
RADAR:	Shoran32 radar system (RB-50F model)

NORTHROP RB-49A

In early 1941, war was raging in Europe and the Japanese were expanding their hold on China. In spring of that year, the US Army Air Corps released a specification for a long-range bomber capable of delivering a 10,000-pound (4,536-kilogram) bomb load on 10,000-mile (16,000-kilometer) mission while cruising at 275 miles per hour (443 kilometers per hour). This design was America's first, true intercontinental bomber, capable of attacking targets in Europe from bases in the United States, if necessary. At the time of its conception, England's collapse under the Nazi onslaught was a real possibility.

Unfortunately, the resulting B-35 and B-49 flying wing programs suffered "teething problems" as well as political pressures that doomed the programs from the start. The B-35s were plagued with engine and propeller vibration issues. The B-49's lack of range due to new, fuel-thirsty jet engines—along with the political desire for Northrop to merge with Convair—spelled trouble for the radical new design. The plan to develop a recon version of the flying-wing bomber was a last-ditch attempt to save the program.

DESIGN

The request for proposals for a new long-range bomber was submitted to Boeing and Consolidated Vultee in April 1941. The following month, Northrop was invited to participate in the proposal process. Northrop responded with a flying-wing design designated the XB-35; Consolidated's proposal was designated XB-36.

To prove the flying-wing concept, the US Army Air Forces (changed from Corps on 20 June 1941) ordered a one-third-scale development aircraft, designated the N-9M. In all, four N-9Ms were built, each having twin engines and a 60-foot (18.3-meter) wingspan. From the lessons learned in testing the N-9M, the XB-35 was designed as an 88,000-pound (39,916-kilogram), all-metal bomber powered by two supercharged 28-cylinder Pratt & Whitney R-4360-17 and two supercharged R-4360-21 radial engines buried within the wing; these drove contrarotating propellers via extension shafts.

The US Army Air Forces ordered 200 B-35s in June 1943; Northrop built two prototype XB-35s and thirteen preproduction YB-35s, and Martin Aircraft was slated to construct the balance of the order.

The XB-35 and YB-49/YRB-49A were not given an official US Army Air Forces or Air Force name.

OPERATIONS

YB-35, serial number 42-102376, was converted from a piston-powered aircraft into the jet-powered YRB-49A long-range recon bomber and fitted with six Allison J35-A-19 engines—four internal, fuselage-mounted (two

YRB-49A 42-102376 near Northrop's Ontario Airport, California. This aircraft, the last of the World War II–era flying wings, was scrapped in November 1953. *Nicholas A. Veronico collection*

Northrop YB-49. *US Air Force photo*

on each side of the fuselage compartment) and two suspended outboard of the main landing gear in underwing pods. A contract for 30 YRB-49As was issued, with Northrop building the prototype and Convair's Fort Worth, Texas, factory slated to construct the balance. Photo-recon equipment was to be installed in the aft fuselage pod where the bomber version's defensive armament had been located.

The sole YRB-49A flew its maiden flight on 4 May 1950. It subsequently made 13 test flights and was then flown to the company's facility at the Ontario Airport in Southern California in spring 1952, where stability modifications were to be incorporated. The aircraft had accumulated only 17 hours, 40 minutes of flight time. While it was on the ground, the air force cancelled the project and moved the money to the B-36 program. YRB-49A 42-102376 never flew again and was scrapped in November 1953.

STATUS

Cancelled. Two XB-35 prototypes were constructed along with 11 preproduction YB-35s. The YB-35s were to be converted from piston power to jet power and two completed the installation. When the YB-49 program was cancelled on 15 March 1950, the remainder of the flying wing fleet was ordered scrapped. ■

—*Nicholas A. Veronico*

BOEING RB-49A

CREW:	6 (pilot, copilot, flight engineer, navigator, radar navigator, camera operator)
ENGINES:	6x Allison J35-A-19 static-thrust engines; 5,000 lbst (2,268 kgst) each
WEIGHTS:	Empty: 88,442 lb (40,117 kg) Combat: 133,559 lb (60,581 kg) Maximum: 193,938 lb (87,969 kg)
LENGTH:	53 ft 1 in (16.2 m)
WINGSPAN:	172 ft (52.4 m)
HEIGHT:	20 ft 1 in (6.1 m)
SPEED:	520 mph (837 kph)
CEILING:	42,000 ft (12,802 m)
RANGE:	Estimated 4,000 miles (6,437 km)
ARMAMENT:	None; photo-recon equipment in lower rear of fuselage
RADAR:	AN/APQ-24 (K-1 navigation and bombing system)

GRUMMAN F9F-2P/F9F-5P PANTHER

The Panther was Grumman's first jet-propelled aircraft, as well as the US Navy's first jet-propelled aircraft to enter combat—and it may have been the world's first jet-propelled aircraft to shoot down another jet. A carrier-based fighter, the Panther saw extensive service in the Korean War.

Small numbers of Panthers were converted to the F9F-2P and manufactured as F9F-5P photorecon aircraft. The Panther evolved into the swept-wing F9F Cougar series (see separate entry on page 181). The few Panthers in service after 1 October 1962 were redesignated in the F-9 series.

DESIGN

The aircraft was initially designed as a two-seat night fighter, designated F9F-1, with four wing-mounted turbojet engines; its design was competitive with the Douglas F3D Skyknight. (Four engines were required because of the low power available with contemporary turbojet engines.) The availability of the British Rolls-Royce Nene engine permitted a complete redesign to a single-engine fighter, the F9F-2 Panther.

The Panther was a low-wing, streamlined aircraft with large intakes for the single engine buried in the wing roots. The wings folded for carrier stowage. The standard fighter configuration had four 20mm cannon, and eight wing pylons could hold up to 3,000 pounds of bombs or six 5-inch rockets.

Wingtip fuel tanks (120 gallons, or 454 liters, each) normally were fitted and could not be jettisoned in flight.

RECON VARIANTS

At the start of the Korean War, the navy's need for photorecon aircraft led to the substitution of oblique and vertical cameras in place of the 20mm nose guns and magazines (760 rounds) in a "small number" of existing F9F-2 aircraft, which were redesignated the F9F-2P. (Available records do not provide the exact number of aircraft.)

Grumman built 36 of the F9F-5P configuration photorecon aircraft. The substitution of vertical and oblique cameras for guns increased the length of the aircraft by just over 1 foot (30.5 centimeters) compared to the standard F9F-5. Other changes were minimal.

Grumman F9F-2P/F9F-5P. *US Navy photo*

GRUMMAN F9F-5P

CREW:	1
ENGINE:	1x Pratt & Whitney J48-P-6 turbojet; 7,000 lbst (3,175 kgst)
WEIGHTS:	Empty: 10,147 lb (4,603 kg) Maximum: 21,245 lb (9,637 kg)
LENGTH:	40 ft (12.2 m)
WINGSPAN:	38 ft (11.6 m)
HEIGHT:	12 ft 3 in (3.7 m)
SPEEDS:	Maximum: 604 mph (972 kph) at sea level Cruise: 481 mph (774 kph)
CEILING:	42,800 ft (13,049 m)
RANGE:	1,300 mi (2,092 km)
ARMAMENT:	None
RADAR:	AN/APG-30

OPERATIONS

Both the F9F-2P and F9F-5P photo aircraft served aboard carriers during the Korean War. The first F9F-2P deployment was with composite squadron VC-61 on board the carrier *Princeton* (CV-37) in December 1950. The F9F-5P went aboard carriers two years later.

STATUS

Retired. The first flight of the XF9F-2 was on 24 November 1947. The first model to enter service was the F9F-3 with fighter squadron VF-51 in May 1949; the first Panthers to enter Marine Corps service were F9F-2s with fighter squadron VMF-115 in August 1949.

Grumman completed a total of 1,385 Panthers, the last being F9F-5/5P aircraft delivered in January 1953. They served in operational US Navy and Marine Corps fighter squadrons until 1956, and then for another decade in support roles.

Argentina's naval air arm acquired 24 refurbished F9F-2s in 1958. They were retired in 1969. ∎

—*Norman Polmar and John Bessette*

BOEING RB-47/EB-47 STRATOJET

The B-47 Stratojet was Boeing's first jet bomber and the first multiengine, swept-wing strategic bomber built in any significant quantity in the world. While not particularly long lived in its bombing role, the B-47 was used to fulfill multiple mission requirements over the years, serving as a testbed, in weather research, and as both photographic and electronic reconnaissance platforms.

Built to be the backbone of the then-new US Air Force and SAC, the B-47 struggled in its early career. It was a large, complex aircraft with a small, three-man crew, and the transition for piston-engine pilots was initially very challenging, leading to a large number of accidents attributed to pilot error. In spite of a somewhat rough start, the B-47 was the mainstay of SAC, and lessons learned from its design led directly to the successes not only of Boeing's follow-on B-52, but of their civilian fleet, starting with the 707, as well.

DESIGN

The Stratojet's roots date to the latter years of World War II, when the USAAF requested a jet-powered medium bomber. Boeing already had a design study based on a smaller version of their successful B-29, but the new cart was designed to be powered by four General Electric TG-180 turbojets. When tested in the wind tunnel, this design, the Model 424, exhibited a great deal of drag. Boeing engineer George S. Schairer had recently inspected a secret R&D facility in Germany just after the end of the war in Europe and took note of a number of German designs on the drawing board. Several had swept wings, and the wind tunnel data gathered by the Germans showed tremendous efficiency.

Schairer was sold on the concept of swept wings, and began work on a number of iterations, leading up to the Model 450. The 450, which also incorporated a fighter-style canopy and Schairer's concept of mounting the turbojet engines in pods under the wings, had one other hurdle in front of it: the landing gear. The thin, swept wings that gave the airplane improved performance offered no space for mounting traditional tricycle landing gear, so Boeing went with an inline bicycle configuration. With the landing gear installed in tandem, it was difficult for pilots to rotate on takeoff,

Boeing RB-47E. *US Air Force photo*

so a simple solution was implemented: redesigning the gear so the airplane was already in a nose-up attitude when sitting level. The USAAF ordered the Model 450 in 1946, and the first prototype, redesignated XB-47, rolled out in 1947.

The first operational variant was the B-47B. Several variants were produced over the years, including the EB-47E used for electronic countermeasures as well as SIGINT and telemetry intelligence, and the RB-47E, with its lengthened nose, built for long-range reconnaissance. All variants were officially known as the Stratojet, though that name never saw widespread adoption. Major General Earl G. Peck, former SAC Chief of Staff, once said that the B-47 "never seemed to acquire any sort of affectionate nickname," and added that it was "often admired, respected, cursed, or even feared, (but) it was almost never loved . . . it tended to separate the men from the boys."

OPERATIONS

While the B-47 technically never saw combat, the RB-47 family came the closest. Boeing began delivering the first of 240 of the long-range reconnaissance platforms to the 55th and 90th Strategic Reconnaissance Wings in 1953. The RB-47 was equipped with multiple optical and radar cameras used to perform surveillance missions deep in the heart of the Soviet Union at the height of the Cold War. Such missions took them over targets like Igarka, 450 miles (724 kilometers) inland in Siberia, and the submarine pens at Murmansk. On one such flight in May 1954, an RB-47E flown by Capt. Hal Austin exchanged fire with multiple Soviet MiG-17s and returned to its base at RAF Fairford in the UK with cannon damage to the left wing. In 1956, an RB-47 was shot down over the Kamchatka Peninsula, and a second was lost in 1960 over the Barents Sea.

Boeing ERB-47H. *US Air Force photo*

The later H variants were built with a pressurized compartment in place of a bomb bay. This was home to two or three electronic warfare officers (EWOs). The space was extremely cramped and poorly insulated, making the life of an EWO (also known as a "Crow") pretty uncomfortable. Other RB-47 variants included the ERB-47H, which focused on ELINT, and the EB-47E, which carried large telemetry pods to capture data from Soviet missile tests.

The RB-47H was retired in 1967 and replaced by Boeing's RC-135. The final EB-47E missions were flown not by the air force but by the US Navy as electronic warfare testbeds until 1977.

STATUS

Retired. About two dozen B-47s of assorted variants are on display in museums. While no flying examples exist, the example at the Castle Air Museum in California was ferried there from the Naval Air Weapons Station in China Lake in June 1986, marking the true final flight for the type. ■

—Hal Bryan

BOEING B-47

CREW:	6 (pilot, copilot, navigator, 3 EWOs)
ENGINES:	6x General Electric J47-GE-25 turbojets; 5,670 lbst (2,572 kgst) each, plus optional jet-assisted takeoff (JATO)
WEIGHTS:	Empty: 89,230 lb (40,474 kg)
	Maximum: 218,728 lb (99,213 kg)
LENGTH:	108 ft 8 in (33.0 m)
WINGSPAN:	116 ft 4 in (35.5 m)
HEIGHT:	28 ft (8.5 m)
SPEEDS:	Maximum: 602 mph (969 kph)
	Cruise: 557 mph (896 kph)
	Loiter: 460 mph (740 kph)
CEILING:	38,850 ft (11,842 m)
RANGE:	3,935 mi (6,333 km) unrefueled
ARMAMENT:	2x M24A1 20mm cannon in a tail turret, remotely operated
RADAR:	AN/ALD-4, AN/APR-17, AN/ASQ-32, AN/ALA-6, QRC-91, and AN/APD-4, among others

Lockheed EC-121. *US Air Force photo*

LOCKHEED CONSTELLATION EC-121

From its initial design to its ultimate withdrawal from service, the Lockheed Constellation and its military derivatives became a mainstay of American aeronautics for almost 40 years. Although the name is most often associated with commercial aviation (the basic design originated with an order from the airline industry), US armed forces also relied on it for cargo, troop movement, and other duties. In fact, the first Constellation flew in January 1943, not as a passenger airplane, but as a military transport (designated C-69). Indeed, not until 1947 did a Constellation built solely as an airliner (Model 649A) grace the skies. Much longer (roughly 95 feet, or 29 meters) and heavier (takeoff weight of 98,000 pounds, or 44,452 kilograms) than the dominant airliner of the previous generation, the Douglas DC-3, the "Connie," along with the McDonnell Douglas DC-6, represented a new age of air travel.

Five years after its introduction, the Constellation was succeeded by the 1049 Super Constellation. Stretched to a total length of 113.5 feet (34.6 meters), it had four 2,800-horsepower Wright Cyclone engines that propelled the aircraft to a cruising speed of 320 miles per hour (515 kilometers per hour). Takeoff weight increased to 120,000 pounds (54,431 kilograms),

and it carried up to 92 passengers. Successive improvements added power, size, and paying customers. The 1049H, which could be converted from a cargo to a passenger aircraft in a few hours, weighed up to 140,000 pounds (63,503 kilograms) on takeoff and accommodated up to 109 travelers. Configured as an airliner, the 1049H, powered by four 3,250-horsepower Wright 3350-EA3 turbo compound engines, had a range of 4,313 miles (6,941 kilometers) with three hours of reserve fuel.

DESIGN

Nine military variants of the 1049 Super Constellation (five air force, four navy) evolved alongside the civilian aircraft. All fuselage shared an all-metal semimonocoque design, a circular cross-section, and a cambered (arched) centerline to improve aerodynamic efficiency. Each low, cantilevered wing carried two engine nacelles. The tail unit consisted of a horizontal tail plane with two outboard vertical fins/rudders and a third on the fuselage centerline.

Most C-121s simply translated the civilian capabilities of the Super Constellation directly to the military requirements of troop and cargo transport. In these roles, the air force relied on the C-121C and the navy on the R7V-1. The VC-121E, a specially outfitted version of the C-121C, served as a nascent Air Force One for the president of the United States.

Aside from these well-known public missions, the two services also used the Constellation for reconnaissance. The navy first tested the WV-1 version of the Super Constellation in this regard, and then ordered for production the WV-2, designed for early-warning radar and high-altitude surveillance. The WV-2 represented a leap in aerial recon sophistication, constituting a flying mission control center. It carried about 5.5 tons (5,000 kilograms) of electronics and radar equipment, including General Electric's height-finding radar concealed beneath a seven-foot high radome mounted atop the plane's fuselage, and GE's surveillance radar in a large radome that protruded from the bottom of the aircraft's fuselage. Inside the WV-2, radar operators sat at five consoles and plotting tables, where they observed and interpreted incoming data. A Combat Information Center (CIC) coordinated the search information and relayed it to other aircraft, military bases, and ships, as needed. Equipped with a galley, bunks, and a repair shop, the WV-2 could fly long missions, sustained by a large crew of 31 that included back up pilots, technicians, and maintenance specialists. The navy also flew the WV-3, a weather reconnaissance variant of the WV-2.

The air force adapted the WV-2 to its own uses in its RC-121C and RC-121D aircraft (later redesignated as the EC-121C and EC-121D). Known collectively as the EC-121 Warning Star, the "D" model improved on the "C" by increasing fuel capacity to 8,750 gallons (33,000 liters), enabling it to fly without interruption for 24 hours. Like the WV-2, the EC-121s had no armament.

OPERATIONS

For the most part, the EC-121D and the WV-2 served during, and in the years leading up to the Vietnam War. Between 1956 and 1965 the WV-2 flew in support of two naval barrier forces, one each stationed off of the US Pacific and Atlantic coasts. A wing of WV-2s flew 6- to 24-hour missions and provided early-warning coverage against Soviet missile or bomber attack as an extension of the Distant Early Warning (DEW) line.

The US Air Force, meanwhile, fielded three wings of EC-121 Cs and Ds from 1954 to 1978: the 551st Airborne Early Warning and Control Wing (AEWCW)

LOCKHEED EC-121

CREW:	31
ENGINES:	4x Wright R-3350-34, 3,400 lbst (1,542 kgst) each
WEIGHTS:	Empty: 69,210 lb (31,387 kg)
	Maximum: 120,000 lb (60,380 kg)
LENGTH:	113 ft 7 in (34.6 m); 116 ft (35.4 m) with nose radome
WINGSPAN:	123 ft (37.4 m)
HEIGHT:	24 ft 9 in (7.6 m)
SPEEDS:	Maximum: 299 mph (481 kph)
	Cruise: 255 mph (410 kph)
CEILING:	25,000 ft (7,619 m)
RANGE:	4,250 mi (6,843 km)
ARMAMENT:	None
RADAR:	Storm warning radar, Loran

based in Otis Air Force Base, Massachusetts; the 552nd AEWCW at McClellan Air Force Base in California; and the 553rd Reconnaissance Wing that operated from Thailand.

Prior to the Vietnam War, the EC-121s contributed to the US Navy's mission of DEW line service under the direction of the Air Defense Command. But starting in April 1965, and running until June 1974, EC-121s played a prominent role in two of the war's main offensives: Operation Rolling Thunder and Operation Linebacker II. These versatile aircraft offered limited air traffic control for American fighter engagements, provided early-warning detection, directed US aircraft to refueling tankers, and guided rescue planes to pilots shot down by enemy fire. They also flew regular surveillance routes over the Gulf of Tonkin and over Laos.

STATUS

Retired in 1978. The USAF ordered 82 EC-131s between 1951 and 1955; these aircraft continued in service until replaced by the E-3 Sentry Airborne Warning and Control System (AWACS). ∎

—*Michael Gorn*

McDonnell Douglas F2H-2P. *NARA 127-GK-1-A349272*

MCDONNELL F2H-2P BANSHEE

The F2H-2P Banshee was the US Navy's and Marine Corps' most versatile photo-recon asset during the 1950s. As a ship-based, tactical reconnaissance platform, the Banshee could fly higher and its camera configuration could cover more ground, more efficiently, than other navy and Marine Corps aircraft of the time.

DESIGN

The basic F2H-2 fighter, which had a fuel capacity increase of 200 gallons (757 liters) over previous models, was converted into a photo-reconnaissance aircraft by reconfiguring the fighter version's gun nose into a camera platform. The nose section was lengthened by nearly 3 feet (1 meter) to accommodate a variety of camera installations. The nose section contained ten camera ports: one forward facing, three oblique (looking straight down), and three ports each on the starboard and port sides. The typical photo-mapping configuration consisted of three K-17C cameras with 6-inch lenses in the aft position with another K-17C with a 6- or 12-inch lens, and a K-17C in the same configuration in the forward bay, with a P-2 strike camera facing forward. For reconnaissance, a combination of K-17C and K-38 cameras could be fitted.

During night photographic missions, the aft camera bay was fitted with either a K-37 or K-47 camera with a 12-inch lens, the middle bay held the flash synchronization unit, and one photo flash pod was carried under each wing. The photo flash pods were capable of firing 20 flash cartridges each. The camera-carrying F2H-2P retained the Banshee name.

OPERATIONS

Composite Squadron Sixty-One (VC-61) was the first to take the photo Banshee into combat in June 1952 with a three-plane detachment sailing aboard the USS *Valley Forge* (CV 45). Three more VC-61 photo Banshees arrived in theater that same month aboard USS *Essex* (CV 9). The squadron sent three more additional detachments to Korea sailing on USS *Kearsarge* (CV 33, operating from 11 August 1952 to 17 March 1953), USS *Oriskany* (CV 34, September 1952 to 18 May 1953), and USS *Boxer* (CVA 21, 30 March to 28 November 1953). VC-61's record for the Korean War saw F2H-2Ps fly more than 5,000 missions.

The US Marine Corps' Marine Photographic Squadron One (VMJ-1) was in the thick of the fighting in Korea as well. The unit operated from the K-3 airfield outside the port city of Pohang, South Korea. VMJ-1 flew more than 25 percent of the reconnaissance and post-strike photo assessment missions for the Fifth Air Force during the war. This unit also flew more than 5,000 missions during the war—5,025 to be exact.

On the other side of the globe, detachments of VC-62 F2H-2Ps supported the US Navy's Cold War operations in the Atlantic, Caribbean, and Mediterranean. VMJ-2 based at Cherry Point, North Carolina, flew the photo Banshee until the type was phased out in favor of the F9F-8P in 1955.

In the Far East, in 1955, F2H-2Ps began making secret photo-recon flights over China. Beginning on 4 May, VMJ-1 photo Banshees began reconnoitering bases in the Fukien Province of mainland China to determine if the Chinese were preparing to mount an invasion of Taiwan. In all, 77 missions were flown by F2H-2Ps over Communist China before the overflights stopped on 13 June 1955.

STATUS

Retired. First flight of the F2H-2P occurred on 12 October 1950. McDonnell Aircraft Corp. converted F2H-2 Buno. 123366 into the F2H-2P configuration and delivered an additional 58 2P photo-reconnaissance Banshees. The last 2P was delivered on 28 May 1952. The type was retired by the end of 1959. ■

—*Nicholas A. Veronico*

MCDONNELL F2H-2P

CREW:	1
ENGINES:	2x Westinghouse J34-WE-34 turbojets; 3,150 lbst (1,429 kgst) each
WEIGHTS:	Empty: 11,146 lb (5,056 kg) Maximum: 22,312 lb (10,121 kg)
LENGTH:	42 ft 10.5 in (13.1 m)
WINGSPAN:	45 ft (13.7 m) with tip tanks
HEIGHT:	14 ft 5.5 in (4.4 m)
SPEED:	532 mph (856 kph) at 10,000 ft (3,048 m)
CEILING:	44,800 ft (13,655 m)
RANGE:	1,475 mi (2,374 km)
ARMAMENT:	None
RADAR:	None

GRUMMAN F9F-6P F9F-8P COUGAR

The carrier-based Cougar fighter was a swept-wing derivative of the Grumman F9F Panther series. When the US Navy awarded Grumman Aircraft the XF9F-2 contract in October 1946, it included a provision for a swept-wing variant. But that concept was delayed due to Grumman's emphasis on development and production of the straight-wing Panther.

With the onset of the Korean conflict, the swept-wing design was expedited. As aviation historian Rene Francillion wrote in *Grumman Aircraft since 1929*,

> Developed in great haste during the Korean War as a stop-gap design to provide the Navy with a fighter having performance comparable to that of the MiG-15, the Cougar was made ready for squadron assignment in a remarkably short time.

Even so, the Cougar arrived to the fleet too late to fly combat missions during the Korean War.

The Cougars in service on 1 October 1962 were redesignated in the F-9 series, with surviving F9F-8P aircraft becoming the RF-9J.

DESIGN

The Cougar retained most features of the Panther, but it was fitted with wings swept back 35 degrees, as well as swept-back horizontal tail surfaces. The aircraft's wings folded for carrier stowage. Other changes included a reduction in fuel capacity (wingtip tanks were not fitted, as in the Panther).

RECON VARIANTS

Sixty F9F-6P aircraft were produced by Grumman between June 1954 and March 1955. They were similar to the F9F-6, except for vertical and oblique cameras fitted in place of the standard four 20mm cannon.

Grumman built 110 F9F-8P photo aircraft, delivered between August 1955 and July 1957. The photo variant had a longer and larger nose than the straight

Grumman F9F-6P. *National Archives and Records Administration*

GRUMMAN F9F-8P

CREW:	1
ENGINES:	1x Pratt & Whitney J48-P-8A turbojet; 6.250 lbst (2,835 kgst)
WEIGHTS:	Empty: 12,246 lb (5,555 kg)
	Maximum: 22,697 lb (10,295 kg)
LENGTH:	44 ft 2 in (13.5 m)
WINGSPAN:	34 ft 6 in (10.5 m)
HEIGHT:	12 ft 3 in (3.7 m)
SPEEDS:	Maximum: 637 mph (1,025 kph) at 5,000 ft (1,525 ft)
	Cruise: 508 mph (817 kph)
CEILING:	41,500 ft (12,650 m)
RANGE:	1,545 mi (1,045 km)
ARMAMENT:	None
RADAR:	AN/APG-30

F9F-8, with forward, vertical, and oblique cameras fitted in place of guns, and with provisions for a fixed refueling probe.

OPERATIONS

These aircraft served aboard navy carriers for a decade of the Cold War.

STATUS

Retired. The first flight of the XF9F-6 took place on 20 September 1951. The first fleet squadron to convert to the Cougar was VF-32 in November 1952.

Three navy reconnaissance squadrons flew the F9F-6P and/or F9F-8P. The last Cougars to serve with a fleet squadron were F9F-8P photo planes with light photograph squadron VFP-62, retired in February 1960. Cougars remained in various navy support roles until the mid-1960s. One Marine Corps utility squadron flew the F9F-6P and one composite utility squadron flew the F9F-8P, VMJ-2, and VMCJ-3, respectively.

Grumman built 1,988 Cougars, the last being delivered in February 1960.

Argentina's naval air arm acquired two F9F-8T two-seat aircraft in 1962; they served until 1971. ■

—*Norman Polmar and John F. Bessette*

DOUGLAS A3D/A-3 SKYWARRIOR

The Skywarrior was the largest carrier-based aircraft to enter US Navy squadron service. Designed as a nuclear strike aircraft, it was employed as a conventional attack aircraft, aerial tanker, and in the electronic and photo reconnaissance roles.

The Skywarrior was in navy squadron service from 1956 to 1991. The US Air Force flew the B-66 Destroyer, an extensive modification of the Skywarrior as a bomber and in special recon roles (EB-66/RB-66; see separate entry on Destroyer RB-66).

The navy aircraft was developed in response to a Bureau of Aeronautics specification for a long-range strike aircraft with a gross weight of about 100,000 pounds. Edward Heinemann, then chief engineer at Douglas, "whittled away" at a design for the aircraft until a 68,000-pound (30,844-kilogram) design was achieved, including a 10,000-pound (45,359-kilogram) bomb load—the weight of a contemporary nuclear bomb.

The aircraft's designation was changed from the A3D series to A-3 on 1 October 1962.

DESIGN

The Skywarrior was a twin-turbojet aircraft with shoulder-mounted wings swept back 36 degrees; the engines were mounted in pods on wing pylons. The wings and 22.75-foot (6.93-meter) tailfin folded for carrier stowage.

Bomb aiming was done with an AN/ASB-1A bomb director/radar. Originally mounting a pair of 20mm M3 cannon with 500 rounds per barrel in a remote-operated tail turret, most aircraft were refitted with an ECM package in place of the guns. The aircraft was fitted for in-flight refueling.

The three-man crew—pilot, bombardier, and navigator/tail gunner—was housed in a pressurized cockpit forward. Because of the state of technology in ejection

Douglas EKA-3B. *US Navy photo*

seats, Heinemann opted for an escape chute from the cockpit, a scheme whose many critics remarked A3D stood for "All 3 Dead." The electronic and training variants could not have accommodated ejection seats in the specialized working space in the modified weapons bay. Only the 12 specialized training aircraft (A3D-2T/TA-3B) had dual controls.

A maximum bomb load of 12,800 pounds (5,806 kilograms) could be carried in the internal weapons bay, including a variety of nuclear weapons, conventional bombs, and mines. The Skywarrior would be able to deliver—in all weather—a nuclear bomb against targets at a distance in excess of 1,000 nautical miles (1,852 kilometers) at altitudes above 40,000 feet (12,192 meters).

Beginning with the 178th aircraft, an A3D-2 built in 1958, all attack variants were delivered with a "tanker package" to permit rapid conversion to in-flight tankers.

For short-run takeoffs from airfields ashore, the aircraft could be fitted with 12 JATO "bottles" to provide an additional rocket thrust of 54,000 pounds (24,494 kilograms) for a four-second takeoff with a run of only 100 yards (91.44 meters). When landing ashore, the A3D could deploy a deceleration chute.

During the Skywarrior program, the navy considered a possible fighter configuration as an "aerial picket" for carrier defense. These planes would have an air-search radar, probably the AN/APS-20, and air-to-air missiles. They would be stationed aloft some 80 to 175 nautical miles (148 to 324 kilometers) from a carrier task force, a concept that was later called "missileer."

RECON VARIANTS

The A3D-2P reconnaissance aircraft were configured with 12 camera stations plus provisions for photo flash bombs and cartridges. These photo Skywarriors flew with the navy's two heavy photographic squadrons, VAP-61 and VAP-62, operating from land bases as well as from carriers. The three-man crew substituted a photo-navigator for the bombardier in the straight A3D, with the third, an enlisted crewman, designated a photo technician-gunner.

The A3D-2Q electronic surveillance aircraft were fitted with intercept gear to collect tactical intelligence on foreign radar emissions. They had seven-man crews. These planes also flew from land bases and from

carriers in fleet air reconnaissance squadrons VAQ-1 and VAQ-2.

OPERATIONS

The Skywarrior squadrons and detachments served ashore and on carriers in Southeast Asia from 1964 to 1974, flying in reconnaissance, electronic countermeasures, electronic surveillance, tanker, and conventional strike roles.

The first use of Skywarriors in the conventional bombing role occurred on 29 March 1965, when six aircraft from the *Coral Sea* (CVA 43) participated in a strike against Bach Long Vi Island in the Gulf of Tonkin. As the war progressed, it became apparent that the aircraft were too large and slow for strikes against defended targets in North Vietnam, while the specialized tankers were more valuable on the limited carrier deck space. The Skywarriors were rapidly retired from the bomber role, and from 1968 to 1970 participated in the war only in special-mission roles.

Photo reconnaissance RA-3B Skywarriors flew from carriers during the Vietnam War, but operated mostly from land bases in Guam and the Philippines, as well as from Don Muang in Thailand and Da Nang in South Vietnam. These were the navy's only aircraft with a cartographic capability in addition to conducting tactical reconnaissance, and were invaluable in updating maps. The RA-3B photo planes roamed up and down the Ho Chi Minh Trail during the day and later, after the loss of two aircraft to small arms fire, at night. Painted black and fitted with infrared sensors as well as a real-time video display, the RA-3Bs would fly 500 feet (152 meters) or lower, seeking hot spots produced by supply trucks and then calling orbiting attack planes to pounce on the traffic. Using special infrared film, their cameras also could detect whether or not vegetation was alive, thus finding cut foliage that was being used for camouflage.

Two electronic surveillance configurations also flew in the war: the EA-3B and EKA-3B.

By the end of the Vietnam War, Skywarriors were succeeded in the electronics role by EA-6B Prowlers, and in photo recon by RA-5C Vigilantes.

Twenty-one A-3s were lost in Southeast Asia—6 combat losses and 15 operational. The combat losses consisted of four RA-3B photo aircraft, all operating from Naval Air Station Cubi Point in the

Philippines and lost over North Vietnam, probably to antiaircraft artillery, and two A-3Bs from the *Kitty Hawk* (CVA 63). The first was probably downed by a MiG over the China Sea while on a ferry flight from Cubi Point, and the second was lost to unknown causes while on a night mining mission over North Vietnam. Of the crews of these combat losses, only one man was recovered.

STATUS

Retired. XA3D-1's first flight took place on 28 October 1952, with the first squadron delivery in 1961 to heavy-attack squadron VAH-1.

Douglas produced 282 Skywarriors for the navy through 1961:

2   XA3D-1 prototypes
1   YA3D-1 prototype
49   A3D-1 attack aircraft (later A-3A)
164   A3D-2 attack aircraft (later A-3B)
30   A3D-2P reconnaissance aircraft
     (later RA-3B)
24   A3D-2Q electronic surveillance aircraft
     (later EA-3B)
12   A3D-2T dual-control trainer aircraft
     (later TA-3B). ■

—*Norman Polmar and John F. Bessette*

DOUGLAS A3D-1P/RA-3A

CREW:	3
ENGINES:	2x Pratt & Whitney J57-P-1 turbojets; 9,500 lbst (4,320 kgst) each
WEIGHTS:	Empty: 37,656 lb (17,081 kg)
	Combat: 58,289 lb (23.718 kg)
	Maximum: 70,000 lb (31,752 kg)
LENGTH:	75 ft 11 in (23.2 m)
WINGSPAN:	72 ft 6 in (22.1 m)
HEIGHT:	23 ft 10 in (7.3 m)
SPEEDS:	Maximum: 612 mph (984.9 kph) at sea level; 623 mph (1,002.6 kph) at 11,000 ft (3,354 m)
	Cruise: 540 mph (869 kph)
CEILING:	44,500 ft (13,567 m)
RANGE:	3,450 mi (5,552 km) high-altitude mission
ARMAMENT:	*Some aircraft* 2x 20mm M3 cannon (1,000 rounds total)
RADAR:	None

NORTH AMERICAN RF-100 SUPER SABRE

The F-100 Super Sabre was designed as the successor to North American's F-86 Sabre and was the world's first operational fighter capable of supersonic speed in level flight. Although it was conceived as a fighter, all basic variants were used primarily as fighter-bombers and were nuclear capable.

In early 1951, North American proposed a day fighter with a 45-degree wing sweep and extensive use of titanium, virtually a first at the time for a production aircraft. These features, plus the new Pratt & Whitney J57 turbojet engine, guaranteed its supersonic capability. By the end of the year this new aircraft was accepted as the F-100, and the USAF ordered two prototypes followed by production F-100As.

Two recon aircraft programs were initiated at the same time, probably to ensure that at least one would be successful. The USAF ordered six RF-100As in 1954 under project name Slick Chick (see the Martin RB-57 entry on page 188 for details on the other program, the RB-57 Heart Throb).

DESIGN

The Super Sabre could carry up to 6,000 pounds (2,722 kilograms) of ordnance on six wing pylons and was fitted with four 20mm cannon.

Extensive flight tests of the prototypes revealed several design deficiencies, especially a yaw instability that came on too fast and resulted in overstress of the aircraft, sometimes with fatal results. This was partially rectified with a larger vertical tail, retrofitted onto the operational F-100As.

Under Project Slick Chick, six F-100As were taken directly from the production line and stripped of guns, ammunition, and other combat material, which were replaced by five cameras: three K-17s in a trimetrogon

North American RF-100. *US Air Force photo*

configuration and two K-38 split-verticals. The fuselage was bulged slightly to accommodate the right and left trimetrogon cameras. Up to four external fuel tanks could be carried by the recon aircraft to permit coverage of more territory (two external tanks were standard on F-100s). The four-tank configuration had an adverse effect on the maximum service altitude, however, which should ideally have been above 50,000 feet (15,240 meters) to evade hostile fighters and antiaircraft weapons of the time. Thus, the Slick Chicks were often flown with only two external tanks.

OPERATIONS

In the early 1950s, responding to the critical need to gather detailed military intelligence on the Soviet Union, its European satellites, China, and North Korea, the United States and Great Britain agreed to a series of careful high-level overflight missions under the so-called Sensitive Intelligence (SENSINT) program. While SAC and the RAF concentrated on the Soviet Union, the theater air commands (US Air Forces Europe and Far East Air Forces) flew recon missions over Eastern Europe, North Korea, and possibly China. Three RF-100s and three pilots were to be assigned to Europe, and three to the Pacific.

On 9 April 1955, the European RF-100 contingent deployed, and on 16 May it arrived at Bitburg Air Base, West Germany. The new unit was designated Detachment One, 7407th Support Squadron.

After becoming operational at Bitburg, the aircraft are known to have flown six overflights of East Europe. These missions had a combat radius sufficient to cover East Germany and western Poland. If deployed to Fürstenfeldbruck Air Base, near Munich, Slick Chick RF-100s could reach western Hungary and northern Yugoslavia. Penetrations into "denied" airspace paid unexpected dividends when the Soviet air defense radar and communications network activated in response to these flights. The Slick Chick's speed and high-altitude capability protected it from Soviet interception.

One pilot, then-Capt. Cecil Rigsby, recalled one of his missions from Bitburg over western Czechoslovakia:

> As I approached my targets I could see through the viewfinder . . . [a] number of fighters scrambling airborne at one of the airfields and others circling over it. When I reversed direction to return to Germany after photographing all of my targets, I had a great deal of company. The [Soviet] fighters were going all out to match my speed and reach my altitude, but they remained at a much lower level. . . . One airplane managed to get in my eight o'clock position, but he was about 20,000 feet [6,096 m] below me. I did not drop my external fuel tanks because I never felt threatened. The fighters broke off when I reached the West German border and I returned safely to Bitburg.

RF-100 overflight missions, like those of the Heart Throb RB-57As, ended in the summer of 1956, when President Eisenhower decided to replace them with CIA-operated U-2 overflights, which began that June. Slick Chicks, however, remained operational in theater, flying photo-mapping and other missions over Western Europe. One RF-100 was lost operationally in October 1956. The operation was shut down in 1958 and the two remaining aircraft were sent to the Pacific.

In June 1955, three Slick Chick RF-100s were deployed to Yokota Air Base, Japan, joining the 6021st Reconnaissance Squadron. One Slick Chick was lost shortly after arrival at Yokota in a flying accident. The two European Slick Chicks arrived at the Yokota-based aircraft by June 1958. All four were placed in storage shortly thereafter and then transferred to Nationalist China on Taiwan in early 1959.

Three of the aircraft reportedly were assigned to the Taiwanese 4th Squadron at Taoyuan Air Base, near the capital city, Taipei. The Taiwanese found that the aircraft were only marginally mission capable and the

NORTH AMERICA F-100A

CREW:	1
ENGINE:	1x Pratt & Whitney J57-P-21; 8,700 lbst (4,000 kgst)
WEIGHTS:	Empty: 18,185 lb (8,266 kg)
	Combat: 25,607 lb (11,640 kg)
	Maximum: 28,971 lb (13,170 kg)
LENGTH:	47 ft 10 in (14.4 m)
WINGSPAN:	38 ft 10 in (11.6 m)
HEIGHT:	15 ft 6 in (4.7 m)
SPEEDS:	Maximum: 740 mph (1,184 kph) at 34,000 ft (10,366 m)
	Cruise: 583 mph (918 kph)
CEILING:	F-100A: 41,100 ft (12,530 m)
	RF-100A: 53,000 ft (16,160 m)
RANGE:	1,300 mi (2,080 km)
	Radii: F-100A: 462 mi (733 km) high-high mission profile
	RF-100A: approx. 350 mi (560 km) at 53,000 ft (16,154 m)
ARMAMENT:	None in recon variant
RADAR:	None

resulting photography was of poor quality. The RF-100s snever flew operational missions from Taiwan and were officially withdrawn from service on 1 December 1960.

STATUS

Retired. The first YF-100A flew on 25 May 1953. The earlier F-100A/Cs served in the air-superiority role before becoming tactical fighter-bombers like the later F-100D/F aircraft. By 1960, they had replaced the Republic F-84F Thunderstreak as fighter-bombers in the USAF and went on to see extensive use in South Vietnam until 1971.

F-100s were flown by several air national guard units until 1979. France, Denmark, Turkey, and Taiwan also flew F-100 fighters. ∎

—*Norman Polmar and John F. Bessette*

Martin RB-57. *US Air Force photo*

MARTIN RB-57 CANBERRA

When the first Martin-built B-57A Canberra took to the skies on its maiden flight on 20 July 1953, it became the first non-US aircraft design to join the ranks of the USAF (née USAAF) since World War II.

Choosing a foreign-designed plane for US service was unusual: as the war in Korea ramped up, the air force looked to find a new all-weather attack bomber to replace aging Douglas B-26 aircraft. When American manufacturers failed to offer a suitable solution, the USAF considered both the Avro Canada CF-100 and the English Electric Canberra to fill their need for a tactical bomber and reconnaissance aircraft.

While the Canberra won the competition, London-based English Electric was consumed with orders for the Royal Air Force. For this reason, the US military chose the Glenn L. Martin Company to build the USAF version, designated B-57. Though the B-57

made a name for itself as a bomber in combat in the skies above Vietnam, over one-quarter of the 403 aircraft constructed in the US were specially equipped for reconnaissance duties. Additional Canberra aircraft were also converted to the important role of photography and data gathering over time.

RB-57's basic and modified mission designation meant "reconnaissance, bomber." RB-57 types followed the model letter of each Canberra model, specially built or modified: RB-57A, RB-57B, RB-57D, RB-57E, and RB-57F. B-57C aircraft were trainers, with no recon versions built.

DESIGN

In many ways, the general arrangement of the B-57 aircraft was quite different from a typical American aircraft design of the era. The Canberra had short, stubby wings and the plane's engines were integrated into the wings. The original versions of the plane had a domelike canopy, later replaced with a fighter-like tandem cockpit.

The first recon version of the aircraft, the RB-57A, carried cameras in its aft bomb bay along with up to 21 flash photo bombs for capturing images at night. The planes flew with a pilot and navigator/camera operator. While only eight B-57A bombers were built, Martin constructed 67 RB-57A aircraft.

The next iteration of the aircraft was the B-57B. Here, Martin and the USAF began to create a version with features that improved upon the English Electric design. A number of the 202 B-57B aircraft built were converted to RB-57Bs.

The RB-57D high-altitude version was built exclusively for reconnaissance. The plane had improved engines, a longer wingspan, and often flew with two K-38 and two KC-1 cameras. The first example flew in November 1955, with 20 of the planes built. This version could operate at altitudes up to 70,000 feet (21,336 meters).

The B-57E (68 built) was specially equipped as a target tug, though around six of the planes were converted to RB-57E aircraft and used during the Vietnam War.

The RB-57F aircraft came into service when RB-57Ds began to experience wing spar failures. General Dynamics built the F-model from older B-57s, heavily modifying the planes to fly with new engines and a 122-foot (37-meter) wingspan. The planes could reach heights up to 82,000 feet (24,994 meters).

OPERATIONS

While the B-57A bomber was not a combat-ready airplane, many RB-57As went into service with tactical reconnaissance units based overseas in the mid-1950s. Flying from bases in France, Germany, and Japan, RB-57A aircraft flew recon missions for the USAF, most notably Operation Heart Throb—shallow penetrations into Soviet Bloc and Chinese territories. The planes were replaced in frontline service by 1958 and turned over to air national guard units, which used them to complete photo and mapping surveys around the United States up to 1971.

RB-57D aircraft were assigned to SAC and flew from bases in Germany, Alaska, Japan, and the Pacific. Flights included additional incursions into Chinese and

MARTIN RB-57A

CREW:	2
ENGINES:	2x Wright J65-W-5 turbojets; 7,220 lbst (3,275 kgst) each
WEIGHT:	48,847 lb (22,157 kg)
LENGTH:	65 ft 6 in (20.0 m)
WINGSPAN:	64 ft (19.5 m)
HEIGHT:	14 ft 10 in (4.5 m)
SPEED:	609 mph (980 kph)
CEILING:	48,350 ft (14.7 m)
RANGE:	2,568 mi (4,133 km)
ARMAMENT:	None
RADAR:	None

Soviet airspace. By 1959, problems with wing fatigue and the availability of the Lockheed U-2 hastened the end of frontline service for D-model Canberras.

Six E-model aircraft were used by a tactical reconnaissance unit over Vietnam and surrounding areas in the Patricia Lynn operation in the 1960s. Two of the planes were lost in combat: the first caught fire after being hit by ground fire in 1965, while the second was also lost to ground fire in 1968. Both crewmen ejected from the plane.

The official duty of RB-57F aircraft was weather recon, though four of the planes served from bases in Germany and Japan, conducting strategic missions. These were commonly high-altitude flights near "hostile" borders.

For a brief time, the USAF loaned RB-57s to the Republic of China Air Force (1959–1964) and the Pakistan Air Force (1965). Both foreign air forces experienced the loss of one of their aircraft while overflying hostile territory.

STATUS

Operational. All B-57 aircraft were retired from USAF service as of 1983. Pakistan used B-57s until 1985. Three WB-57F aircraft were still used by NASA for high-altitude atmospheric research as of 2016. ∎

—*Cory Graff*

C-130A modified for COMINT collection, Norway, 1958. *George Pittelkau via John F. Bessette*

LOCKHEED C-130/EC-130/RC-130 HERCULES

Shortly after the first C-130As began rolling off Lockheed's Murietta, Georgia, assembly line in 1956, spyplane conversions were taking place. One prototype (54-1632) and 15 production (57-0520 to 57-0524) Hercules were modified to RC-130A photo-mapping configuration. These early aircraft circled the globe, collecting photographic intelligence. They were phased out of service in the late 1970s as more specialized recon versions of the Hercules came on line.

Lockheed developed the EC-130H "Compass Call" version of the tested C-130 Hercules design to serve as tactical jammers capable of defeating an enemy's C3 (command, control, and communications) infrastructure. Jamming these systems prevents an enemy from coordinating a response to the actions of air or ground attacks. Recent Compass Call upgrades have enabled the aircraft to defeat hostile early-warning and target-acquisition radars, playing a vital role in suppression of enemy air defenses (known as SEAD) during the wars in Iraq and Afghanistan.

DESIGN

Fourteen aircraft have worn the EC-130H Compass Call designation (64-14859, 64-14862, and 73-1580, -1581, -1583-1588, -1590, -1592, -1594 and -1595), and the type reached its initial operating capability in 1983. Through the years, these aircraft have undergone a series of upgrades; today, half of them fly in EC-130H Block 30 and the balance in Block 35 configuration. As technology improves, the Compass Call Hercules has received upgraded software, reconfigured workstation positioning on the mission deck, additional jamming capabilities across a greater range of frequencies, digital signal processors, and the ability to interrogate and jam newer generations of early-warning radar.

The Tactical Radio Acquisition and Counter-measures Subsystem (TRACS-C) was introduced to upgrade some of the Compass Call's existing systems. TRACS-C enables operators to acquire target signals faster, and the unit is reprogrammable to adapt to the changing threat environment.

The EC-130H is also fitted with underwing pylons that can house the Special Emitter Array (SPEAR) pod, one under each wing, which communicates with the TRACS-C system. Inside the SPEAR pod are 24 antennas that form four independently controlled jamming beams from each pod. The pod's antennas are on the outward facing side, pointing away from the aircraft.

The official designation of these highly modified electronic jamming Hercules is EC-130H Compass Call.

OPERATIONS

During Operation Desert Storm, Compass Calls disrupted Iraqi air defense networks, preventing command and control centers from directing antiaircraft fire. This was accomplished with the Compass Call aircraft flying outside of Iraqi airspace and safely away from enemy surface-to-air missiles.

EC-130Hs often operated with navy EA-6B Prowlers. The Compass Call's linguists would listen to Iraqi radio traffic and observe radar emissions, then direct the Prowlers to jam large networks while the EC-130Hs targeted different frequencies. Compass Calls were also used to combat improvised explosive devices (IED) planted by Iraqi insurgents. Operators on board Compass Call aircraft jammed various frequencies used to detonate the IEDs, or broadcast false signals to detonate them.

During the campaign, Compass Call C-130s flew 450 sorties, which gave 24-hour jamming of Iraqi tactical communications for 44 days in a row. Since 2002, Compass Calls have flown more than 26,000 hours in support of Operation Iraqi Freedom.

In September 2015, it was announced that a cyber-warfare-modified EC-130H had successfully demonstrated its ability to hack into a target computer network from the air. Future aircraft, possibly modified Compass Calls, will play a major role in the air force's cyber warfare operations.

STATUS

Operational. Deliveries of the EC-130H Compass Call began in 1982. Today, the fleet of 14 EC-130Hs are part of Air Combat Command's 55th Wing (Offutt AFB, Nebraska) and are operated by the 55th Electronic Combat Group's 41st and 43rd Electronic Combat Squadrons based at Davis-Monthan AFB, Arizona. ■
—*Nicholas A. Veronico*

Lockheed EC-130H. *US Air Force photo*

LOCKHEED EC-130H

CREW:	13 (2 pilots, navigator, flight engineer, 2 electronic warfare officers, mission crew supervisor, 4 cryptologic linguists, acquisition operator. airborne maintenance technician)
ENGINES:	4x Allison T56-A-15 turboprops; 4,910 shp each
WEIGHT:	107,000 lb (48,534 kg)
LENGTH:	97 ft 9 in (29.8 m)
WINGSPAN:	132 ft 7 in (40.4 m)
HEIGHT:	38 ft 3 in (11.7 m)
SPEED:	300 mph (483 kph) at 20,000 ft (6,096 m)
CEILING:	25,000 ft (7,620 m)
RANGE:	2,295 mi (3,693 km)
ARMAMENT:	None
RADAR:	Various

Lockheed RB-69A. *US Air Force photo*

LOCKHEED RB-69A NEPTUNE

During the Cold War's unsung battles with the Communist regimes in the Soviet Union and China, the United States made every attempt to gather up-to-the-minute intelligence. The shootdown of Francis Gary Powers in a CIA-operated, US Air Force–marked U-2 spyplane ended overflights of Communist territory. However, the collection of signals, or ELINT, remained a constant task. ELINT yields order of battle information, location of radar, sensor types, and the capabilities of each.

ELINT can be acquired without violating a sovereign nation's airspace, by flying outside its borders. As the recon aircraft flies near the target nation's border, the enemy will interrogate the aircraft with radar and communicate with its air defense infrastructure about the intruder's path and estimated intentions. The target nation's electronic communications are then recorded by the reconnaissance aircraft for interpretation either in the air or upon landing.

In the mid-1950s, the US Air Force and Navy had ELINT collection programs, and the CIA sought a suitable platform that could meet its needs. The CIA acquired seven Lockheed P2V-7 Neptunes under the codename Project Wild Cherry. The Project Wild Cherry aircraft were given a US Air Force cover story, serial numbers, and the designation RB-69. The RB-69s were overall sea blue with white US Air Force titles under the cockpit windows. In addition to collecting electronic intelligence, Neptunes were capable of dropping agents and leaflets, and one was outfitted for photo-reconnaissance missions.

DESIGN

Based on the proven Lockheed P2V Neptune, the RB-69 was externally the same as the navy's P2V-7, featuring a shoulder-mounted wing with two R-3350 engines and a pair of pod-mounted Westinghouse J34 jet engines under the wings. The fuselage was notable for its large belly-mounted radome housing an AN/APS-20 search radar antenna and extended tail-mounted MAD boom fairing.

OPERATIONS

Most likely owned and operated by the CIA, these aircraft flew with US Air Force markings. To make the air force cover story seem plausible, the Air Force Materiel Command gave these seven aircraft the RB-69A designation.

Operations of the RB-69 will remain classified until 2022, when the CIA is expected to release details of the type's operations with Taiwan. What is known is that the CIA flew a pair of RB-69s in Europe, collecting ELINT along the border of the Soviet Union and its satellite nations. In 1959, all of the RB-69s were brought together in Taiwan, where they joined the Republic of China Air Force's 34th Squadron engaged in collecting intelligence along the border of mainland China. Two RB-69s were known to have crashed in South Korea, and three are believed to have been shot down near the Chinese border.

STATUS

The RB-69s were acquired in 1954 and operated in the late 1950s in both Europe and the Pacific until being transferred to the Republic of China Air Force (Taiwan). The Taiwanese are reported to have flown the type until 1966, when the remaining RB-69s were returned to the US Navy and converted to P2V-7 anti-submarine aircraft. ■

—*Nicholas A. Veronico*

DOUGLAS RB-66 DESTROYER

The Douglas RB-66 was a land-based tactical reconnaissance aircraft delivered to the US Air Force in January 1956. The RB-66B was later reconfigured with electronic countermeasures equipment and redesignated EB-66E. The aircraft proved its worth during the Vietnam War when EB-66s escorted bombers over North Vietnam. The electronic countermeasures versions of the B-66 were used to confuse enemy radar, making them unable to determine the size and strength of the attacking squadrons, render them useless in directing MiG fighters to intercept the formations, and blinding surface-to-air missile and radar-directed anti-aircraft cannon fire.

DESIGN

During the height of the Korean War, the US Air Force was flying a mixed fleet of World War II–vintage piston-powered light bombers, such as the B-26 and RB-26 Invader. The air force needed an airframe that could serve as both a bomber and a reconnaissance aircraft. It had to be fast, carry a 10,000 pound (4,536 kilogram) payload with a radius of 1,000 nautical miles (1,852 kilometers), and be capable of carrying a suite of jammers to defeat enemy air defense radars.

In the fall of 1951, the air force was shown the then-under-development concept for the navy's XA3D-1 Skywarrior. Designers at Douglas removed all the equipment necessary for aircraft carrier operations—arresting gear, catapult launch capabilities,

LOCKHEED RB-69A

CREW:	Typically 5 (pilot, copilot, navigator, 2 electronics/recon equipment operators)
ENGINES:	2x Wright R-3350-32W jet engines, 3,500 hp each; and 2x Westinghouse J34-WE-34 turbojets, 3,250 lbst (1,474 kgst) each
WEIGHT:	77,850 lb (35,312 kg)
LENGTH:	91 ft 4 in (27.8 m)
WINGSPAN:	104 ft (31.7 m)
HEIGHT:	29 ft 4 in (8.9 m)
SPEED:	353 mph (568 kph)
CEILING:	22,000 ft (6,706 m)
RANGE:	4,350 mi (7,000 km)
ARMAMENT:	None
RADAR:	AN/APS-20 S-band search radar plus various electronic intelligence-gathering receivers

wing-fold mechanisms, etc.—and modified the design to suit the air force's needs for a low-altitude, high-speed aircraft capable of penetrating heavily defended airspace. The design converted to air force specifications became known as the B/RB-66 Destroyer. The B-66A models were used to solve the aircraft's teething troubles—wing vibrations at high speed, pitch-up tendencies, and underperforming 9,000 pounds static thrust (4,082 kilograms static thrust) Allison J71-A-9 engines.

The B-66B model was equipped with Allison J71-A-13 engines rated at 10,200 pounds static thrust (4,536 kilograms static thrust), which decreased the aircraft's takeoff roll and clearance over a 50-foot (15.2-meter) obstacle by 40 percent. Although the uprated engines solved some problems and provided more speed and greater range, their exhaust output caused a number of structural fatigue issues in the aircraft's flying surfaces: flaps, ailerons, elevators, and rudder. The fix attempted by the air force caused greater problems; however, most were addressed in the "Little Barney" modernization program (May 1958 to 1960). Subsequently, modernized B-66Bs and RB-66Bs planes were modified for the electronic countermeasures role, and were designated

Douglas EB-66E, originally delivered as an RB-66B. *US Air Force photo*

DOUGLAS RB-66

CREW:	3
ENGINES:	2x Allison J71-A-13 turbojets; 10,200 lbst (4,627 kgst) each
WEIGHTS:	Empty: 43,476 lb (19,720 kg) Combat: 49,400 lb (22,407 kg) Maximum: 83,000 lb (37,648 kg)
LENGTH:	75 ft 2 in (22.9 m)
WINGSPAN:	72 ft 6 in (22.1 m)
HEIGHT:	23 ft 7 in (7.2 m)
SPEEDS:	Maximum: 631 mph (1,016 kph) at 6,000 feet (1,829 m) Cruise: 525 mph (845 kph)
CEILING:	43,000 ft (13,106 m)
RANGE:	805 mi (1,491 km)
ARMAMENT:	RB-66B/C: 2x 20mm tail-mounted cannons
RADAR:	Active and passive tunable ECM jammers

EB-66B or 66E with the removal of the tail turret and installation of jammers, ferret (electronic snooper), and infrared sensors. What was unique at the time was that the new jammers were tunable, enabling the sensor operator to jam different types of radar.

All versions of the Douglas B/RB/EB-66 were called the Destroyer.

OPERATIONS

Tactical Air Command began RB-66 operations with the 9th Tactical Reconnaissance Squadron (TRS) of the 363rd Tactical Reconnaissance Wing (TRW) in January 1956 at Shaw AFB, South Carolina. Deployments were made to Europe and Japan, and RB-66s were used to gather intelligence about Cuba and its military operations during and after the Cuban Missile Crisis of October 1962.

For the Vietnam War, tactical planners made great use of the EB-66 aircraft. Escorting strike packages into contested airspace, the EB-66s were able to suppress enemy air defenses and direct fighters and bombers around radar sites, limiting losses to antiaircraft fire and enemy fighters. EB-66 operations were flown by the 41st and 42nd Tactical Electronic Warfare Squadron (TEWS), 355th Tactical Fighter Wing at Takhli, Thailand. During the Vietnam War, one EB-66 was shot down by an enemy MiG fighter, five were downed by surface-to-air missiles, and eleven were lost in accidents.

STATUS

Retired. Although the B/RB-66 was underpowered and the program suffered from funding cuts along the way, the air force took delivery of 294 aircraft in total. Five were preproduction RB-66As that served as test platforms for the development of the RB-66B, of which 145 were accepted. A further 72 bomber versions of the B-66B were purchased, and 36 each of the RB-66C and WB-66D also flew with the air force. The first flight of first RB-66A, serial number 52-2828, took place on 28 June 1954. The last of the electronic warfare B-66s were withdrawn from use at the end of the Vietnam War in 1973. WB-66D serial number 55-0390, the last B-66 to ever fly, was used until 1975 by Westinghouse as an airborne testbed. ■

—*Nicholas A. Veronico*

McDonnell RF-101. *National Archives and Records Administration*

MCDONNELL RF-101 VOODOO

The F-101 Voodoo fighter was conceived shortly after World War II as a long-range bomber escort, with a secondary ground-attack role. The initial result was the XF-88, which lacked power for supersonic flight.

In the early, 1950s McDonnell redesigned the aircraft around two Pratt & Whitney J57 engines, and the air force accepted it as an escort fighter for SAC bombers. As bomber penetration tactics changed, SAC decided escort fighters were no longer needed, and the aircraft were moved to TAC.

TAC saw the Voodoo as both a penetrating fighter-bomber and a tactical reconnaissance platform. F-101s eventually equipped a USAF Europe fighter-bomber wing, and two-seat variants equipped both US and Canadian air defense squadrons. But the Voodoo's premier tactical function was low-level reconnaissance as the RF-101.

DESIGN

The F-101 featured a swept-back wing and tail, hydraulic flight controls, all-movable stabilizer, anti-fatigue autopilot, and in-flight refueling using either the probe-and-drogue or the flying boom method. Providing two J57 jet engines permitted design improvements and McDonnell strengthened the internal structure of the F-101A, increasing the maneuvering load factor and resulting in the F-101C.

The fighter-bomber F-101A and C could carry a nuclear weapon, and the air-defense F-101B had nuclear air-to-air missiles. Like the F-101A/C, the RF-101 had a central weapon station equipped to carry a nuclear weapon, and at least one unit, the Europe-based 66th Tactical Reconnaissance Wing, trained for nuclear delivery.

The recon Voodoo had a forward-firing, two split-vertical, and three tri-metrogon cameras, all in an extended nose. A 1964 modification improved the Voodoo camera system, with the more capable version prepared for the RF-4C Phantom II.

OPERATIONS

In 1957, both the air force and navy strove to break coast-to-coast flying records. A navy F8U-1 Crusader set a new record on 15 July 1957 (see the Chance Vought RF-8 Crusader entry). McDonnell Aircraft Corporation and the air force quickly sought to break that mark and at the same time showcase their new RF-101. Operation Sun Run was an attempt to fly round-trip, nonstop Los Angeles–New York–Los Angeles. Captain Robert Sweet accomplished this feat in 6 hours, 46 minutes on 27 November 1957 (and broke the east-to-west record in the process). Lieutenant Gustav Klatt set the new west-to-east record, both flights being refueled by new SAC KC-135 tankers.

MCDONNELL RF-101C

CREW:	1
ENGINES:	2x Pratt & Whitney J57-P-13 turbojets; 8,700 lbst (4,000 kgst) each
WEIGHTS:	Empty: 26,136 lb (11,855 kg) Combat: 36,586 lb (16,630 kg) Maximum: 51,000 lb (23,133 kg)
LENGTH:	69 ft 4 in (21.1 m)
WINGSPAN:	39 ft 8 in (12.1 m)
HEIGHT:	18 ft (5.5 m)
SPEEDS:	Maximum: 1,012 mph (1,619 kph) at 35,000 ft (10,666 m) Cruise: 254 mph (kph)
CEILING:	53,300 ft (16,855 m)
RANGE:	2,143 mi (3,430 km) Combat radius: 850 mi (1,360 km) high-low-high mission profile
ARMAMENT:	None in recon variants
RADAR:	None

Following this activity, TAC incorporated the RF-101 into its Composite Air Strike Force (CASF) "packages," one of which was sent in 1958 to the eastern Mediterranean in response to a crisis in Lebanon. Later that year, a CASF package—including RF-101s—was sent to the western Pacific when China threatened war in the Taiwan Straits. And, in August 1961, in response to the erection of the Berlin Wall, the United States sent significant land and air reinforcements, including Voodoos, to Europe.

On 21 October 1962, the day before President Kennedy alerted the world to the Soviet missile deployments in Cuba, the 363rd Tactical Reconnaissance Wing was alerted to deploy RF-101 and RB-66 Destroyer aircraft to MacDill AFB, Florida. However, initial testing showed that the Voodoo's cameras and supporting gear could not provide good photo coverage at the required low-altitude, high-speed flight needed in the Cuban threat environment. KA-45 and KA-46 cameras like the navy had on its RF-8

Crusaders were made available, and the air force flew its first successful, low-level mission on 26 October.

The 363rd Voodoos and the navy VFP-62 Crusaders flew low-altitude missions over the Soviet missile and troop sites in Cuba on alternate days. Sorties continued into November, monitoring Soviet withdrawal of missiles and support equipment. The 363rd flew 83 combat missions, receiving the Air Force Outstanding Unit Award personally from President Kennedy. Fifteen 363rd pilots were awarded the Distinguished Flying Cross.

There were sporadic USAF recon efforts in Southeast Asia as early as 1960, but, as the conflict heated up in October 1961, Japan-based RF-101s were deployed to Vietnam and then to Thailand to provide low-level recon of Viet Cong activity and North Vietnamese troop movements. These flights gradually increased, with the first Voodoo loss (to ground fire) occurring in November 1964. From then until 1970, the RF-101s flew an estimated 35,000 recon sorties, suffering 39 losses, 33 in combat, including one lost to a North Vietnamese MiG-21.

In October 1959, eight RF-101As were transferred to the Republic of China Air Force on Taiwan. Augmented by six RF-101C aircraft in 1962, they flew missions over and along the Chinese mainland. Three Taiwanese Voodoos were shot down, on 2 August 1961, 18 December 1964, and 18 March 1965. The last known Taiwanese flights occurred in 1965, with the remaining Voodoos departing Taiwan by 1970.

STATUS

Retired. The first YF-101A flew on 29 September 1954. Once structural improvements were made in the mid-1950s, the aircraft was cleared for both fighter-bomber and tactical recon roles.

McDonnell produced 804 F-101s, 201 of which were specialized RF-101s, plus 83 recon aircraft converted from other variants. The first were delivered in summer 1957, replacing obsolescent Republic RF-84Fs. In turn, the RF-101 was replaced by the McDonnell Douglas RF-4 Phantom beginning in 1965.

The last operational air force RF-101s were taken out of service on 12 November 1970, with some remaining in air national guard units in Arkansas, Kentucky, and Nevada until 1979. ∎

—*Norman Polmar and John F. Bessette*

CHANCE VOUGHT F8U-1P/RF-8 CRUSADER

The F8U-1P Crusader—often called the Photo Crusader—was the US Navy's last specialized photo plane in a lineage of specialized reconnaissance aircraft that extended back to the beginning of World War II. The aircraft was adapted from the F8U Crusader, a high-performance, single-seat day fighter.

The efficacy of the basic F8U design led the navy to select it for the photorecon role; the 32nd F8U-1 was converted to recon prototype (YF8U-1P), which in turn was followed by F8U-1P production. The aircraft could perform photo missions both day and night, and from treetop levels up to approximately 35,000 feet (10,668 meters).

Designation changed from the F8U series to F-8 on 1 October 1962.

DESIGN

Faced with the challenge of creating a Mach 1+ fighter with good carrier-landing characteristics, Chance Vought designers gave the Crusader a wing that raised 7 degrees during landing and takeoff, thus providing the angle-of-attack necessary for a 130 miles per hour (209 kilometers per hour) landing speed and still have the fuselage in a near-horizontal attitude for maximum pilot visibility. The outer wing sections folded for carrier stowage.

In the photo planes the fighter's four 20mm cannon and magazines were deleted, more fuel was carried, and the nose was reconfigured with up to six cameras. (The F8U-1 fighter carried 1,273 gallons (4,819 liters), compared to 1,497 gallons (5,667 liters) in the F8U-1P, that is, a 15 percent increase.)

The types and arrangement of cameras periodically were changed, with four cameras fitted in the forward fuselage. The cameras were controlled by an electronic arrangement that enabled the pilot to manually take photos or to use an automatic mode in which he would dial in the plane's speed and altitude.

The important role of the aircraft was recognized when 73 RF-8As were upgraded to permit continued service with the designation RF-8G.

OPERATIONS

The speed and range of the F8U-1P was demonstrated in July 1957 when marine Maj. John H. Glenn piloted an F8U-1P from California to New York in 3 hours, 28 minutes, 50 seconds, for an average speed of 723.517 miles per hour (1,164.39 kilometers per hour), a cross-continent record. On three occasions, Major Glenn had to descend from his optimum altitude and slow to 350 miles per hour (563 kilometers per hour) to fuel from AJ-2 Savage tankers, but he still maintained an average speed of Mach 1.1 for the flight. (Glenn subsequently became the first American astronaut to orbit the earth and later served as a US senator.)

The Photo Crusader entered combat in October 1962 during the Cuban Missile Crisis. While the high-flying U-2 spyplanes had provided the first photographs of the Soviet weapons buildup on the Caribbean island, the Kennedy administration needed low-level, detailed photos of the sites. Six navy F8U-1P photo planes, flying from Key West, Florida, undertook the first US low-level overflights of Cuba on 23 October 1962, under Operation Blue Moon. As they began their photo runs over Cuba, the planes flew at speeds 400 miles per hour (644 kilometers per hour) at altitudes of a few hundred feet.

Led by Cmdr. William B. Ecker, commanding officer of photo squadron VFP-62, navy and marine pilots flew 80 low-level sorties during the crisis, providing

Chance Vought RF-8. *National Archives and Records Administration*

CHANCE VOUGHT RF-8A

CREW:	1
ENGINES:	1x Pratt & Whitney J57-P-4 turbojet with afterburning; 10,200 lbst (4,627 kgst) each
WEIGHTS:	Empty: 16,796 lb (7,619 kg)
	Combat: 23,752 lb (10,774 kg)
	Maximum: 27,822 lb (12,620 kg)
LENGTH:	54 ft 6 in (16.6 m)
WINGSPAN:	35 ft 8 in (10.9 m)
HEIGHT:	15 ft 9 in (4.8 m)
SPEEDS:	Maximum: 983 mph (1,582 kph) at 35,000 feet; 730 mph (1,175 kph) at sea level
	Cruise: 569 mph (916 kph)
CEILING:	42,350 ft (12,912 m)
RANGE:	2,000 miles (3,219 km)
ARMAMENT:	None
RADAR:	None

the Pathet Lao by China or the Soviet Union, fired at the aircraft. One of these first recon flights, flown by Lt. Charles F. Klusmann on 21 May, was struck by ground fire. The Crusader burned in the air for 20 minutes en route back to the *Kitty Hawk*, nevertheless landing safely aboard the ship. On 6 June, ground fire again struck Lieutenant Klusmann's plane over Laos. This time, the damage was severe and he ejected, parachuting safely to the ground. Nearby communist troops captured Klusmann, but almost three months later he escaped his captors and reached safety.

Immediately after the Gulf of Tonkin incident in August 1964, carrier-based navy and marine Photo Crusaders overflew Southeast Asia. These missions brought back photos of Viet Cong and North Vietnamese troop and supply movements, identified potential targets, and conducted post-strike reconnaissance. On 5 April 1965, an RF-8A from the *Coral Sea* brought back photographs of the first positively identified SA-2 Guideline surface-to-air missile (SAM) site. Discovery of the SA-2 site, 15 miles (24 kilometers) southeast of Hanoi, was of major significance for the air war over North Vietnam.

The Photo Crusaders flew throughout the Vietnam conflict. Twenty were lost to enemy antiaircraft fire; none were lost to missiles or MiG fighters.

detailed intelligence on the Soviet activities in Cuba. The F8U-1Ps were joined from 26 October by air force RF-101 Voodoo photo planes. The low-level missions also had a harassment value, as Soviet officials could have no doubt that the Americans knew precisely what was happening, and that the photo planes would likely be followed by strike aircraft. Neither Soviet nor Cuban weapons were fired at Commander Ecker's planes.

The VFP-62's accomplishments were recognized when President Kennedy personally awarded the squadron the first peacetime Navy Unit Citation. Additionally, 12 navy and 4 marine pilots were awarded the Distinguished Flying Cross for the Blue Moon missions.

During the early 1960s, US warships patrolled off South Vietnam, with carrier-based Photo Crusaders performing regular reconnaissance overflights of the area. During late May 1964, the attack carrier *Kitty Hawk* (CVA 63), steaming in the South China Sea off the coast of Vietnam, launched recon missions over Pathet Lao territory in an effort to aid the Laotian Neutralist regime. The RF-8A Crusaders crisscrossed the communist-held areas. Occasionally, light antiaircraft guns, provided to

STATUS

Retired. The XF8U-1 first flew on 25 March 1955, exceeding Mach 1 on its first flight. A production F8U-1 later set an international speed record of 1,015.428 miles per hour (1,634.17 kilometers per hour).

The F8U-1 began entering navy and marine fighter squadrons in 1957. The US Navy procured 1,072 F8U fighters in addition to 2 XF8U-1 prototypes. Another 42 F-8E Crusaders were produced for the French Navy for operation from their carriers *Clemenceau* and *Foch*. The French aircraft were retired in 1999.

The first flight of the YF8U-1P occurred on 17 December 1956. One hundred forty-four F8U-1P aircraft were built, with 73 upgraded to the RF-8G configuration. Photo Crusaders were in service with active navy and Marine Corps photo and utility squadrons from 1957 to 1976. Reserve navy photo squadrons flew the RF-8G variant until 1986. Their last carrier deployment of Photo Crusaders was on board the *Coral Sea* (CV 43), ending in June 1980. ∎

—*Norman Polmar and John F. Bessette*

LOCKHEED CL-282

Lockheed's CL-282 was an unproduced design for a high-altitude reconnaissance aircraft that grew out of Lockheed's famed Skunk Works designer Clarence "Kelly" Johnson's study on how to modify the company's F-104 Starfighter to serve as an extremely high-altitude intelligence-gathering platform. In March 1954, Johnson sent his ideas to the USAF, which responded by asking for a specific proposal. At that time, the CL-282 was to be based on the fuselage of the F-104, with a long, high-aspect-ratio wing like a sailplane and, to save weight, no landing gear.

DESIGN

Lockheed formally submitted their proposal in April 1954, but the command of the Strategic Air Command at the time, the legendary General Curtiss LeMay, reportedly dismissed it out of hand, claiming "no interest in a plane with no wheels and with no guns." While the air force wasn't immediately interested, and chose to invest in the RB-57 instead, the Central Intelligence Agency was. Johnson met with CIA Director Allen Dulles, among others, and stunned them with his

Lockheed CL-282

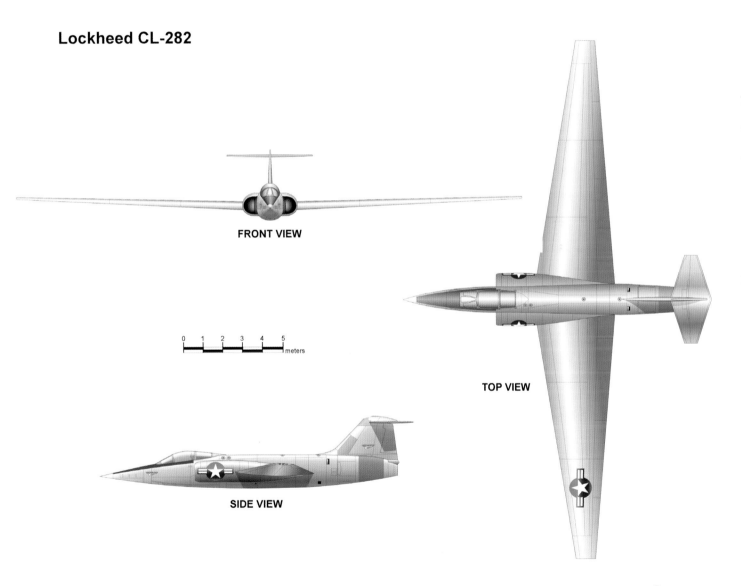

FRONT VIEW

TOP VIEW

SIDE VIEW

G. DE CHIARA ⓒ - 2016

Lockheed CL-282 concept rendering. *Giuseppe de Chiara*

LOCKHEED CL-282 (PLANNED)

CREW:	1
ENGINE:	1x one General Electric J73 turbojet
WEIGHT:	undetermined
LENGTH:	44 ft (13.4 m)
WINGSPAN:	70 ft 8 in (21.5 m)
HEIGHT:	18 ft 4 in (5.6 m)
SPEEDS:	Maximum: Undetermined, planned to be capable of transonic flight for short periods Cruise: 430 mph (690 kph)
CEILING:	70,000+ ft (21,336 m)
RANGE:	1,400 mi (2,253 km)
ARMAMENT:	None

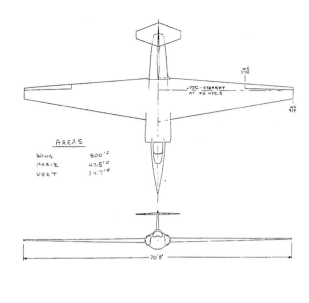

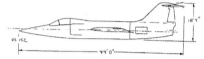

Lockheed CL-282. *Lockheed Martin photo*

promise to build 20 airplanes for around $22 million—and that the first one would fly in just eight months.

The CIA's interest was only emboldened when one of their technological committee members, Edwin Land, best known for inventing the Polaroid instant camera, championed the project. President Eisenhower became a believer, too, and approved the concept in November 1954 as a joint project, known to the CIA as Aquatone and to the USAF as Oilstone. The original idea of basing the new airplane on the F-104 was set aside in short order, and the CL-282 was reborn as a clean-sheet design that would become better known as the Lockheed U-2. ∎

—Hal Bryan

LOCKHEED U-2 DRAGON LADY

Undoubtedly the world's best-known spyplane, the U-2 photo and electronic recon aircraft has been in US service since 1956, continuing in frontline US service into the twenty-first century and outlasting its planned successor, the Lockheed SR-71 Blackbird.

U-2 development began about 1953 as a "black" program with codename Aquatone. It was sponsored by the CIA, with Deputy Director Richard M. Bissell as program manager. Clarence (Kelly) Johnson, the head of the Lockheed "Skunk Works," was the chief designer. President Eisenhower, who personally approved the production of 30 U-2 aircraft, supported the U-2 because of concerns that Soviet strategic nuclear weapon developments could threaten the United States with a surprise attack.

The U-2 was to fly over Soviet territory at altitudes above 60,000 feet (18,288 meters). Essentially a powered glider, it had "such a unique configuration that there was little chance of its being mistaken for a bomber," according to Eisenhower's memoir, *Waging Peace, 1956–1961* (1963).

When the U-2 was built, it was estimated that it would be able to fly over the Soviet Union for two years before the Soviets would detect it and have the capability to shoot it down. Nevertheless, all of the estimated 24 overflights of the Soviet Union between 1956 and 1960 were tracked by Soviet radar.

Then, on 1 May 1960, the U-2B flown by CIA pilot Francis Gary Powers was shot down by a Soviet SA-2 surface-to-air missile near the industrial center

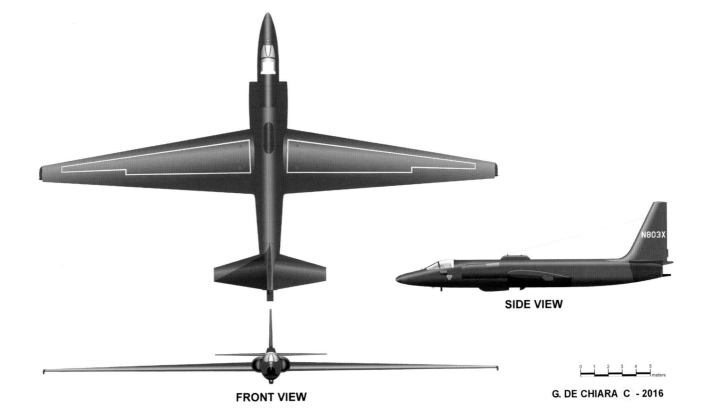

SIDE VIEW

FRONT VIEW

G. DE CHIARA Ⓒ - 2016

Lockheed U-2A concept rendering. *Giuseppe de Chiara*

of Sverdlovsk in central Russia. Powers had taken off from Peshawar, Pakistan, and had intended to cross the Soviet Union and land in Bödo, Norway, in a 9.5-hour flight covering 3,788 miles (6,096 kilometers), of which 2,919 miles (4,698 kilometers) would be over the Soviet Union. Eight or nine SA-2 missiles were fired by the air defense unit commanded by Major M. R. Voronov. The U-2 seems to have suffered an engine problem and, as it lost altitude, it was severely damaged by an SA-2 missile. (One of the other missiles shot down a Soviet MiG-19 that was attempting to intercept the U-2.)

Powers' aircraft was fitted with a plastic explosive linked to a delayed timing switch that he was to initiate prior to ejecting from the aircraft. The explosive was intended to destroy the camera but not the aircraft. Powers was unable to initiate the destruct mechanism,

Lockheed U-2. *National Archives and Records Administration*

U-2S (formerly TR-1A). *Denny Lombard photo, Lockheed Martin*

though he parachuted from the aircraft and was captured upon landing. The wreckage of his crashed U-2 was placed on display in Gorky Park in Moscow, and later moved to a museum.

The Powers incident occurred 15 days before a scheduled summit conference of major world leaders in Paris. As a result, Soviet Premier Nikita Khrushchev demanded an apology at the conference from President Eisenhower, causing the collapse of the conference and a worsening of American-Soviet relations. Following the incident, U-2s were no longer flown over the Soviet Union, but they did continue overflights of other areas of interest to the United States.

The U-2 was flown exclusively by the CIA until the USAF 4080th Strategic Reconnaissance Wing received its first U-2 on 11 June 1957. (The name Dragon Lady was used by the air force, not by the CIA.)

The CIA's U-2 program was terminated on 1 August 1974, after which all U-2/TR-1 aircraft were operated exclusively by the USAF. (The TR-1s were redesignated U-2R or U-2S in 1992.)

The air force has plans to retire its remaining U-2s by 2020.

DESIGN

The U-2 design—a lightweight aircraft that could reach high altitudes while carrying a heavy load of fuel for long-range flights—presented numerous challenges. Thus, the U-2 was in many respects a powered glider. The larger, more capable U-2R variant—referred to as a "big wing" aircraft—was manufactured from the late 1960s.

The early U-2s had a turbojet engine with a maximum speed of 430 miles per hour (692 kilometers per hour); a more powerful engine increased this to 528 miles per hour (850 kilometers per hour) in the later U-2C, while the subsequent U-2R had a top speed of 510 miles per hour (821 kilometers per hour). The U-2's ceiling originally was some 60,000 feet (18,288 meters), and 85,000 feet (25,908 meters) for the U-2C and 90,000 feet (27,432 meters) for the U-2R. The early U-2s had a range of 2,200 miles (3,541 kilometers), extended to 3,000 miles (4,828 kilometers) in the U-2C, and 3,500 miles (5,633 kilometers) in the U-2R. A few U-2C aircraft were fitted for in-flight refueling to extend their range.

The U-2S upgrades of the 1990s provided a lighter engine (General Electric F-118-101) that burned less fuel, increased power, and reduced overall weight. The first U-2S was delivered in October 1994.

Because of the high altitudes flown, the pilot wears a full pressure suit.

The reconnaissance systems were regularly updated; the U-2B of the early 1960s had a camera fitted with a 944.7mm lens that could take 4,000 paired photos of a strip of land 125 miles by 2,174 miles (200 kilometers by 3,500 kilometers). In addition to cameras, the early U-2s had a miniaturized ELINT system, more advanced than any previously built, to collect Soviet radar signals.

At least two U-2R COMINT aircraft were fitted with a large, airfoil-shaped radome on a short dorsal pylon to relay COMINT data by satellite; several U-2s—and the two TR-1B models—had a second pilot position for training.

U-2S (formerly TR-1A). *Denny Lombard photo, Lockheed Martin*

A number of efforts were undertaken to reduce the radar cross section of U-2 aircraft (for example, Project Rainbow), but with limited success.

Several U-2G aircraft were fitted with arresting hooks for carrier operation, with shipboard trials having been conducted as Project Whale Tale. One operational mission was flown from a carrier.

In late 2014, Lockheed Martin proposed an unmanned U-2 variant with greater payload capacity, but the concept was not pursued.

OPERATIONS

The U-2 overflights were initially to be flown from the Royal Air Force base at Lakenheath, England, but because of political problems, the aircraft instead were based at Wiesbaden, near Frankfurt, West Germany. The first operational U-2 mission took place on 20 June 1956, when an aircraft overflew Poland and East Germany.

The first U-2 overflight of the Soviet Union took place on 4 July 1956, with Moscow as the primary target. The second overflight occurred the following day. In 1957, a U-2 was reported to have looked down on the first Soviet intercontinental missile on its launcher at Tyuratam, east of the Aral Sea. The flights over the Soviet Union were piloted by civilian pilots under contract to the CIA, actually on loan ("sheep-dipped") from the air force.

To get U-2 bases closer to their targets, the "European" U-2s were based at Incirlik Air Base near Adana, Turkey, with some of their flights taking off from remote airfields in Pakistan.

The last U-2 flight over the Soviet Union occurred on 1 May 1960, when Powers's aircraft was shot down.

British pilots also trained to fly the U-2, and in 1958 President Eisenhower persuaded Prime Minister Harold Macmillan to have RAF pilots overfly the Soviet Union. Operating out of Adana, Turkey, RAF pilots in late 1959 and early 1960 flew two highly successful missions over Soviet missile test facilities. RAF pilots also flew high-altitude weather missions over Britain as part of their cover story.

Most RAF U-2 missions were over the Middle East, however, where British pilots flew 27 missions in the two years that they participated.

U-2s were also flown extensively over Cuba, with the first flight, personally authorized by President Eisenhower, made on 27 October 1960, by a CIA aircraft. On the night of 13–14 October 1962, air force pilots began making the Cuba overflights. The U-2s revealed the buildup of Soviet weapons on the Caribbean island, precipitating the Cuban Missile Crisis.

On 27 October 1962, a U-2 piloted by air force Maj. Rudolf Anderson Jr. was shot down over Cuba by a Soviet SA-2 surface-to-air missile, killing Anderson.

U-2 FOLLOW-ON

In 2015 the Lockheed Martin "Skunk Works"—which designed and developed the U-2—proposed a spyplane that the firm labeled the UQ-2 or RQ-X. This proposal came more than six decades after the debut of the U-2, which continued in US service as this volume went to press.

The proposed aircraft would carry many of the same sensors as the U-2, with the same F118 engine, and would operate at 70,000 feet (21,336 meters) or higher. The new plane would feature a new, low-observable body design and have increased endurance.

Although the air force had not requested a follow-on design for the U-2, the program manager at the Skunk Works, Melani Austin, said that she sees a future need for such capabilities and that Skunk Works would be remiss not to have something in development. "With funding and a clear and stable environment, Skunk Works could again rapidly deliver a next-generation aircraft with far more capability than either the U-2 or Global Hawk," she said.

—*Norman Polmar and John F. Bessette*

Far Eastern U-2 operations initially were flown from the US air base at Atsugi, Japan. U-2 flights over China flown by Nationalist pilots from Taiwan began on 13 January 1962, with 101 more flights occurring over the next six and a half years.

The first Taiwanese U-2 loss occurred in September 1962, and China eventually claimed to have shot down a total of nine Taiwanese U-2s during the 1960s. While four have been confirmed by western sources, only seven U-2s were transferred to Taiwan.

Other unusual U-2 missions included spy flights over China made by US pilots flying from India, in 1962, when, following another Chinese-Indian clash, the Delhi government turned to the West for military assistance (while continuing to procure arms from the Soviet Union). After lengthy negotiations, in early 1964 the Indian government agreed to the CIA using the Charbatia Air Base near Cuttack, on the eastern coast of India. A single U-2 made two or three overflights of China and Tibet—the first in May 1964 and the last probably in December 1964—shortly after the first Chinese nuclear test at Lop Nor. Intelligence about Chinese military forces in the border region was shared with the Indian government in this highly secret operation.

The last U-2 flight over China was made in June 1974.

Meanwhile, Middle East operations, primarily over Israel and Egypt, flew from West Germany, the RAF

	LOCKHEED U-2	LOCKHEED U-2R
CREW:	1	1
ENGINE:	1x Pratt & Whitney J57-P-37 turbojet; 10,200 lbst (4,627 kgst)	1x Pratt & Whitney J75-P-13B turbojet; 17,000 lbst (7,711 kgst)
WEIGHT:	24,150 lb (10,954 kg)	40,000 lb (18,144 kg)
LENGTH:	49 ft 8.5 in (15.1 m)	63–69 ft* (19.2–21 m)
WINGSPAN:	80 ft 2 in (24.4 m)	103 ft (31.4 m)
HEIGHT:	15 ft 2 in (4.6 m)	16 ft (4.9 m)
SPEED:	430+ mph (692+ kph)	470+ mph (756+ kph)
CEILING:	72,000 ft (21,951 m)	74,000 ft (22,561 m)
RANGE:	2,950 mi (4,747 km)	3,000 mi (4,828 km)
ARMAMENT:	None	None
RADAR:	None	None

*Varies with sensor package installed.

base on Cyprus, and from Adana, Turkey. The first such flight, taking off from Wiesbaden, was on 29 August 1956, during the Suez crisis. More flights followed during the 1956 crisis.

Following the 1973 Yom Kippur War, by agreement with both Israel and Egypt, USAF U-2s flying from Cyprus carried out truce verification missions over the Sinai Peninsula and the Suez Canal, an operation that has continued into the twenty-first century.

During the Gulf War of 1991, U-2s were flown in Saudi Arabian airspace to provide real-time intelligence on Iraq. The U-2s subsequently monitored the "no-fly zones" of Iraq, briefly flew over Iraq under the aegis of the United Nations to seek out illegal weapons; they provided valuable intelligence again in the Gulf War of 2003.

U-2s were first assigned to the air force in June 1957; from 1974, all strategic recon U-2s were assigned to the air force. The 9th Strategic Reconnaissance Wing at Beale AFB, California, took over U-2 operations.

One CIA-piloted mission took off from the US aircraft carrier *Ranger* (CVA 61) in the mid-Pacific in May 1964. That U-2G successfully photographed the island of Mururoa, part of French Polynesia, to spy on French atomic bomb tests being conducted there.

The navy flew two U-2R variants with special radar to evaluate an ocean surveillance role (designated EP-X), but the program was cancelled.

In 1981, NASA began flying two ER-2s (Earth Resources) survey missions. On 27 January 2000, an ER-2 entered Russian airspace with Russian government permission as part of a multinational ozone research project. NASA participation in the project also included a modified DC-8 transport and balloons carrying research instrumentation.

Once the existence of the U-2 was revealed to the public, the aircraft established several world records. In the 1980s, Lockheed pilots flying a U-2C on loan to NASA from the air force since 1971, set 15 altitude and time-to-climb records. Among these was a horizontal flight altitude of 73,700 feet (22,464 meters).

STATUS

Operational. The prototype U-2 flew for the first time on 1 August 1955. The U-2R first flew in 1967 and the TR-1A in 1981.

Forty-nine aircraft of the basic U-2 series were built from 1955 to 1969. These were periodically modified and updated before the last was retired in 1989. Six U-2D variants were produced from spare parts ordered to support these aircraft.

The 47 "big-wing" U-2R and TR-1 aircraft were delivered from 1979 to 1989. The TR-1, similar to the U-2R, was developed to provide surveillance over European battlefields. NASA received two similar ER-2 variants. NASA also flew several earlier U-2s.

A total of 104 U-2s were produced:

20	U-2
29	U-2A
6	U-2D
20	U-2R (most to U-2S; 2 to Navy EP-X)
25	TR-1A (later U-2R/S)
2	TR-2B (later U-2R/S)
2	ER-2 (NASA)

In 2016, the USAF had 27 operational U-2s in its inventory. ∎

—*Norman Polmar and John F. Bessette*

BOEING EC-135/RC-135 STRATOTANKER

A chameleon in its wide variety of configurations and missions, the RC-135 followed in the tradition of the RB-50 and its successor, the B-47, as big aircraft converted from their primary missions for global eavesdropping.

In its search for a new jet tanker/transport suited to the rigors of the Cold War, the air force selected the Boeing Model 367-80 prototype (similar to the 707 airliner, but smaller in size, weight, and fuselage diameter). Designated the KC-135A, it made its maiden flight in August 1956 and entered the air force inventory in June 1957. On its upper deck, it offered long-range transportation to 80 passengers, 25 tons of cargo, or a combination of the two. Below deck, it satisfied the tanker role by carrying refueling equipment, including the rigid, pivoting flying boom, later modified with trailing drogues for modern tactical aircraft. Subsequent models differentiated the cargo from the tanker roles, reflected in their names: the C-135 Stratolifter had no refueling apparatus, but carried up to 126 troops (or 44 stretchers and 54 seats for the wounded); while the

Boeing RC-135. *US Air Force photo*

BOEING RC-135V

CREW:	26 (2 pilots, 2 navigators, 22 equipment operators)
ENGINES:	4x Pratt & Whitney TF33-P-9 non-afterburning turbofans; 18,000 lbst (8,165 kgst) each
WEIGHTS:	Empty: 102,300 lb (46,403 kg)
	Combat: 299,000 lb (135,626 kg)
	Maximum: 322,500 lb (146,000 kg)
LENGTH:	140 ft 6 in (42.8 m)
WINGSPAN:	130 ft 10 in (39.9 m)
HEIGHT:	41 ft 8 in (12.7 m)
SPEEDS:	Maximum: 600 mph (966 kph)
	Cruise: 532 mph (856 kph)
CEILING:	40,600 ft (12,375 m)
RANGE:	5,655 mi (9,100 km)
	Combat radius 2,675 mi (4,305 km)
ARMAMENT:	None
RADAR:	Advanced array inside nose radome for surveillance; side-looking airborne radar array (SLAR); long range air-to-navigation (LORAN)

KC-135 Stratotanker concentrated solely on refueling. Additionally, many models underwent structural strengthening and engine replacement for higher thrust and improved fuel economy.

Rather than ordering the immense production run of 820 KC/C-135s in big batches, the air force chose to buy many small blocks of specialized models from the Boeing factories and also authorized conversions of existing aircraft to satisfy new missions. Consequently, at least 34 KC/C-135 variants have flown. Among these, 12 have been dedicated to reconnaissance. Designated the RC-135, they initially bore the nickname "Ferret" due to their ability to "sniff" hostile activities.

DESIGN

Spacious, stable, and capable of tremendous range, the KC/C-135s and RC-135s all benefited from the same basic platform. Although the exteriors of the C-135B and the RC-135 looked almost alike (barring the RC-135S, V, and W's elongated, thimble noses and the RC-135U, V, and W's prominent cheek fairings), the insides differed strikingly. The RC-135 cockpit featured four seats: two for the pilots and two for navigators who made clear the boundaries of enemy airspace. Crews could be accommodated in bunks at the back of the cabin (aerial refueling enabled the RC-135s to stay aloft for extended periods as they conducted missions far inside the borders of hostile powers).

Each RC-135 variant had an interior at least somewhat distinct from all others, suited specifically for the types of reconnaissance that it pursued. In general, though, highly sensitive electronics equipment sat up on racks at the front, while in the rear operators worked at their stations. Signals intelligence (SIGINT) variants of the RC-135s accommodated seven technicians on the starboard side and special equipment on the port side. Aircraft designed to gather COMINT carried foreign-language experts capable of eavesdropping on enemy communications and also sending false ones. And radiation intelligence (RINT) equipment picked up signals from dormant radar, power lines, and engine ignitions.

OPERATIONS

Originally, ten RC-135s entered air force service during the 1960s with SAC's 55th Strategic Reconnaissance Wing. Until 1992, these and all subsequent RC-135s saw action under SAC, but in that year the 55th migrated to Air Combat Command (ACC) at Offutt AFB, Nebraska, with forward operating locations around the world. In total, ACC fielded 22 aircraft in three versions: RC-135S (codename Cobra Ball), RC-135U (Combat Sent), and RC-135V/W (Rivet Joint).

RC-135s have the distinction of serving in nearly every US armed conflict that has arisen during its long service life, including the Vietnam War, Grenada, Panama, the Balkans, the Gulf War, and the Iraq War.

Boeing RC-135W interior. *Department of Defense photo*

Moreover, RC-135s flew missions on the borders of Russia, around the Middle East, and in association with the War on Terrorism.

STATUS

Operational. Active in the 55th Wing, Air Combat Command. ■

—*Michael Gorn*

CONVAIR RB-58 HUSTLER

Convair's B-58 was the US Air Force's first supersonic strategic bomber, forming one leg of America's nuclear deterrent strategy triad—bombers, submarine-launched ballistic missiles, and intercontinental ballistic missiles (ICBMs). Although the B-58 "Hustler" was not capable of extended-duration missions like the B-52, it was designed to fly to its target supersonically, drop its ordnance, then exit the target area at supersonic speeds.

The Hustler's four General Electric J-79-GE-5A turbojets consumed a large amount of fuel, a commodity the aircraft was not designed to carry. Convair's solution was to transport the required fuel and ordnance in a two-piece strike pod suspended under the fuselage;

the lower section contained fuel and was dropped when empty as the bomber flew to the target, while the top half contained ordnance. In the reconnaissance role, the pod was modified with forward-facing cameras and side-looking sensors.

DESIGN

Incorporating data from the National Advisory Council on Aeronautics (NACA) and captured reports of swept- and delta-wing research from Nazi Germany, Convair engineers designed the B-58 medium-range bomber. Using a 60-degree delta wing with four, pod-mounted General Electric J79-5A engines, the B-58

Convair RB-58. *National Archives and Records Administration*

CONVAIR RB-58

CREW:	3 (pilot, bombardier/navigator, defensive systems/electronic countermeasures operator)
ENGINES:	4x General Electric J-79-GE-5A turbojets; 15,600 lbst (7,076 kgst) each; 10,400 lbst (4,717 kgst) each in afterburner
WEIGHTS:	Empty: 55,550 lb (25,197 kg) Maximum: 163,000 lb (73,936 kg)
LENGTH:	96 ft 9 in (29.5 m)
WINGSPAN:	56 ft 10 in (17.3 m)
HEIGHT:	31 ft 5 in (9.6 m)
SPEED:	1,321 mph (2,126 kph) at 63,150 ft (19,248 m)
CEILING:	63,150 ft (19,248 m)
RANGE:	Combat radius 1,750 mi (2,816 km), extendable with aerial refueling
ARMAMENT:	1x General Electric T-171E3 Vulcan 20mm tail cannon
RADAR:	Hughes AN/APQ-69 side-looking; Goodyear AN/APS-73 synthetic aperture

was capable of sustained speeds at Mach 2.0 or greater. The type made its first flight on 11 November 1956.

The air force ordered 30 preproduction test aircraft: 2 XB-58A prototypes and 28 YB-58A-CFs (Convair, Fort Worth), of which the final 17 YB-58As were delivered as RB-58As (58-1007 to -1023). In 1963, an additional 28 B-58As were given the capability to carry the Main Line I reconnaissance pod. In total, 45 aircraft were modified to use these photographic reconnaissance pods by installing the system's operating avionics into the defensive systems/electronic countermeasures operator's cockpit and installing fuselage connections for the pod. All told, Convair built 116 B-58s.

OPERATIONS

Under Project Quick Check, B-58A serial number 55-0668 was fitted with a special MB-1 pod that carried a Raytheon-built, forward-looking radar and a Goodyear AN/APS-73 synthetic aperture radar. Using the Quick Check pod, 55-0668 flew a reconnaissance mission over Cuba during the Cuban Missile Crisis in October 1962. This was the B-58's only operational mission overflying hostile territory.

The Quick Check pod modifications led to the Main Line I and II photo-reconnaissance pods. Main Line I saw the installation of Fairchild KA-56 low-level panoramic cameras for high-speed (Mach 0.92), low-level (300 to 500 feet altitude; 90 to 150 meters) reconnaissance flights. MB-1C pods modified for the KA-56 camera installation were redesignated LA-331 pods. The pods also carried Hughes AN/APQ-69 side-looking radar or Goodyear

AN/APS-73 synthetic aperture radar in addition to the film camera. Ten pods were modified into this configuration and 45 aircraft were configured to fly with the LA-331 pods. Main Line II was slated to serve as an upgrade to the LA-331 pods, but only one pod was configured with new cameras and electronics. LA-331 pods were used by SAC B-58s to photograph the devastation left in the wake of the 9.2-magnitude Anchorage, Alaska, earthquake that occurred on 27 March 1964.

STATUS

Retired. The B-58 fleet was retired in January 1970, after only ten years of service. The majority were delivered to the Military Aircraft Storage and Disposal Center (MASDC) at Davis-Monthan AFB, Tucson, Arizona, and subsequently scrapped. Today, only eight examples of America's first supersonic bomber remain. ■

—*Nicholas A. Veronico*

MCDONNELL DOUGLAS F4H-1P/RF-4 PHANTOM

At times, one military service will observe the capabilities of an aircraft in a sister service and adapt it to its own needs. The famous F-4 Phantom began not with the air force but rather as a long-range, all-weather, fleet air defense fighter, purchased by the navy from McDonnell Aircraft in October 1954. With its projected mission changed to attack fighter, it had its maiden prototype flight in May 1958 and, in December 1960, it entered operational service as the navy F4H-1 Phantom II. But air force officials jumped at the chance to procure some when they saw ground trials that proved the Phantom's ability to detect and destroy targets within radar range *without the assistance of ground radar*. Despite a tradition that put the purchase of navy planes off-limits, USAF officials placed an

order for aircraft known in air force parlance as the F-4C Phantom.

Impressed by the F-4's performance, the air force further realized its potential as a replacement for the aging RF-101 Voodoo for tactical reconnaissance. Accordingly, the prototype YRF-4C made its initial flight in August 1963, followed by the RF-4C's first production flight in May 1964. Once begun, the assembly lines stayed open for nine and a half years, by the end of which 505 RF-4Cs had been built.

DESIGN

Since 1960, no jet aircraft built outside of Russia has been fabricated in numbers to rival those of the F-4. In all, 5,195 had been constructed when manufacturing

McDonnell Douglas RF-4C. *National Archives and Records Administration*

MCDONNELL DOUGLAS RF-4E

CREW:	2
ENGINES:	2x General Electric J79-GE-17 turbojets; 17,900 lbst (8119 kgst) each
WEIGHTS:	Empty: 31,110 lb (14,111 kg) Maximum: 52,836 lb (23,966 kg)
LENGTH:	63 ft (19.2 m)
WINGSPAN:	38 ft 5 in (11.7 m)
HEIGHT:	16 ft 6 in (5.0 m)
SPEEDS:	Maximum: 898 mph (1,445 kph) at sea level Cruise: 585 mph (940 kph)
CEILING:	62,250 ft (18,975 m)
RANGE:	1,885 mi (3,034 km) Combat radius 711 mi (1,145 km)
ARMAMENT:	None
RADAR:	APQ-102 side-looking and APQ-99 forward-looking

stopped in 1979. That number reflects the high value placed on the F-4's design and engineering. Its semi-monocoque fuselage had three parts: forward, center, and aft sections, with the keel and rear fabricated extensively from steel and titanium. The cantilever wings, mounted low on the fuselage, had a 45-degree sweepback. Its powerplant consisted of two General Electric J79 engines, each rated at 17,900 pounds of thrust (8,119 kilograms static thrust), with inlet ducts monitored by an air data computer.

Although similar in overall structure to the standard F-4, the RF-4 aircraft differed significantly in its internal placements. The US versions—as opposed to those flown by many foreign governments—carried no conventional armament; and, aside from the ability to deliver nuclear weapons, the RF-4 had the sole role of conducting reconnaissance in support of air and ground forces. To accomplish this mission, engineers at Holloman Air Force Base tested different sensor configurations during 1964, eventually arriving at the RF-4's package. To adapt it to the F-4's airframe, McDonnell technicians

lengthened its nose by almost three feet and, where the guns had been, they installed a number of new features. These included forward- and side-looking radar, which provided high-definition film images on both sides of the flight path; an infrared detector to spot enemy forces day or night by registering exhaust gases and heat sources; and photographic equipment, including forward- and side-looking KS-87 cameras and panoramic KA-55 and KA-56 models equipped with moving lens elements capable of capturing horizon-to-horizon vistas. The weapons systems operator in the rear cockpit controlled all of these devices in flight.

OPERATIONS

Tactical Air Command's 33rd Tactical Reconnaissance Training Squadron took possession of the initial production RF-4Cs in September 1964, followed in August 1965 by the 16th Tactical Reconnaissance Squadron, which became the first unit to prepare it for wartime conditions. The combat opportunity presented itself just two months later, when the RF-4Cs joined the fight in Southeast Asia. By the end of 1965, 20 had been dispatched to Tan Son Nhut Air Base in the Republic of Vietnam. During these forays, as in others, the RF-4s and their crews from broad aerial surveillance to concentrate on pinpoint targets—bridges, airfields, massed vehicles, gun emplacements, and so on—captured as the planes dashed overhead at high speeds and low altitudes.

By October 1967, about 100 RF-4Cs had been sent to Pacific Air Forces Command for service in four squadrons supporting operations in South Vietnam from Tan Son Nhut and in Thailand from Udorn Air Base. Eventually, a total of 84 RF-4Cs went down in Southeast Asia.

The RF-4C also saw action with the US Air Forces in Europe Command, including a wing at RAF Alconbury and a squadron at Ramstein Air Base. Additionally, the Marine Corps contracted with McDonnell for 56 RF-4Bs, the first of which saw action at Da Nang, South Vietnam.

STATUS

Retired. They remained active during Operation Desert Shield/Storm. The Alabama Air National Guard cleared the last operational RF-4C from its inventory in 1994. ■

—*Michael Gorn*

North American RA-5C. *US Navy photo*

NORTH AMERICAN A3J-3P/RA-5C VIGILANTE

The Vigilante was developed as a supersonic (Mach 2+), carrier-based, all-weather nuclear strike aircraft, the nominal successor to the A3D/A-3 Skywarrior. However, soon after entry into service as attack aircraft, all Vigilantes were converted for combination reconnaissance-strike roles (although subsequently employed only as recce aircraft). Significantly, the Vigilante was retired more than a decade before the Skywarrior, the aircraft that it was intended to replace.

The Vigilante flew in the heavy attack role from 1961 to 1964, and in the reconnaissance role from 1963 to 1979.

A high-performance interceptor variant for land-based operation by the air force was considered from 1959 onward; that proposal included a liquid-fuel rocket

North American A3J-3P. *US Navy photo*

installed in the weapons bay to boost high-altitude performance. Later, a variant with three turbojet engines was proposed. These air-defense concepts were not pursued.

On 1 October 1962, the Vigilante's designation was changed from the A3J series to A-5.

DESIGN

The Vigilante was a swept-wing aircraft, with a mid-fuselage wing mounted above distinctive, square air intakes for the aircraft's twin turbojet engines. The engines were housed in large nacelles that extended to the tail of the aircraft; they were fitted with variable-geometry intakes, the first such feature on a production aircraft.

The attack aircraft had a unique, tunnel-like, linear weapons bay in the fuselage (between the engine nacelles); payloads were ejected rearward. The nuclear bomb was fitted in a spherical container that was rigidly linked to a pair of 275-gallon (1,041-liter) fuel tanks, with all three being ejected from the rear of the aircraft over the target area.

Weapons (including nuclear) and fuel tanks also could be carried on two or—in later aircraft—four wing pylons, each of which had a 2,500-pound (1,134-kilogram) capacity. The pylons could carry conventional or nuclear bombs, or four 400-gallon (1,514-liter) fuel tanks. The Vigilante's wings and tailfin folded for carrier stowage.

RECON VARIANT

The recon variant, RA-5C, was fitted with three fixed tanks in the weapons bay, containing 885 gallons (3,350 liters); an ECM package could be fitted in place of one of these tanks. A sensor "canoe" installed under the fuselage contained five cameras, side-looking aircraft radar (SLAR), infrared mapping, and passive ECM. Pods containing chaff and strobe flashers, as well as fuel tanks (or weapons), could be carried on the wing pylons. No guns were fitted.

All reconnaissance information collected by an RA-5C was instantaneously recorded on magnetic tape which, together with exposed photographic films, was fed into the carrier's Integrated Operational Intelligence Center (IOIC) as soon as the plane landed aboard ship. The IOIC rapidly processed the large amount of data obtained by the aircraft and then produced integrated presentations for the force commander and his staff.

NORTH AMERICAN A3J-3P/RA-5C

CREW:	2 (pilot, bombardier-navigator)
ENGINES:	2x General Electric J79-GE-8 turbojet with afterburners; 17,000 lbst (7,711 kgst) each
WEIGHTS:	Empty: 37,498 lb (17,009 kg)
	Combat: 55,617 lb (25,228 kg)
	Maximum: 79,588 lb (36,091 kg)
LENGTH:	76 ft 6 in (23.3 m)
WINGSPAN:	53 ft (16.2 m)
HEIGHT:	19 ft 4 in (5.9 m)
SPEED:	Maximum: 1,319 mph (2,123 kph) at 40,000 ft (12,195 m)
	Cruise: 573 mph (922 kph)
CEILING:	47,700 ft (14,543 m)
RANGE:	3,029 mi (4,875 km) high-altitude mission
	2,776 mi (4,467 km) hi-lo-hi mission
ARMAMENT:	4x nuclear bombs (Mark 28, Mark 43) or 4x 2,000 pound (907 kg) bombs
RADAR:	AN/ASB-12 inertial bomb/nav

The first IOIC became operational in the carrier *Saratoga* (CVA 60) in November 1962, with a total of nine carriers fitted with an IOIC.

OPERATIONS

The aircraft's large size and high landing speed, and the need for a sophisticated shipboard intelligence center, restricted it to larger US carriers of the *Forrestal* (CVA 59) and later classes. (Significantly, the heavier A3D/ A-3 Skywarrior could operate from smaller carriers.)

The Vigilante established several performance records, perhaps the most impressive being a world altitude mark for aircraft carrying a 2,204-pound (1,000-kilogram) payload, reaching 91,450.8 feet (27,874.2 meters) on 13 December 1960. The previous record was 67,096 feet (20,451 meters) set by a Soviet aircraft.

A small number of RA-5C recon flights were made over Cuba in 1963 and 1964.

Arriving off Vietnam in August 1964, the carrier *Ranger* (CVA 61) brought the navy's first reconnaissance heavy attack squadron—RVAH-5—to the conflict with six RA-5C Vigilante aircraft. During the conflict the aircraft flew pre-strike, post-strike, reconnaissance, and aerial mapping sorties. During early deployments, the aircraft's systems were difficult to maintain.

The RA-5C suffered the highest loss rate of any type of navy aircraft in the Vietnam War. The navy's last aircraft loss of the conflict was on 28 December 1972, when an RA-5C from the carrier *Enterprise* (CVAN 65) was shot down by a North Vietnamese MiG-21 firing an Atoll air-to-air missile. The navy pilot ejected and became a prisoner; the naval flight officer died in the shootdown. (North Vietnamese records do not show an RA-5C shot down by a MiG on that date.)

This also was the last of 18 RA-5C Vigilantes lost in the Vietnam conflict: 11 were downed by antiaircraft fire, 2 by SA-2 missiles, 1 by a MiG-21, and 4 lost due to unknown causes—probably gunfire or SA-2 missiles. Another five Vigilantes were lost in accidents during the conflict.

STATUS

Retired. First flight YA3J-1 on 31 August 1958; squadron delivery of the A3J-1 began in June 1961. First flight RA-5C on 30 June 1962. The RA-5C became operational in June 1963.

One hundred fifty-six Vigilantes were produced, a relatively small number for a significant US naval aircraft. The last aircraft was delivered in November 1970. Vigilante production consisted of:

2 YA3J-1 prototypes

47 A3J-1 attack aircraft (later A-5A)

6 A3J-2 attack aircraft (later A-5B)

91 A3J-3P reconnaissance aircraft (later RA-5C)

In addition to the new-build reconnaissance aircraft, starting in 1964, North American converted 1 prototype, 45 A3J-1, and 6 A3J-2 aircraft to the RA-5C configuration, for a total of 143 RA-5Cs.

The last RA-5C was retired from the fleet in November 1979. ■

—*Norman Polmar and John F. Bessette*

LOCKHEED EP-3 ORION

The Orion has been the principal maritime patrol and anti-submarine aircraft of the US Navy and 17 other navies and air forces since the mid-1960s. The Harpoon missile and other weapons can provide the Orion with antiship capability.

The US Navy and Japan Maritime Self-Defense Force (JMSDF) have modified Orions for intelligence collection roles. The Orion also has been flown as a research platform for various reconnaissance systems and in a number of other research roles, including as an Airborne Early Warning (AEW) platform. During the US wars in Iraq and Afghanistan beginning in 1991, the basic P-3, as well as recon-configured aircraft, were widely employed over land as communications and intelligence collection aircraft. It also has been flown by the US Customs Border Patrol for antidrug and immigrant surveillance,

and by the Commerce Department and National Oceanics and Atmospheric Administration.

The Orion succeeded the Lockheed P2V/P-2 Neptune in the maritime patrol role. The Boeing P-8 Orion is replacing Neptune in the maritime patrol role in the US Navy and several foreign services.

The Orion as developed as the P3V and changed to the P-3 on 1 October 1962.

DESIGN

The basic Orion design was adapted from the commercial Electra transport with a lengthened fuselage, internal weapons bay, and many other design modifications. A straightforward, low-wing design, the Orion is powered by four turboprop engines. The fuselage was lengthened, provided with a radome

Lockheed EP-3E. *National Archives and Records Administration*

nose, an internal weapons bay, and a distractive MAD "stinger" in the tail.

Up to 15,000 pounds (6,804 kilograms) of rockets, missiles, mines, anti-submarine torpedoes, or nuclear depth bombs can be carried in the internal weapons bay and on ten wing pylons. The US P-3C aircraft are fitted to carry the Harpoon, SLAM-ER, and Maverick air-to-surface missiles. (In the early 1970s, some P-3B/C variants were fitted to carry the Bullpup missile.) The basic aircraft also has 48 external (fuselage) sonobuoy chutes, plus 4 in-flight reloadable (internal) chutes; a total of 84 buoys are normally carried. No defensive gun armament was provided in any variant, although Sidewinder air-to-air missiles were tested and installed in three Taiwanese P-3A "black" recon aircraft.

While on patrol, one or two engines can be shut down to increase range and endurance. Patrol missions of ten hours or more are standard. A New Zealand P-3 established a record flight of 21.5 hours.

Numerous mission-enhancing updates have been provided to US and foreign aircraft.

A planned P-3G maritime patrol/anti-submarine warfare aircraft for the US Navy was to have had new engines and updated avionics. That aircraft was incorrectly identified as a P-3F in some official documents; six P-3F variants were produced for Iran. The procurement of 125 P-3G models in fiscal years 1990–1995 was envisioned, although the navy did not pursue the option because only Lockheed responded to the navy's request for a proposal, and the new-design P-7 LRAACA was planned in its place, though never developed.

RECON VARIANTS

There have been several ELINT collection variants and upgrades of the Orion.

Several P-3A aircraft were modified as the EP-3A for electronic research roles, including one for ELINT experiments. Special equipment was installed, with its MAD boom removed.

Two P-3A aircraft were modified as the EP-3B for ELINT collection under the Batrack program, with a variety of electronic equipment installed. A modified tail boom was retained to house electronic equipment. A "canoe" housing was installed atop the fuselage, as was a (smaller) ventral canoe and a retractable radome under the forward fuselage. From June 1969, the aircraft were operated by fleet air reconnaissance

squadron VQ-1, with some missions flown from Da Nang Air Base in South Vietnam. The aircraft were subsequently upgraded to EP-3E standards.

Ten P-3A Orions were modified under the Airborne Reconnaissance Integrated Electronic System (ARIES) program to the EP-3E configuration. These were among the most sophisticated ELINT platforms of the era. The electronic recon/surveillance gears were housed in dorsal and ventral canoes and a modified tail boom.

With the two EP-3B upgrades, these aircraft provided six EP-3Es to each of the navy's ELINT squadrons (VQ-1 in the European-Mediterranean areas, and VQ-2 in the western Pacific). As these 12 aircraft reached the end of their airframe life in the 1990s, they were replaced by 12 P-3C Orions, which were modified to EP-3E standard under the ARIES II program. Subsequently, after the loss of 1 EP-3E in a mishap, 7 more P-3Cs were converted to EP-3Es to provide a stable of 16 aircraft and to ensure a deployable force of 12 aircraft.

SPECIAL PROJECTS

There have been various upgrades of the EP-3E aircraft over the ensuing years. Since about 1967, the navy has maintained two "special projects" patrol squadrons—VPU-1 and VPU-2—which have operated extensively modified Orions on "special projects." The aircraft have been modified with specialized surveillance gear and cameras, and generally fly with fake identification (bureau) numbers and unit markings. By the start of the twenty-first century, each squadron had five modified P-3C aircraft.

There are unconfirmed reports that the squadrons have been consolidated into a single squadron at Kaneohe Bay, Oahu.

ACS AIRCRAFT

The successor to the EP-3E was to be the US Army's Aerial Common Sensor (ACS) aircraft. The Lockheed Martin entry, the Embraer RJ145, was selected and the navy planned to purchase 19 aircraft before the program was cancelled in January 2006 because the airframe was considered inadequate for its requirements. A follow-on navy program—the EPX—was cancelled in February 2010 as too expensive. The follow-on ELINT aircraft probably will be a variant of the Boeing P-8 Poseidon maritime patrol/ASW aircraft.

PROJECT AF

From 1964 to 1967, three P-3A aircraft were operated under a "black" recon project, with the aircraft modified for clandestine operations. They were fitted with special equipment, including SLAR and provisions for Sidewinder air-to-air missiles, and they were painted black. (There had rumors that one of the aircraft shot down a MiG fighter during an operation.)

These aircraft may have operated over China as well as the South China Sea and Southeast Asia, flying mainly from Okinawa. In 1966, two and possibly all three of the aircraft were transferred to Taiwan for operations under the aegis of the CIA.

JAPANESE PROJECTS

Kawasaki modified two Japanese-built P-3C aircraft to EP-3C configurations for evaluation by the JMSDF beginning in 1991. Three additional EP-3 aircraft have been acquired by Japan.

OPERATIONS

During the Cold War, the EP-3E Orions flew reconnaissance flights along the periphery of the Soviet Union, China, North Korea, and other target counties, carefully remaining beyond the 12-mile (19.3-kilometer) territorial limit. They have also been used in counterinsurgency surveillance operations in Colombia and have been used extensively in support of intelligence operations in Afghanistan, Iraq, and Libya.

Periodically, the Orions have been "buzzed" by foreign aircraft. This practice became particularly common off the coast of China in the late 1990s. On 1 April 2001, a pair of Chinese J-8 fighters approached an EP-3E flying off Hainan Island. One fighter veered into the EP-3E, causing a midair collision. Heavily damaged, the fighter fell into the sea, killing its pilot. The EP-3E, also heavily damaged, turned toward Hainan Island. While the technicians hastily destroyed equipment and recordings, the pilots fought to retain control of the aircraft and were able to bring it down at a Chinese airfield.

The 24 US Navy personnel (21 men and 3 women) were detained but treated well by the Chinese; the EP-3E was searched, but not ransacked. After 11 days, the crew was released. Following lengthy negotiations, the United States was allowed to send technicians to Hainan to partially disassemble the aircraft, which was then flown out in a Russian An-124 cargo plane, as the Chinese refused permission for US military aircraft to land on Hainan.

The aircraft was rehabilitated and resumed service on 15 November 2002.

STATUS

Operational. First flights were 19 August 1958 (aerodynamic airframe); 25 November, 1959 (prototype YP-3A); and 15 April 1961 (P-3A). The aircraft has been operational in US patrol squadrons from August 1962.

A total of 624 Orion and foreign Aurora/Arcturus variants were produced in the United States by Lockheed, of which 551 went to the US Navy, with the last a P-3C delivered in April 1990. The last Lockheed California-built aircraft was a CP-140A Arcturus for the Canadian forces, completed in May 1991; eight P-3C aircraft for South Korea were delivered in 1995 by the Lockheed-Martin facility at Marietta, Georgia.

Japan took delivery of three US-built P-3Cs, and Kawasaki in Japan assembled five airframes produced by Lockheed and, under license, built 102 additional aircraft for the JMSDF: 93 P-3C, 5 EP-3, 1 UP-3C, and 3 UP-3D. ∎

—*Norman Polmar and John F. Bessette*

LOCKHEED EP-3E

CREW:	15
ENGINES:	4x Allison T56A14 turboprops; 4,910 hp each
WEIGHTS:	Empty: 61,491 lb (27,892 kg)
	Maximum: 142,000 lb (64,411 kg)
LENGTH:	116 ft 10 in (35.6 m)
WINGSPAN:	99 ft 8 in (30.4 m)
HEIGHT:	33 ft 8.5 in (10.3 m)
SPEEDS:	Maximum: 473 mph (761 kph) at 15,000 ft (4,573 m)
	Cruise: 380 mph (611 kph) at 25,000 ft (7,620 m)
CEILING:	28,300 ft (8,628 m)
RANGE:	1,550 mi (2,493 km) with 13 hours on station
ARMAMENT:	None
RADAR:	AN/APS-115

North American XB-70A. *NASA photo*

NORTH AMERICAN XB-70 VALKYRIE

The North American Aviation–designed and –built XB-70 Valkyrie was, like the Convair B-58 Hustler supersonic bomber, conceived in the early 1950s at a time when US strategy envisioned a fleet of Mach 3+ bombers that could penetrate an enemy's radar and antiaircraft defenses, drop nuclear bombs, then exit the target area at greater than three times the speed of sound and return to base. This strategic bombing concept was viable through the decade of the 1950s and to the middle of the 1960s, when the Soviet Union was seen as America's prime enemy.

Air combat in Vietnam demonstrated the need for a more versatile force, one that could operate trans-sonically, yet have supersonic capabilities. Most of the supersonic aircraft designed for strategic warfare in the mid-1950s were unable to fulfill the needs of a ground force that had to be supported by tactical aircraft.

As the Vietnam War escalated, there was still a need for a strategic deterrent; however, that role was dominated by the US Air Force's fleet of 740 B-52 Stratofortresses. The B-52's domination of the strategic bomber role, coupled with the dramatic improvement of Soviet air defenses in the late 1950s and early 1960s, forced the US Air Force to reevaluate its bomber needs. The threat environment changed as Soviet air defense fighters were improving and its antiaircraft missile technology became a serious threat. Now B-52s would penetrate Soviet airspace flying low, nape-of-the-earth, terrain-following flights and sneaking in under enemy radar.

By the time the six-engine, Mach 3+–capable XB-70 flew for the first time on 21 September 1964, it was an aircraft in search of a mission. The US Air Force had moved away from a supersonic penetrator and its nuclear-capable force had become part of the deterrent triad of bombers, missile-launching submarines, and ICBMs.

To keep the XB-70 viable, the reconnaissance role was pitched and the concept was designed RB-70H. President John F. Kennedy cancelled the B-70 program on 28 March 1961 and, although there were efforts to revive the program, it was over. Two aircraft were contracted for to explore the aerodynamic and materials technologies necessary for flight at speeds in excess of Mach 3. Note that this contract was cancelled at a time when Lockheed's A-11 and A-12 Mach 3+ spyplanes were being built but had not flown.

DESIGN

The XB-70 Valkyrie had a delta-wing planform with canards at the forward end of the fuselage behind the cockpit. The outer wing panels could be folded down 65 degrees in flight, providing increased longitudinal stability at high Mach numbers while changing the wing's center of lift. Six 19,000-pound-static-thrust General Electric YJ93-GE-3 turbojet engines (28,000 pounds of thrust with afterburner) were mounted under the wing at the rear of the fuselage.

OPERATIONS

As test aircraft, the XB-70s achieved a number of program milestones: highest sustained speed, 2,020 miles per hour, on 12 January 1966; longest flight at Mach 3, 32 minutes, on 19 May 1966; greatest Mach number, Mach 3.08; accumulating 108 minutes at Mach 3 during ten flights.

STATUS

Retired. XB-70A serial number 62-0001 is now on display at the National Museum of the United States Air Force at Wright-Patterson AFB, Ohio. This aircraft was flown from Edwards AFB, California, to the museum on 4 February 1969.

The second XB-70A, serial number 62-0207, was involved in a midair collision on 8 June 1966, during a formation photo flight of air force aircraft powered by General Electric engines. Due to wake vortices from XB-70's wingtips, test pilot Joe Walker's F-104 rolled over and impacted the rear of the Valkyrie inverted, killing him instantly. XB-70 pilot Al White and copilot Carl Cross both ejected; Cross did not survive and White sustained serious injuries. ■

—*Nicholas A. Veronico*

NORTH AMERICAN XB-70

CREW:	2 (pilot and copilot)
ENGINES:	6x General Electric YJ93-GE-3 turbojets; 19,000 lbst (8,618 kgst) each; 28,000 lbst (12,701 kgst) each with afterburners
WEIGHTS:	Empty: 251,635 lb (114,140 kg)
	Maximum: 581,025 lb (263,549 kg)
LENGTH:	196 ft 6 in (59.9 m)
WINGSPAN:	105 ft (32.0 m)
HEIGHT:	30 ft 8 in (9.2 m)
SPEEDS:	Maximum: 2,250 mph (3,621 kph) at 75,550 ft (23,028 m)
	Cruise: 1,254 mph (2,018 kph) at 35,000 ft (10,668 m)
	Landing: 184 mph (296 kph)
CEILING:	79,500 ft (24,231 m)
RANGE:	Combat radius 4,750 mi (7,644 km)
	Ferry range: 12,445 mi (20,028 km)
ARMAMENT:	Up to 65,000 lb (29,484 kg) of bombs or missiles

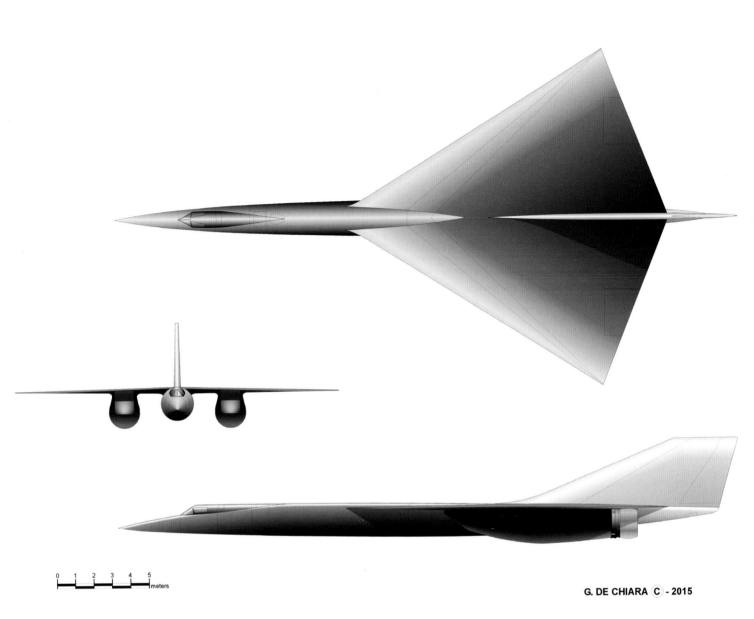

G. DE CHIARA Ⓒ - 2015

Lockheed A-11. *Giuseppe de Chiara*

LOCKHEED A-11 ARCHANGEL

As early as the summer of 1956, when the U-2 high altitude reconnaissance aircraft made its first over-flights of the Soviet Union, the CIA, the US Air Force, and American aircraft industries had already begun to contemplate a successor. They estimated that only 18 to 24 months separated these initial U-2 flights from a time when improved air defenses would render it susceptible to antiaircraft attack. Indeed, US intelligence determined that the Soviets had been able to detect and track even these preliminary forays.

President Dwight Eisenhower keenly appreciated the importance of aerial reconnaissance to verify Soviet military activities, and after he expressed concern about the U-2's vulnerability to radar detection, in August 1957 the CIA embarked on a crash program to field a follow-on spyplane.

Because Lockheed's Skunk Works had designed and fabricated the U-2, it found itself in the running for a successor—but not without competition from the Convair Division of General Dynamics.

Lockheed A-11. *US Air Force photo*

DESIGN

In all, it took only one year for the Skunk Works team led by Clarence "Kelly" Johnson to draft nine successive concept designs for the U-2 successor before arriving at the winning candidate. Under the CIA code name Project Gusto, preliminary specifications required a 500-pound (227-kilogram) reconnaissance payload capacity, 2,000-nautical-mile (3,700-kilometer) mission range, and a 90,000-foot (27,400-meter) cruising altitude. In April 1958 Johnson made his first pencil sketch of an aircraft with a pointed nose and a thin, tapered, cylindrical fuselage, twin engine pods on the fuselage, and stubby wings mounted about midpoint on the aircraft. The concept measured roughly 167 feet (50.9 meters) long and 50 feet (15.2 meters) at its wingspan, with a gross weight of roughly 102,000 pounds (46,266 kilograms). Equipped with two J58 turbojet engines, the proposal described a Mach 3 aircraft capable of flying to an altitude of between 83,000 and 93,000 feet (25,300 and 28,350 meters,

respectively) and operating within the 2,000-mile (3,200-kilometer) range required by the CIA Originally called the U-3, the team renamed it the Archangel, designated the A-1.

Eight months later, having considered seven other Archangel designs, Johnson and his engineers proposed the A-11 to the CIA, which at the same time also had under evaluation the Convair FISH (First Invisible Super Hustler), a ramjet-powered aircraft launched from the B-58 Hustler bomber.

The A-11 broke new ground. Presented to the CIA in March 1959, it had clean, sleek lines and a polished profile. It had double delta wings, each with a long engine nacelle slung under it, and its slender fuselage drew down to a sharply tapered nose. The A-11's projected performance matched its appearance; its twin J58 turbojets with afterburners enabled the proposed aircraft to cruise at Mach 3.2, reach an altitude of 93,500 feet (28,500 meters), and fly within the 2,000-mile mission profile.

LOCKHEED A-11

CREW:	1
ENGINES:	2x Pratt & Whitney J58 turbojets with afterburners
WEIGHTS:	Empty: 36,800 lb (16,692 kg) Maximum: 92,130 lb (41,789 kg)
LENGTH:	116 ft 8 in (35.6 m)
WINGSPAN:	56 ft 8 in (17.3 m)
HEIGHT:	21 ft (6.4 m)
SPEEDS:	Maximum: 2,455 mph (3,951 kph) Cruise: 2,436 mph (3,920 kph)
CEILING:	93,500 ft (28,500 m)
RANGE:	3,200 mi (5,150 km)
ARMAMENT:	None

But it had one flaw—one that Kelly Johnson thought might disqualify it. After six months of trying to reconcile the CIA's formidable radar-evasion requirements, Johnson could only report that no aircraft foreseeable in the next three to five years would be able to evade radar. In fact, the A-11 had such a prominent radar signature that Johnson feared it might be mistaken for a bomber—hardly ideal for a spyplane meant to operate in secret.

The agency reviewed the Skunk Works and Convair FISH proposals in July. Its evaluators rejected Convair's use of the B-58 launch platform and told the contractor to design an aircraft that flew at the required speed and altitude without assistance. They instructed the Lockheed group to reduce the radar cross-section of the A-11, in exchange for which the spy agency would accept lower cruise altitude.

The next month, the CIA made its choice. Convair proposed a bigger FISH called the Kingfish, which took off on its own power, flew at Mach 3.25, and reached an altitude of 125,000 feet (38,100 meters). The evaluation panel thought the performance of this aircraft superior to that of the Lockheed candidate—now called the A-12—but riskier to achieve. For their part, Johnson and his engineers hardly proposed a conservative alternative. In the crucible of making a high-performance design that also defeated radar, they produced the radical, blended planform that later distinguished the SR-71. Lockheed won a four-month contract to prove the radar-evading properties of the new design. Once done, the A-12 proceeded under the CIA's Project Oxcart. ∎

—*Michael Gorn*

LOCKHEED CL-400 SUNTAN

In 1956, the United States Air Force was unpleasantly surprised to learn that the Soviets were able to track U-2s during their high-altitude overflights, in spite of intelligence estimates suggesting Soviet radar wasn't up to the task. This development, alongside a number of research and development studies the USAF was conducting into liquid hydrogen as a fuel source, led the legendary Kelly Johnson of Lockheed's Skunk Works to propose the CL-400, often referred to as "Suntan," the name of the USAF request to which Skunk Works was responding.

DESIGN

Johnson proposed an airplane that could fly at an altitude of 100,000 feet (30,500 meters) and a speed of Mach 2.5, with a range of more than 2,500 miles (4,000 kilometers). Johnson also promised that he could deliver the first of two flyable prototypes in just eighteen months. The airplane was to be powered by Pratt & Whitney engines designated 304-2, engines that Pratt & Whitney did eventually produce and test. Lockheed's design was understandably sleek, looking at least superficially like a big F-104 Starfighter, though the tip-mounted engines were a notable difference. Later iterations moved the engines to varying locations under the wings and added a small canard toward the front of the fuselage.

By 1957, Johnson had drastically reduced his predictions for the aircraft's range, becoming convinced, based on the efficiency of liquid hydrogen, that the airplane was only likely to manage about 1,300 miles (2,100 kilometers) without refueling—and refueling wasn't an option. His counterparts

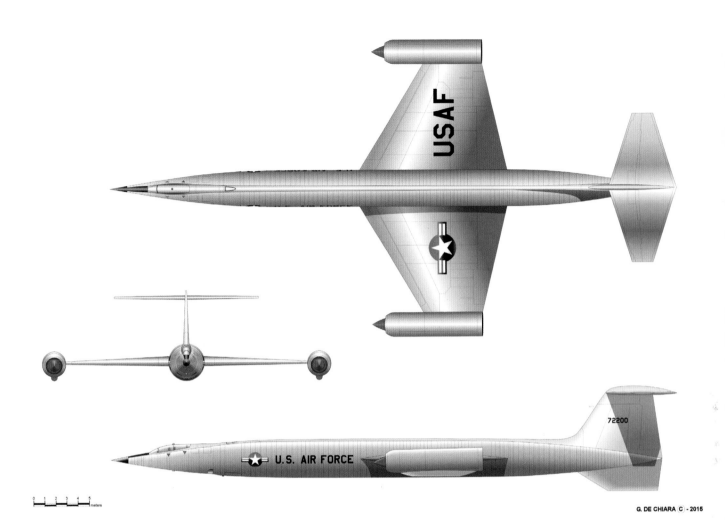

G. DE CHIARA (C) - 2015

Lockheed CL-400 concept rendering. *Giuseppe de Chiara*

were convinced that the design could fly up to 1,700 miles, (2,700 kilometers)—and that it would have to in order to be considered a success. Both sides maintained their position until, with costs exceeding $100 million ($250 million according to some), the project was cancelled in 1958. Johnson didn't protest, having recommended cancellation himself, telling the Secretary of the Air Force "I'm afraid I'm building you a dog." Most reports indicate that Lockheed returned the bulk of the funding to the USAF.

In addition to the design of the aircraft itself, significant effort went into developing procedures to deal with the production and handling of liquid hydrogen, research that provided direct value to the burgeoning US space program, just as research on the CL-400 itself contributed directly to the A-12 and SR-71. ■

—*Hal Bryan*

LOCKHEED CL-400

CREW:	2
ENGINE:	1x liquid hydrogen–powered Pratt & Whitney 304-2
WEIGHTS:	Empty: 178,500 lb (80,966 kg)
	Maximum: 358,500 lb (162,613 kg)
LENGTH:	290 ft (88.4 m)
WINGSPAN:	98 ft (29.9 m)
HEIGHT:	52 ft 3 in (15.9 m)
SPEEDS:	Maximum: Undetermined
	Cruise: Mach 2.5 (1,700 mph, 2,750 kph) at 100,000 ft (30 km)
CEILING:	100,000 ft (30,480 m)
RANGE:	1,300 mi (2,092 km)
ARMAMENT:	None

Lockheed A-12. *US Air Force photo*

LOCKHEED A-12/SR-71 BLACKBIRD

The SR-71 Blackbird stands alone among reconnaissance aircraft. Designed expressly for overflight during the height of the Cold War, its different varieties assumed unique roles for the agencies it served: the CIA, the US Air Force, and the National Aeronautics and Space Administration (NASA).

All variants derived from the successive concept designs proposed for the CIA by the Lockheed Skunk Works as the Archangel aircraft series. Archangel models 1 to 11 did not meet the intelligence agency's needs but, with the A-12, the CIA found its candidate. The project entered the production phase under the codename Project Oxcart.

The A-12 looked much like the later YF-12 and SR-71 in overall planform, although many small but significant differences distinguished them. Onlookers who saw the A-12 for the first time during its maiden flight in April 1962 must have been astonished—it looked like nothing that had ever flown before. Conceived for high performance, the aircraft's long, low, blended contours greatly reduced its side profile, a quality essential for radar evasion. Progressing backward from the strongly tapered nose, the forebody of the aircraft had chines that flared outward from the sides of the fuselage. The tips of the engine inlet spikes extended roughly to the middle of the fuselage. And, at midwing, the nacelles of the J58 engines had twin vertical fins mounted atop them. Fabricated from titanium, 13 AF-12s entered the CIA's inventory and flew (in secret) between 1962 and 1968.

Lockheed SR-71. *US Air Force photo*

Even before delivery of the first A-12, in 1960 the US Air Force entered discussions with Lockheed for an air-defense interceptor version, equipped with launch bays for three AIM-47 missiles and a place behind the pilot for a second crewman, who would serve as a fire-control officer. The nose of this new aircraft differentiated it from the A-12: in the air force variant, the nose chines were taken off to accommodate the fire-control radar equipment. The service ordered three units, designated the YF-12A. These served as test prototypes, but when Defense Department officials decided not to proceed with a production F-12 interceptor, the air force transferred the three aircraft to NASA, where, from 1969 to 1979, they participated in various flight research projects that required sustained cruising speeds of around Mach 3.

DESIGN

Early in the development and production of the A-12 and YF-12A projects, Skunk Works chief engineer Clarence (Kelly) Johnson began to think about the economies possible if the needs of the CIA and the air force could be met by a single airframe. He called such an aircraft the R-12 Universal, capable of reconnaissance, strike, and interceptor roles. By early 1963, the air force and the CIA agreed to share the costs for an initial six R-12s, followed by an additional 24. As a consequence, the A-12 fell to the budgeter's ax.

Lockheed SR-71B. *NASA photo*

To accommodate the three roles envisioned for the R-12, its design deviated significantly from that of the A-12. Like the YF-12A (and unlike the single-seat A-12), it had a second crewmember—the reconnaissance systems operator—positioned behind the pilot. It differed from the YF-12A in having a slightly longer fuselage—for significantly more fuel storage—and it had greater range and heavier weight. More obvious to the observer, Skunk Works engineers broadened the chines at the nose to improve high-speed cruise qualities. Ultimately, none of the SR-71s or variants carried armament.

President Lyndon B. Johnson announced the R-12 to the public in July 1964 (in the context of a new reconnaissance aircraft for SAC). As it turned out, he misread his briefing notes, erroneously calling it the SR-71. The name stuck. At the end of the year, an SR-71

flew for the first time; by late 1967, Lockheed delivered the last of 32 SR-71s.

In order to conduct strategic reconnaissance, the SR-71 had photographic, infrared, and electronic sensors embedded in the forward sections of the wing and body chine fairings—specifically, at four underfuselage bays and in the nose. The aircraft offered a wide assortment of overflight options, from common battlefield surveillance systems to high-performance equipment for interdiction, reconnaissance, and strategic observation. For example, in a one-hour flight, the SR-71 could survey roughly 60,000 to 100,000 square miles (155,400 to 259,000 square kilometers) of terrain. It accomplished this using a variety of technologies, including panoramic and long-range oblique optical cameras (commonly with large, 66-inch focal lengths or more), side-looking radar, infrared linescan, and ELINT antennae and receivers.

OPERATIONS

Because the SR-71 conducted its reconnaissance operations under the cloak of secrecy, its service history has been difficult to unravel. The air force SR-71 unit (SAC's 9th Strategic Reconnaissance Wing [SRW] at Beale AFB, California) became operational in June 1966. During the 1960s and 1970s, it covered such targets as North Korea, North Vietnam (after the cessation of bombing in 1973), and Cuba. SR-71s may also have overflown the Suez Canal region in 1970, the People's Republic of China before 1971, and the Middle East after the Yom Kippur War in late 1973. In the pursuit of its observations, the SR-71s provoked over 1,000 surface-to-air missile attacks, none of which resulted in losses.

With the Beale operations established, two forward detachments of the 9th SRW opened, one at Kadena AFB, Okinawa (Detachment 1) and the other at Mildenhall Royal Air Force Base, United Kingdom (Detachment 4)—both in good locations to send Blackbirds to international hot spots. During the SR-71's first ten years of service, air force planners assumed that two squadrons staffed with 20 personnel and ten aircraft each would be required. In 1976, thinking had changed: punished by the rigors of high-altitude and high-speed flight, the aircraft were put on a limited mission rotation, which mean that no more than ten could serve at a single time. The rest cycled into the active inventory on an eight-year basis, thus preserving their airframes and providing spare parts for the J58 engines.

Commonly, SR-71 pilots engaged in one of two missions: broad-based general surveillance or specific target acquisition as directed from Washington, DC, by National Command Authorities and the Joint Chiefs of Staff. Whether the flight instructions came in sealed envelopes from the nation's capital or from more standard assignments at the squadron level, pilots had to exercise extreme care when carrying out their missions. As one pilot commented, "We have to be totally aware of where we are at any given moment, as we cover *thirty miles every minute*." Reprimands and diplomatic incidents followed failure to observe this rule.

During the 1980s, as the focus of world conflicts shifted, Detachment 4 assumed the bulk of missions, concentrating on flights over North Africa and the

LOCKHEED SR-71A

CREW:	2
ENGINES:	2x Pratt & Whitney J58 afterburning turbojets; 23,000 lbst (10,433 kgst) each dry, 32,500 lbst (14,742 kgst) each with afterburning
WEIGHTS:	Empty: 60,000 lb (27,216 kg)
	Normal: 145,000 lb (65,772 kg)
	Maximum: 170,000 lb (77,112 kg)
LENGTH:	107 ft 5 in (32.7 m)
WINGSPAN:	55 ft 7 in (17.0 m)
HEIGHT:	18 ft 6 in (5.6 m)
SPEEDS:	Maximum: 2,309 mph (3,715 kph)
	Cruise: 1,981 mph (3,187 kph)
CEILING:	Above 80,000 ft (24,400 m)
RANGE:	2,982 mi (4,800 km)
	Operational radius: 1,200 mi (1,930 km)
ARMAMENT:	None
RADAR:	High-resolution side-looking airborne radar (SLAR)

Persian Gulf and flying up to 450 total hours per year from Mildenhall. Additionally, in its final years, the SR-71s devoted about 90 percent of their operating time on behalf of the US Navy, monitoring Soviet naval maneuvers in the South China, Baltic, and Black Seas. In addition, national security assignments often directed the Blackbirds to fly to the edges of—or even enter—hostile airspace to map military installations and test the reactions of Cuban, North Korean, Middle Eastern, and Soviet radar defenses.

Although officially decommissioned in January 1990, the air force transferred an SR-71B to NASA in 1991, where it served as a flight research platform until 1997. At the same time, Congress appropriated $100 million to return three air force SR-71s to operational status; these flights ended in 1997. NASA flew the last SR-71 mission at the Edwards AFB open house in October 1999.

STATUS

Retired. ■

—*Michael Gorn*

Lockheed Martin ES-3As. *US Navy photo*

LOCKHEED MARTIN ES-3A SHADOW

The S-3 Viking served on board US Navy aircraft carriers as an anti-submarine/surveillance/strike/tanker aircraft from 1975 to 2009. From 1993, the S-3B variant was considered a "sea control" aircraft vice ASW, and in the mid-1990s the ASW equipment and operators were removed. Thus configured, they were employed in ocean surveillance, antishipping (with Harpoon and Maverick air-to-surface missiles), and aerial tanking (with external drogue pod and fuel tanks). The last role was particularly significant because of the demise of the KA-6D Intruder tanker and the relatively short range of the large numbers of F/A-18 Hornets embarked in US carriers.

Lockheed Martin converted 16 S-3A aircraft to the ES-3A electronic recon configuration, replacing the long-serving EA/EKA-3B Skywarriors. Sometimes labeled TASES (Tactical Airborne Signal Exploitation System), the aircraft's missions were (1) electronic warfare reconnaissance, (2) over-the-horizon targeting, and (3) airborne tactical command, control, communications, and intelligence. One or two ES-3As normally operated from each forward-deployed aircraft carrier.

The Navy Department's 1998 report, *Naval Aviation: Forward Air Power . . . From the Sea*, stated that the aircraft supports "all facets of Navy, Marine Corps, and joint operations," seeking out electronic emissions from potential hostile radars and intercepting communications. And, "the ES-3A has already demonstrated tremendous reliability and safety, as well as a robust mission capability." Shortly thereafter, the decision was made to retire the aircraft to save operating funds.

The Viking was built as an ASW aircraft to replace the S2F/S2 Tracker as the navy's ship-based, fixed-wing ASW aircraft.

DESIGN

The S-3 was designed to be within the approximate dimensions of the piston-engine Tracker, but to be faster, and to carry more advanced ASW equipment; it was a high-wing, twin turbojet. The sensors included radar, sonobuoys, and MAD. The internal weapons bay, sized to hold four lightweight ASW torpedoes, could carry 2,400 pounds (1,089 kilograms) of weapons or auxiliary fuel tanks. There also were two wing pylons, which in the S-3B were upgraded to carry the Harpoon antiship missile.

From December 1987, 160 Vikings upgraded to the S-3B standard rejoined the fleet. These aircraft had an improved acoustic processor and the APS-137 Inverse

Synthetic Aperture Radar (ISAR). A major avionics upgrade program for 124 S-3B aircraft began in 1995.

The ES-3A conversion included replacing the weapons bay with avionics racks and sensors. The MAD tail boom was replaced by electronic antennas. An electronics "canoe" and other antennas were placed in the dorsal position.

The wings and tailfin folded for carrier stowage.

(Five preproduction S-3A aircraft were modified to a US-3A cargo configuration for operation from carriers in the western Pacific and Indian Ocean; these planes were taken out of service in the early 1990s. A KS-3 tanker configuration was proposed as well as pod tanks and drogue system for the US-3A variant; however, no development of a specialized tanker was undertaken.)

DESIGNATION

The ES-3A aircraft were generally called Shadow or Sea Shadow, although the names were not officially assigned.

OPERATIONS

These aircraft were operated by electronic reconnaissance squadrons VQ-5 and VQ-6, in the western Pacific and the Atlantic-Mediterranean areas, respectively. Carrier deployments began in 1993.

Upon retirement of the ES-3A carrier, battle group commanders employed land-based recon aircraft, primarily the EP-3E ARIES II flown by squadrons VQ-1 and VQ-2.

STATUS

Retired. First flight of the YS-3A took place on 21 January 1972. Lockheed produced 187 S3A aircraft through August 1978. The last fleet S-3B squadron—VS-24—was deactivated on 31 March 2007. Six S-3Bs were retained in service with squadron VX-30 as range control aircraft, and two serve in test roles with NASA.

The first flight prototype ES-3A conversion (NS-3A aerodynamic prototype) took place on 7 September 1989; first flight of the second conversion—the first with full electronics suite—occurred on 21 January 1992. The 16 ES-3A conversions were delivered to the fleet from May 1992 through September 1993. The last ES-3A aircraft was taken out of service in 1999. ∎

—Norman Polmar and John F. Bessette

Lockheed Martin ES-3A. *US Navy photo*

LOCKHEED MARTIN ES-3A

CREW:	4
ENGINES:	2x General Electric TF34GE400 turbofans; 9,275 lbst (4,207 kgst) each
WEIGHTS:	Empty: 26,783 lb (12,149 kg) Maximum: 52,539 lb (23,832 kg)
LENGTH:	53 ft 4 in (16.3 m)
WINGSPAN:	68 ft 8 in (20.9 m)
HEIGHT:	22 ft 9 in (6.9 m)
SPEEDS:	Maximum: 506 mph (814 kph) at sea level Cruise: 400+ mph (644 kph)
CEILING:	40,000 ft (12,195 m)
RANGE:	2,645+ mi (4,260 km)
ARMAMENT:	None
RADAR:	APS-137 ISAR

BEECHCRAFT RC-12 GUARDRAIL/MC-12W LIBERTY

The Beechcraft RC-12 and MC-12 are reconnaissance and SIGINT versions of the C-12 Huron, one of only a few aircraft types employed by the US Army, US Air Force, US Navy, *and* the US Marine Corps. The C-12 grew out of the army's need for a light transport aircraft and was first pressed into service in 1974. The navy and marines deployed the UC-12B five years later, and the air force followed suit as well.

More than two dozen variants of the C-12 have served a variety of roles, including logistics, VIP and other light transport, and training. But the type's utility in reconnaissance and intelligence gathering, coupled with its relatively low cost and short-field capabilities, keep it employed after more than 40 years in service.

The RC-12 (*R* for "reconnaissance") is referred to as the Guardrail by the US Army, while the US Air Force knows the MC-12W (*M* for "multirole") as the Liberty.

DESIGN

Based originally on the civilian King Air 200, then on the larger King Air 350, the C-12 is a family of low-wing, tricycle-gear, twin-engine turboprops. The King Air design's first flight was in 1963, but the C-12s are derived from what was initially known as the Super King Air, starting with the 200 series. With a crew of 2, a standard C-12 could seat as many as 13 passengers, but the spyplane variants trade seats for sensors—a sophisticated and largely classified suite of electronics—and operate with as few as two sensor operators in addition to the pilots.

The King Air 200, first flown in 1972, featured a longer wing, an improved cabin pressurization system, and increased fuel capacity. The biggest visual change from the earlier models was the introduction of the T-tail, a design element still in use today. The 300 series

Beechcraft MC-12W. *Drwooden, CC Attribution-Share Alike 3.0*

BEECHCRAFT MC-12

CREW:	4+ (2 pilots and 2 or more sensor operators)
ENGINES:	2x Pratt & Whitney PT6A-60A turboprops; 1,050 shp each
WEIGHTS:	Empty: 12,500 lb (5,670 kg) Maximum: 16,500 lb (7,484 kg)
LENGTH:	46 ft 8 in (14.2 m)
WINGSPAN:	57 ft 11 in (17.7 m)
HEIGHT:	14 ft 4 in (4.4 m)
SPEEDS:	Cruise: 312 ktas (359 mph; 578 kph) Loiter: 235 ktas (270 mph; 435 kph)
CEILING:	35,000 ft (10,668 m)
RANGE:	Approximately 2,400 nmi (3,862 km)
ARMAMENT:	None

brought more powerful engines, and the 350, introduced in 1990, was created by stretching the fuselage by 3 feet (nearly 1 meter) and adding winglets, among other improvements.

OPERATIONS

The first RC-12s saw service with the US Army in Stuttgart, Germany, in the 1980s, while the MC-12 Liberty was developed and deployed for combat operations beginning in 2009, flying out of Balad Air Base in Iraq as part of Operation Iraqi Freedom. MC-12s have been deployed extensively in Afghanistan, alongside civilian contractor-flown counterparts as part of Operation Enduring Freedom.

Typical MC-12 missions can last up to eight hours and usually involve the airplane loitering over a particular area of operations while the sensor operators—one focused on SIGINT, the other on video—gather and report their intelligence data, which commanders on the ground receive in real time, providing both a figurative and literal bird's-eye view of the battlefield. In addition to the onboard operators, these missions are supported by crews on the ground in command centers, as well as Joint Terminal Attack Controllers (JTAC) in the field, collecting the reconnaissance information for analysis and further distribution.

The aircraft carry a sophisticated multisensor payload that supports high-zoom, full-motion video with night- and thermal-imaging capabilities, as well as laser range finders and laser designators and illuminators that allow the crew to specify targets for a variety of manned and unmanned weapons systems. At the same time, the SIGINT operator can listen in on—and jam—all manner of the adversary's voice and data communications.

According to a US Air Force report published in late 2014, the MC-12W had flown more than 400,000 combat hours in Afghanistan and Iraq, and "aided in the kill or capture of more than 8,000 terrorists, discovered more than 650 weapons caches, helped divert convoys around improvised explosive devices, provided over watch for large numbers of coalition forces, and saved coalition lives."

STATUS

Operational. As of this writing, approximately 300 C-12s are flying in US military service, along with an undisclosed number operated by civilian contractors in support of US forces. The army reports 44 RC-12s in their inventory, and they're expected to assume control of at least some of the air force's MC-12s as part of a divestiture program, while 13 MC-12s have been transferred to the Oklahoma Air National Guard.

As of November 2015, the US Army had begun soliciting preliminary proposals to replace its C-12s with a commercial off the shelf (COTS) aircraft that could be adapted for military use. In the meantime, Northrop Grumman has developed an upgrade program called the RC-12X that is expected to extend the type's service life through 2025. ■

—Hal Bryan

AURORA

The Aurora probably doesn't exist, and presumably never did. Still, a couple of tantalizing reports from credible eyewitnesses—along with almost three decades of rumor, conjecture, and intrigue—leave more than a little room for doubt.

DESIGN

In 1985, the published US budget included a line item allocating $455 million for top-secret aircraft development called "Aurora." Five years later, in 1990, *Aviation Week and Space Technology* magazine reported the story, along with a follow-up indicating that the budget for Project Aurora, whatever that actually was, had grown to more than $2.5 billion. Even though *AW&ST*

reported that the term Aurora seemed to refer to an overall project (as opposed to a specific aircraft type), a legend was born.

Rumors of a replacement for the SR-71 Blackbird had been swirling since the mid-1980s. While these rumors were purely conjecture, with the Blackbird's age, not to mention its own clandestine history, it stood to reason—and still does—that the USAF might certainly be developing or even already flying something faster and far more mysterious. Starting in late 1989, a number of eyewitness reports surfaced that added fuel to the speculative fire.

The first was a sighting of a triangular aircraft in formation with two F-111s and a KC-135 over the

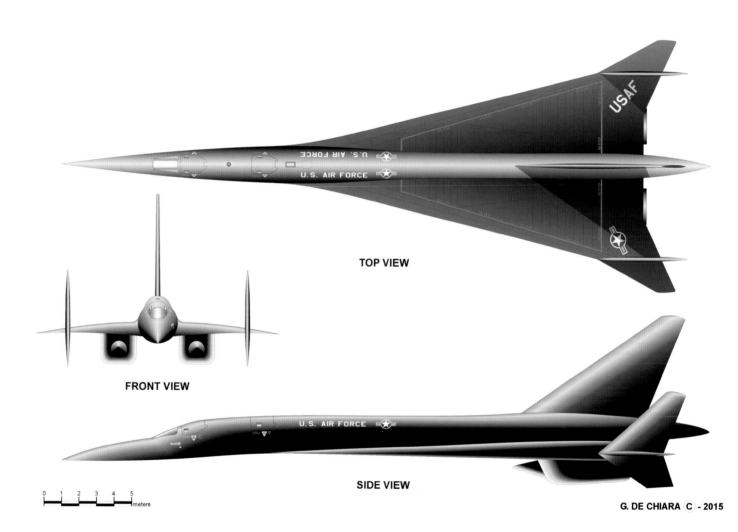

TOP VIEW

FRONT VIEW

SIDE VIEW

0 1 2 3 4 5 meters

G. DE CHIARA ⓒ - 2015

Aurora concept rendering. *Giuseppe de Chiara*

North Sea. This report came from someone almost peculiarly well qualified: an engineer named Chris Gibson, who was a member of the Royal Aircraft Observer Corps, a group that had regularly won awards for their ability to recognize different aircraft types. Other reports throughout the southwestern US included unattributable sonic booms and sightings of a distinctive contrail pattern dubbed "donuts on a rope."

As early as 1994, Ben Rich of Lockheed's famed Skunk Works had declared that Aurora was simply the codename for the proposal that ultimately led to the B-2 Stealth Bomber. In spite of this, speculation continued for many years, largely petering out after the turn of the century, though reports of odd-looking and odd-sounding aircraft continue to this day. ∎

—*Hal Bryan*

AURORA

CREW:	Unknown
ENGINES:	Unknown
WEIGHT:	Unknown
LENGTH:	Unknown
WINGSPAN:	Unknown
HEIGHT:	Unknown
SPEED:	Unknown (presumably hypersonic)
CEILING:	Unknown
RANGE:	Unknown
ARMAMENT:	Unknown (presumably none if it's truly a replacement for the unarmed SR-71)

BOEING/NORTHROP GRUMMAN E-8 JOINT SURVEILLANCE TARGET ATTACK RADAR SYSTEM (JOINT STARS)

The US Air Force/US Army E-8 (Joint Surveillance Target Attack Radar System; Joint Stars or JSTARS) is an airborne battle management and intelligence, surveillance, and reconnaissance (ISR) platform. Operations are based on the aircraft's AN/APY-7 radar, which has five operating modes: wide-area surveillance, fixed-target indicator, synthetic aperture radar, moving-target indicator, and target classification. On board the aircraft, 1 operator sits at the navigation and defensive systems station, and 17 others process information for flight-path planning, cartographic data, radar management, surveillance and threat analysis, jammer locations, and the pairing of airborne weapons to ground targets. This information can be sent through a secure satellite link to ground stations, or, using the Joint Tactical Information Distribution System (JTIDS), to tactical aircraft or to AWACS planes. The JSTARS antenna can scan a 120-degree field of view under the aircraft and detect targets out to more than 150 miles (241 kilometers).

The air force took delivery of the first E-8C, serial number 92-3289, on 22 March 1996. Since its delivery, the E-8C fleet has undergone a number of upgrade programs as radar receiver and target identification resolution has improved.

DESIGN

The E-8C fleet is based on commercial Boeing 707-300 jetliner airframes that have been extensively modified by Northrop Grumman (airframe overhauls are accomplished at Lake Charles, Louisiana) and then flown to the company's Melbourne, Florida, facility for avionics installations.

OPERATIONS

Two preproduction E-8s supported US forces in Operation Desert Storm in 1991. During the battle, the E-8s were able to track convoys and monitor enemy staging areas as well as their paths of retreat. The E-8s flew 42 sorties, during which they demonstrated the need to track moving targets on the ground and the ability to datalink target information to field commanders and airborne attack aircraft.

Four years later, they were flying in the skies over Bosnia as part of Operation Joint Endeavor. Since its

Boeing/Northrop Grumman E-8 JSTARS. *Northrop Grumman Corp.*

BOEING/NORTHROP GRUMMAN E-8

DESIGN:	Boeing (aircraft), Northrop Grumman (systems)
CREW:	Typically 21 (pilot, copilot, flight engineer, 18 mission specialists); sometimes 40 (2 pilots, 2 copilots, 2 flight engineers, 34 mission specialists) for extended-endurance missions
ENGINES:	4x Pratt & Whitney TF-33-102C turbojets; 19,200 lbst (8,709 kgst) each
WEIGHTS:	Empty: 171,000 lb (77,564 kg) Maximum: 336,000 lb (152,407 kg)
LENGTH:	152 ft 11 in (46.6 m)
WINGSPAN:	145 ft 9 in (44.4 m)
HEIGHT:	42 ft 6 in (13.0 m)
SPEED:	0.84 Mach
CEILING:	42,000 ft (12,802 m)
RANGE:	9 hours (20 hours with inflight refueling)
ARMAMENT:	None
RADAR:	AN/APY-7 active electronically scanned array capable of wide area surveillance (WAS), fixed target indication (FTI), ground moving target indicator (GMTI) and synthetic aperture radar (SAR) modes

introduction, the E-8C fleet has flown more than 85,000 combat hours in support of Operations Enduring Freedom (Afghanistan 2001–2014), Iraqi Freedom, New Dawn (Iraq), Odyssey Dawn (Libya), and Unified Protector (NATO, Libya, 2011).

STATUS

Operational. There are 16 E-8C JSTARS in the US Air Force's inventory, all jointly operated by the Ninth Air Force's 461st Air Control Wing and the Georgia Air National Guard's 116th Air Control Wing located at Robbins AFB.

In March 2016, Raytheon and Northrop Grumman were awarded contracts to study the development of a JSTARS follow-on surveillance radar. The new radar will be mounted onto a large commercial jet aircraft. That platform will be supplied by Boeing (offering the P-8 version of its 737-800ERX), Bombardier (offering a modified Global 6000), Embraer (possibly an ERJ-145), or Gulfstream (its G550 business jet), each competing for the follow-on contract. The JSTARS replacement is slated to enter service in 2022. The business jet platform will reduce the sensor operator crew from 18 to 10. ∎

—*Nicholas A. Veronico*

LOCKHEED SR-72

The final curtain call for the SR-71 was long and complex. Although decommissioned in 1990, it served as a flight-research platform for NASA until 1997. The US Congress voted in 1994 to reactivate three SR-71s for the air force. The final USAF flight occurred in 1997, and in 1999 NASA made a last flyover during its annual Edwards AFB open house.

But public interest in secret, high-altitude, high-speed aircraft refused to die with the SR-71. Even before the Blackbird left the tarmac for good, media reports speculated whether strange sounds and contrails in the skies over the western US meant that American military and intelligence services had developed a successor aircraft, known by the codename Aurora.

Whether Aurora existed or not, in November 2013 the Lockheed Martin Skunk Works unveiled to *Aviation Week and Space Technology* a plan for a next-generation SR-71. In releasing its concept, Lockheed pinpointed the specific role of a demonstrator that it called the SR-72: an armed, hypersonic, uncrewed aircraft capable of reacting to flashpoints around the world more quickly than satellites or subsonic aircraft. In a time of unpredictable acts of terrorism—and in an environment in which US satellites could be tracked and airspace fortified against American incursions—Lockheed argued that its candidate vehicle could evade detection, get to targets more rapidly, and strike at adversaries before they had a chance to escape.

DESIGN

In its announcement, the Skunk Works revealed that it had been collaborating with the Aerojet Rocketdyne Company since 2006, with the goal of arriving at a breakthrough in "air-breathing" (ramjet) propulsion technology that would enable the SR-72 to travel at Mach 6—more than 4,500 miles per hour (7,240 kilometers per hour).

Some significant steps had been taken in the years between the last NASA SR-71 flight and the Lockheed Martin/Aerojet Rocketdyne merger of interests in 2006. The Defense Advanced Research Projects Agency (DARPA) had sponsored research for the Falcon Project, which focused on developing

LOCKHEED SR-72	
CREW:	Uncrewed, though a demonstrator might be piloted
ENGINES:	2x F100 or F110 turbines integrated with a modified ramjet
WEIGHT:	Unknown
LENGTH:	Over 100 feet (30.5 m), about the size of the F-22 stealth fighter
WINGSPAN:	Similar to SR-71 (55 ft 7 in; 17 m)
HEIGHT:	Similar to SR-71 (18 ft 6 in; 5.6 m)
SPEED:	4,604 mph (7,409 kph)
CEILING:	Unknown
RANGE:	Same as the SR-71 (2,982 mi; 4,800 km)
ARMAMENT:	Strike capability likely
RADAR:	Unknown

*All specifications were provisional at time of publication

a reusable hypersonic cruise vehicle. After NASA cancelled research on its successful X-43C scramjet demonstrator in 2004, DARPA folded it into Falcon. (The scramjet proven by NASA worked with no moving parts. At sufficient speed, the engine compressed the supersonic airflow as it entered the aircraft's inlet, mixed it with propellant, and ignited it. Most of the heated exhaust that poured from the nozzles drew air from the atmosphere—hence, an air-breathing engine). Lockheed participated in these studies, gaining critical knowledge about—but as yet no solution for—the necessary propulsion transition from turbojet to ramjet and back again.

When the Lockheed Martin and Aerojet Rocketdyne engineers met to push development forward, the key problem still involved how to bridge this handover between the turbine engine, which propelled the aircraft from takeoff to Mach 2.5, and the ramjet, which became effective between Mach 3 and 3.5. Clearly, a yawning speed gap existed between the two technologies. Lockheed's air-breathing hypersonics manager Brad Leland revealed in the

SR-72 announcement that the two sides had found a way to close the difference between Mach 2.5 and 3 and to integrate the two propulsion systems. It involved using a standard jet engine like the F100 or F110 and a modified ramjet capable of producing thrust at a lower speed, through which it could take over seamlessly from the turbine engine. Leland did not elaborate on the mechanisms of the ramjet modification.

The dramatic planform of the SR-72 features chines blended into a delta that extends backward from about the midpoint of the fuselage. It has deep, underwing nacelles mounted close inboard and a humpbacked fuselage.

Following these public revelations, NASA officials decided in December 2014 to transfer over $892,000 to the Skunk Works for a feasibility study of the SR-72, after which (in March 2016) Lockheed Chief Executive Officer Marillyn Hewson predicted that her firm could fabricate an SR-72 demonstrator for less than $1 billion. Because the US Department of Defense planned to build a hypersonic weapon during the 2020s, Lockheed foresaw potential SR-72 production during the 2030s.

STATUS

In development. Lockheed proposed the fabrication of a flight demonstrator aircraft (with an optional piloted version) starting in 2018, with flight testing to begin by 2023. ∎

—*Michael Gorn*

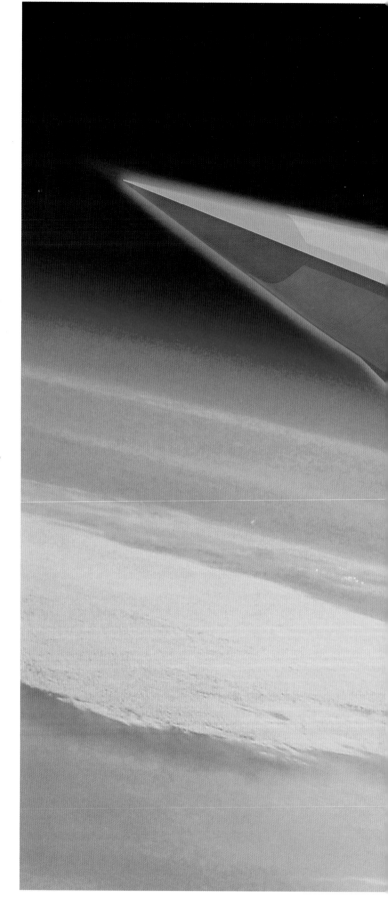

Lockheed SR-72 concept rendering. *Lockheed Martin photo*

ENDNOTES

1. Jon Guttman, *Reconnaissance and Bomber Aircraft Aces of World War 1* (Oxford [UK]: Osprey, 2015) p. 6.
2. Ken Delve, "The Eye in the Sky: Reconnaissance in the Royal Air Force, Part 1," *Air International* (May 1995), pp. 281–285.
3. Charles Coulson Gillespie, *Science and Polity in France: The Revolutionary and Napoleonic Years*, pp. 372–373, quoted in "French Aerostatic Corps," https://en.wikipedia.org/wiki/French_Aerostatic_Corps retrieved September 25, 2015.
4. Jeffrey T. Richelson, *A Century of Spies: Intelligence in the Twentieth Century* (New York: Oxford University Press, 1995), p. 17.
5. Delve, p. 282.
6. Quoted in Col. Terrance J. Finnegan, USAFR (Ret), *Shooting the Front* (Stroud: History Press, 2011), p. 13.
7. Ibid.
8. David Kahn, *Hitler's Spies* (New York: Macmillan, 1978), p. 35.
9. Lt. Col. George A. Larson, USAF (Ret), "Early Aerial Reconnaissance 1912 Connecticut War Games," *Air Force Museum Friends Journal* (summer 2004), p. 40.
10. The German World War I–era army air force—the *Luftstreitkraefte*—was disbanded under the terms of the Versailles Treaty; Adolf Hitler established a military air arm, the *Luftwaffe*, on February 26, 1935.
11. Andrew J. Brookes, *Photo Reconnaissance* (London: Ian Allan, 1984), p. 38.
12. F. H. Hinsley, *British Intelligence in the Second World War: Its Influence on Strategy and Operations* (London, 1979), Vol. 1, Appendix 2, pp. 496–499.
13. Kahn, *Hitler's Spies*, pp. 114–135, 449–450. Also Col. Roy M. Stanley II, USAF, *World War II* Photo Intelligence (New York: Charles Scribner's Sons, 1981), pp. 43-51.
14. "Kawanishi's Parasol Patroller," *Air International* (December 1985), pp. 293–305.
15. Jonathan Garraway, "Dark Horse," *FlyPast* (June 2013), pp. 46–47.
16. Robert Forsyth and Eddie J. Creek, *Messerschmitt Me 264: Amerika Bomber*, (Hersham, Surrey: Ian Allan, 2006), pp. 116–120.
17. Engineer-Col. L. Safronov, Soviet Air Forces (Ret.), "Strategy and Operational Art: from the Experience of Photoreconnaissance during the Great Patriotic War," *Voyenno-Istoricheskiy Zhurnal* (No. 5, 1979), pp. 20–23.
18. Wesley Frank Craven and James Lea Cate, *The Army Air Forces in World War II*, Vol. I, *Plans and Early Operations, January 1939 to August 1942* (Washington, D.C.: Office of Air Force History), pp. 189-190.

19. Bill Cahill, "War in the Ether" *FlyPast* (March 2011), pp. 114–119.
20. John F. Kreis, Ed., *Piercing the Fog* (Washington, D.C.: Air Force History and Museum Program, 1996), pp. 94–99; and Larry Tart, *Freedom Through Vigilance: History of US Air Force Security Service, Volume IV, Airborne Reconnaissance Part I* (West Conshohocken, Penna.: Infinity Publishing, 2012), pp. 1710–1764.
21. Alfred Price, *The History of US Electronic Warfare*, (Fairfax, Va.: Association of Old Crows, 1989), Vol. 2, pp. 33–34.
22. John T. Farquhar, *A Need to Know: The Role of Air Force Reconnaissance in War Planning, 1945–1953* (Maxwell AFB, Ala.: Air University Press, 2004), pp. 40–41.
23. 23 The PB4Y-2 Privateer was an extensively modified variant of the Liberator with a tall tail fin replacing the familiar twin-tail configuration of the B-24. The PB4Y-2 also had a seven-foot fuselage extension forward of the wing to carry additional electronic equipment and operators and other major changes, especially the fitting of Pratt & Whitney R-1830-94 engines (without turbo-superchargers) for low-altitude operations.
24. James E. Wise Jr., and Scott Baron, *Dangerous Games: Faces, Incidents, and Casualties of the Cold War* (Annapolis Md.: Naval Institute Press, 2010), pp. 41–45.
25. Rear Adm. Lewis L. Strauss, USNR (Ret), *Men and Decisions* (London: Macmillan, 1963), p. 204.
26. Ibid., p. 205.
27. William B. Scott, "Sampling Missions Unveiled Nuclear Weapon Secrets," *Aviation Week & Space Technology* (3 November 1997), p. 54.
28. Walton S. Moody, *Building a Strategic Air Force* (Washington, D.C.: Air Force History and Museums Program, 1996), p. 252. This is an excellent study of the development of SAC's bomber and reconnaissance force.
29. Cahill, "The Korean War and the Maturation of SAC Reconnaissance," p. 41.
30. R. Cargill Hall, "The Truth about Overflights," *MHQ* [Military History Quarterly] (Spring 1997), pp. 30–31.
31. A.L. George, *Case Studies of Actual and Alleged Overflights, 1930–1953*, Rand Corp. Study RM-1349 (Santa Monica, Calif.: Rand, 1955). Arthur S. Lundahl and Dino Brugioni, interview by Donald E. Welzenbach, CIA, tape recording, Washington, D.C., December 14, 1983. Recordings, transcripts, and notes for the interviews conducted for this study are on file with the DCI History Staff. Also see Donald E. Hillman and R. Cargill Hall, "Overflight: Strategic Reconnaissance of the USSR," *Air Power History* (Spring 1996), pp. 28–39. In 1952 Hillman was deputy commander of the 306th

Bombardment Wing, the only B-47 wing in the Strategic Air Command at the time, and commanded the lead B-47.
32. For a description of these early RAF flights see Paul Lashmar, *Spy Flights of the Cold War* (Gloucestershire [UK]: Sutton Publishing, 1996), pp. 65ff.
33. Cargill Hall, "The Truth about Overflights," p. 29.
34. Paul Lashmar, *Spy Flights of the Cold War*, pp. 77–83; Cargill Hall, "The Truth about Overflights," pp. 33–34. Aviation historian Chris Pocock has unsuccessfully searched for evidence that these flights occurred; he tentatively concludes that they did not.
35. Ben R. Rich and Leo Janos, *Skunk Works: A Personal Memoir of My Years at Lockheed* (Boston: Little, Brown, 1994), p. 124.
36. Bill Gunston, *Bombers of the West* (New York: Charles Scribner's Sons, 1973), p. 126.
37. R. Cargill Hall: "Strategic Reconnaissance in the Cold War," *Prologue, the Journal of the National Archives & Records Administration* (Summer 1996), p. 113.
38. Lt. Col. William Cahill, USAF, "The Korean War and the Maturation of SAC Reconnaissance." *Air Power History* (Autumn 2012), pp. 42, 47.
39. USAF photo reconnaissance in the Korean conflict is detailed in Robert Frank Futrell, *The United States Air Force In Korea, 1950–1953* (New York: Duell, Sloan, and Pearce, 1961), pp. 509–521.
40. E. A. Gillespie, as quoted in Richard A. Morley, "E. A. 'Ed' Gillespie, the World's Oldest Test Pilot?" *American Aviation Historical Society Journal* (Summer 2001), p. 93.
41. These China overflights were led by Lt. Col. Marion Carl, USMC; see Carl, *Pushing the Envelope: The Career of Fighter Ace and Test Pilot Marion Carl* (Annapolis, Md.: Naval Institute Press, 1994), pp. 81–85.
42. Hall, "The Truth about Overflights," p. 38.
43. R. Cargill Hall & Clayton D. Laurie, ed.: "Early Cold War Overflights Symposium Proceedings, Vol. 1: Memoirs," p. 112.
44. On 1 January 1957, FEAF was reorganized and officially was renamed Pacific Air Forces (PACAF).
45. Capt. William C. Chapman, USN (Ret.), "Steve Brody and the Banshee," *Foundation* [Museum of Naval Aviation] (Spring 1993), pp. 44–48; and author Norman Polmar's discussions and correspondence with Chapman in 1998. Steve Brody was a New York saloonkeeper who, in 1886, jumped off the Brooklyn Bridge to win a wager. "To pull a Brody" instantly became a term for doing a dangerous stunt.
46. Dino A. Brugioni, *Eyes in the Sky: Eisenhower, the CIA, and Cold War Aerial Espionage* (Annapolis, Md.: Naval Institute Press, 2010), p. 148.
47. Dino Brugioni, *Eyes in the Sky*, p. 158.

48. Richard M. Bissell Jr., Interview with Donald E. Welzenbach, quoted in Michael Beschloss, *Mayday: Eisenhower, Khrushchev, and the U-2 Affair* (New York: Harper & Row, 1986), p. 140, and Norman Polmar, *Spyplane: The U-2 History Declassified* (Osceola, Wisc.: MBI Publishing, 2001), p. 106.

49. Gregory W. Pedlow and Donald E. Welzenbach, *The CIA and the U-2 Program, 1954–1974* (Washington, D.C.: Central Intelligence Agency, 1998), pp. 317–318.

50. Allen W. Dulles, "Statistics Relating to the U-2 Program," CIA, August 19, 1960, as mentioned in Brugioni, *Eyes in the Sky*, p. 356. These numbers are not cumulative; a single U-2 mission might have flown over portions of both the Soviet Union and China, as well as over, for example, India.

51. JCS 2150/29, referenced in "Memorandum of Discussion on All Forms of Aircraft Intelligence Reconnaissance Platforms . . . ," p. 5. White House Office of the Staff Secretary, undated (summer 1960), via the Eisenhower Library and BACM Research, accessed 5 May 2011: http://www.paperlessarchives.com/FreeTitles/Eisenhower/AerialIntelligence.pdf

52. Dave Forster and Chris Gibson, *Listening In: RAF Electronic Intelligence Gathering Since 1945* (Manchester [UK]: Hikoki, 2014), pp. 44–49, 82–83.

53. Dave Forster and Chris Gibson, *Listening In*, pp. 50–63,176.

54. Kevin Wright and Peter Jefferies, *Looking Down the Corridors: Allied Aerial Espionage over East Germany and Berlin 1945–1990* (Stroud, Gloucestershire [UK]: History Press, 2015). The British effort is described on pp. 85–105, and French missions are covered on pp. 106–122.

55. Chris Pocock, *50 Years of the U-2*, pp. 72–73.

56. Chris Pocock, *50 Years of the U-2*, pp. 67–70.

57. Michael Dobbs, *One Minute to Midnight: Kennedy, Khrushchev, and Castro on the Brink of Nuclear War* (New York: Alfred A. Knopf, 2008), pp. 69ff, 210.

58. Dobbs, *One Minute to Midnight*, pp. 63–65, 139–140. Also Pocock, *50 Years of the U-2*, p. 174.

59. Norman Polmar, *Spyplane*, p. 195.

60. Japan had occupied the island in 1895 and renamed it Formosa, Portuguese for "beautiful island."

61. Chris Pocock, *The Black Bats: CIA Spy Flights over China from Taiwan 1951–69* (Atglen Penna.: Schiffer Publishing, 2010), pp. 12-28.

62. Chris Pocock, *The Black Bats*, pp. 29–40.

63. Chris Pocock, *The Black Bats*, p. 47.

64. Zhang Lei and Qiao Songbai, "U-2 Terminator," *China Armed Forces* (April 30, 2014), pp. 92–93. The Chinese credited the missile battalion commander with destroying five Nationalist U-2s over time, thus his title, "U-2 Terminator."

65. Chris Pocock, *The Black Bats*, pp. 119-123; *50 Years of the U-2*, pp. 246-252.

66. Chris Pocock, *50 Years of the U-2*, p. 204.

67. Paul F. Crickmore, *Lockheed SR-71 Operations in the Far East*, Osprey Combat Aircraft 76 (Oxford [UK]: Osprey Publishing, 2008), pp. 6–9.

68. Ibid., pp. 11–13.

69. USS *Pueblo* (AGER 2) was the US Navy intelligence collector ("spyship") captured in international waters in the Sea of Japan, 22 January 1968.

70. Paul Crickmore, *Lockheed SR-71 Operations in the Far East*, pp. 31–50.

71. Paul F. Crickmore, *Lockheed SR-71 Operations in Europe and the Middle East*, (Oxford [UK]: Osprey Publishing, 2009), pp. 14–19.

72. "Forty Years On and Still Going Strong: The Boeing C-135 Stratotanker Series," Part 2, *Air International* (February 1998), pp. 94–101.

73. Col. Thomas P. Ehrhard, USAF (Ret), *Air Force UAVs: The Secret History* (Arlington, Va.: Mitchell Institute for Aerospace Studies, July 2010), p. 12.

74. Ibid., pp. 29-38.

75. Bruce Cunningham, "Douglas A3D-2 Versions, Part III," *Journal of the American Aviation Historical Society* (Summer 2008), pp. 139–140.

76. Chris Pocock, *50 Years of the U-2*, p. 264.

77. Paul Crickmore, *Lockheed SR-71 Operations in the Far East*, pp.15–19, 26–46, 61.

78. Lt. Col. John Kovacs, USAF (Ret), et al., "SAC Reconnaissance in the Vietnam War," *Friends [of NMUSAF] Journal* (Summer 2012), pp. 16–17.

79. Thomas Ehrhard, *Air Force UAVs*, pp. 25-29.

80. "Alone, Unarmed, and Unafraid," *FlyPast* (June 2013) pp. 124–129.

81. "Plane Facts: Soviet Strategic Reconnaissance," *Air International* (February 1977), p. 98. Also "Tsybin RSR," Wikipedia http://en.wikipedia.org/wiki/Tsybin_RSR, retrieved February 25, 2015.

82. "Bear Tracks in Germany: The Soviet Air Force in the former German Democratic Republic," *Air International* (November 1992), p. 253.

83. Stefan Buettner and Alexander Golz, "Foxbat Finale," *Combat Aircraft* (March 2014), pp. 66–71.

84. Dr. Dave Sloggett, "Defending the Skies: British Air Defence in the Cold War," *Jets* (March–April 2013), p.56.

85. Volker Liebscher, *Geheime Aufklarungsfluege 'Relais': Die MfS-Spezialfunkdienste in Zusammenarbeit mit NVA und Sowjetarmee* [Secret Reconnaissance Flights 'Relais': The GDR Stasi Special SIGINT Service in Cooperation with the GDR and Soviet Armed Forces] (Berlin: Aerolit, 2008), pp. 56–72.

86. Vice Adm. G. E. Miller, USN (Ret.), "Some Thoughts about Soviet Aircraft Over Flights of U. S. Aircraft Carriers during the Cold War," working paper, November 20, 2003. Miller had successively commanded the Second Fleet in the Atlantic and the Sixth Fleet in the Mediterranean.

87. Dave Forster and Chris Gibson, *Listening In*, pp. 138–149, 176–178.

88. Gerard Casius, "The P-51D/K Mustangs of the Royal Netherlands East Indies Air Force," *American Aviation Historical Society Journal* (winter 2010/2011), pp. 298ff.

89. Jan Forsgren, "Sweden's Spitfires in the Cold War," *Aeroplane Monthly* (March 2015), pp. 60–65.

90. Lennart Anderson, "Softly, Softly: Swedish SIGINT Operations against the USSR," *Air Enthusiast* (March/April 2004), p. 22.

91. Dave Forster and Chris Gibson, *Listening In*, pp. 179–180. Also Wing Comdr. Sidney Edwards, RAF, *My Secret Falklands War* (Hove [UK]: The Book Guild, 2014), pp. 45–61.

92. Chris Pocock, *50 Years of the U-2*, pp. 289–290.

93. David E. Hoffman, *The Dead Hand: The Untold Story of the Cold War Arms Race and its Dangerous Legacy* (New York: Doubleday, 2009), pp. 73–79.

94. Ehud Yonay, *No Margin for Error: The Making of the Israeli Air Force* (New York: Pantheon Books, 1993), pp. 66–70, 190.

95. Quoted in Brian Cull, *Wings Over Suez* (London: Grub Street, 1996), p. 198.

96. Ibid.

97. Ibid., p. 237.

98. Isabella Ginor and Gideon Remez, *Foxbats Over Dimona* (New Haven, Conn.: Yale University Press, 2007), pp. 121–137.

99. Noam Hartoch, "The Boeing Stratocruiser/Stratofreighter in Israeli Service," *Journal of the American Aviation Historical Society* (Winter 1985/86), pp. 307–314.

100. Shlomo Aloni, "F-4E(S) Shabool: Israel's Special Reconnaissance Phantoms," *International Air Power Review* (Winter 2005/06), p. 168.

101. Chris Pocock, *50 Years of the U-2*, pp. 306ff.

102. Central Intelligence Agency, *The Significance of Soviet Tu-95 Bear-D Deployments in West Africa*, NI IIM 77-010C [Washington, D.C.: April 1977], p. 3.

103. "Bear Briefing," *Air Power Journal* [Spring 1990], p. 104.

Quarto is the authority on a wide range of topics.

Quarto educates, entertains and enriches the lives of our readers—enthusiasts and lovers of hands-on living.

www.quartoknows.com

First published in 2016 by Voyageur Press, an imprint of Quarto Publishing Group USA Inc., 400 First Avenue North, Suite 400, Minneapolis, MN 55401 USA. Telephone: (612) 344-8100 Fax: (612) 344-8692

quartoknows.com
Visit our blogs at quartoknows.com

Voyageur Press titles are also available at discounts in bulk quantity for industrial or sales-promotional use. For details contact the Special Sales Manager at Quarto Publishing Group USA Inc., 400 First Avenue North, Suite 400, Minneapolis, MN 55401 USA.

10 9 8 7 6 5 4 3 2 1

ISBN: 978-0-7603-5031-7

Library of Congress Cataloging-in-Publication Data

Names: Polmar, Norman, author. | Bessette, John, author
Title: Spyplanes : the illustrated guide to manned reconnaissance and surveillance aircraft from World War I to today / by Norman Polmar and John F. Bessette; with Hal Bryan, Alan C. Carey, Michael Gorn, Cory Graff, and Nicholas A. Veronico.
Other titles: Spy planes | Illustrated guide to manned reconnaissance and surveillance aircraft from World War I to today
Description: Minneapolis, MN : Voyageur Press, an imprint of Quarto Publishing Group USA Inc., [2016] | Includes bibliographical references and index.
Identifiers: LCCN 2016033862 | ISBN 9780760350317 (hc)
Subjects: LCSH: Reconnaissance aircraft--History. | Reconnaissance aircraft--Pictorial works.
Classification: LCC UG1242.R4 P65 2016 | DDC 358.4/583--dc23
LC record available at https://lccn.loc.gov/2016033862

Acquiring Editor: Dennis Pernu
Project Manager: Caitlin Fultz
Art Director: James Kegley
Cover Designer: James Kegley
Page Design: Mayfly Design
Layout: Simon Larkin

Printed in China

MIX
Paper from responsible sources
FSC® C101537

ACKNOWLEDGMENTS

Mr. Polmar and Mr. Bessette wish to acknowledge the following: Dana Bell, historian, author, and researcher par excellence; George Cully of the US Air Force Historical Research Agency; Robert F. Dorr, aviation historian; John D. Gresham, historian and author; R. Cargill Hall, retired US Air Force and NRO historian; Peter Jefferies and Chris Halsall of the UK Medmenham Association; Yvonne Kincaid and Terry Kiss of the US Air Force History Support Office; and Bret Stolle and Jeffrey Duford of the National Museum of the US Air Force.

Mr. Gorn recognizes Karl A. Bender, senior librarian at the NASA Armstrong Flight Research Center, Edwards, California, and Kaylynn M. Clark, Armstrong Library technician, for their thoughtful and thorough research assistance.
Mr. Bryan thanks Sue Lurvey, librarian and archivist at the Experimental Aircraft Association (EAA) for her help with research, and EAA's director of publications, Jim Busha, for his encouragement and support. Mr. Bryan also thanks his wife, Muffy Bryan, for muddling through without him while he typed away in his home office.